SHAKESPEARE AND MODERNISM

Artists and writers in early twentieth-century England engaged in a variety of ways with the cultural traditions of Shakespeare as a means of defining and relating what they understood to be their own unique historical experience. In *Shakespeare and Modernism*, Cary DiPietro expands upon the established studies of this field by uncovering the connections and contexts which unite a broad range of cultural practices, from theatrical and book production, including that of Edward Gordon Craig and Harley Granville-Barker, to literary constructions of Shakespeare by high modernists such as T. S. Eliot, James Joyce and Virginia Woolf. Important contexts for the discussion include Marxist aesthetic theory contemporary with the period, the Nietzschean and Freudian contexts of English modernism, and early twentieth-century feminism. An original and accessible study, this book will appeal to students and scholars of both Shakespeare and modernism alike.

CARY DIPIETRO is currently a lecturer in English language and literature at Kyoto University. He has published a number of articles on theatre, Shakespeare and Anglo-Irish modernism in academic journals including *New Theatre Quarterly*, and is one of the contributors for the forthcoming *Shakespeare Survey 59* to be published in 2006 (Cambridge).

SHAKESPEARE AND MODERNISM

CARY DIPIETRO

 CAMBRIDGE
UNIVERSITY PRESS

CAMBRIDGE UNIVERSITY PRESS
Cambridge, New York, Melbourne, Madrid, Cape Town, Singapore, São Paulo

Cambridge University Press
The Edinburgh Building, Cambridge CB2 2RU, UK

Published in the United States of America by Cambridge University Press, New York

www.cambridge.org
Information on this title: www.cambridge.org/9780521845397

First published 2006

Printed in the United Kingdom at the University Press, Cambridge

A catalogue record for this publication is available from the British Library

Library of Congress cataloguing in publication data

DiPietro, Cary, 1971-
Shakespeare and modernism / Cary DiPietro. – 1st edn.
p. cm.
Includes index.
ISBN-13: 978-0-521-84539-7 (hardback)
ISBN-10: 0-521-84539-4 (hardback)

1. Shakespeare, William, 1564–1616 – Criticism and interpretation – History – 20th century.
2. Shakespeare, William, 1564–1616 – Stage history – 1800–1950.
3. Shakespeare, William, 1564–1616 – Stage history – England.
4. Shakespeare, William, 1564–1616 – Appreciation – England.
5. Shakespeare, William, 1564–1616 – Influence.
6. Modernism (Literature) – England. I. Title.
PR2970.D57   2006
822.3′3–dc22   2005022420

ISBN-13 978-0-521-84539-7 hardback
ISBN-10 0-521-84539-4 hardback

Contents

Illustrations

SOURCES AND PERMISSIONS

British Film Institute, London: 3.1. Ohtani Women's University, Osaka: 3.2(a) and (b), 3.4. Bodleian Library, Oxford: 3.3. The Shakespeare Centre Library, Stratford-upon-Avon: 3.5, 3.6(a), 3.7. Bibliothèque Nationale de France: 3.6(b). Mills Special Collections, Birmingham: 4.1, 4.2, 4.3, 4.4.

Acknowledgements

This book developed out of research and writing begun as a graduate student at the Shakespeare Institute, University of Birmingham. I owe my appreciation to the teaching, library and support staff there. John Jowett, who was consistently encouraging and conscientious as my graduate supervisor, was indispensable in offering advice throughout the many stages of early draft writing. For their advice after reading earlier versions of the current work, I would like to thank Russell Jackson, Peter Holland, Alan Sinfield and Nick Walton. For their help at the later stages, I also thank Sarah Stanton of Cambridge University Press, and the anonymous readers of the Press, *New Theatre Quarterly*, in which a part of chapter 3 appears, and *Shakespeare Survey*, who offered advice on chapter 4. Special mentions must go to Hugh Grady and Carol Chillington Rutter, both of whom offered invaluable commentary and needed encouragement in bringing the final draft to completion.

Research staff at the Universities of Birmingham, Oxford, McMaster, Toronto, and Kyoto have all been consistently helpful in response to nearly endless enquiries. I would also like to thank the British Film Institute, Ohtani Women's University in Osaka, The Bibliothèque Nationale de France in Paris, The Edward Gordon Craig Estate and the Shakespeare Centre Library in Stratford-upon-Avon for their help in acquiring and allowing me to reproduce illustrations here.

I would like to thank my colleagues at Kyoto University. Most importantly, I owe my gratitude to my family for their continued support and understanding through this and all endeavours.

Introduction

Shakespeare and modernism – the one, an early modern playwright, and the other, separated by about three hundred years, a cultural situation of late modernity – are arguably antithetical. We think of Shakespeare as the affirmation of what heights creative genius can achieve in the exploration of human themes, writing in the renaissance, an allegorical concept suggestive of the rebirth of classical antiquity at the beginning of a new historical epoch, modernity. Shakespeare's dramatic characters, in their mimetic capacity, would seem to demonstrate the potential for the intellectual and emotional life of the individual in post-feudal civilization. They communicate to us, in slightly antiquated language, their essential modernity, the stage an always self-conscious metaphor for our lived experience. By comparison, we think of modernism as a broadly defined literary paradigm, linked to the 'early modern' within the framework of modernity, but characterized by fragmentation and dissociation, the de-centring of the humanist tradition. Modernist artworks would seem to communicate an altogether different ethos, a disconnectedness to modernity, an inability to relate to or make sense of the modern experience. A waste land, an end game, modernism occupies the opposite ontological category.

Yet modernists, like their Victorian predecessors, read Shakespeare. They wrote copious volumes of literary criticism. They discussed and debated his biographical details and personal character. They produced his plays in the theatre and introduced them to the cinema. They studied his texts and applied current scientific methodologies to help explicate and understand them. They appropriated his life and works in their literature. They also protested against Shakespeare. They disparaged the style of nineteenth-century essay writing characteristic of popular literary appreciation and established academic institutions for literary criticism. They denounced the stagnant traditions associated with Shakespeare's performance in the theatre and heralded the arrival of a new drama and

avant-garde aesthetic movements. They rebelled against the central position of Shakespeare in the English literary canon and even denounced
his plays as artistic failures, antiquated relics, and bastions of bourgeois
commercialism. In late nineteenth and early twentieth-century English
culture, the numerous appropriations, allusions, denunciations and discussions – this engagement with Shakespeare across a range of cultural
practices – served to define, mediate and relate the modernist experience.

The purpose of this book is to explore the modernist engagement with
Shakespeare, the ways in which artists and writers read and interpreted,
re-imagined and re-configured Shakespeare as a canon, an author, a
literary archetype; and in so doing, the ways in which they read and
interpreted, theorized and canonized their own work and that of their
contemporaries. The suggestion of both Shakespeare's mutability and
modernism's narrativity here suggests a familiar problematization of these
two literary categories; indeed, who were modernists, and what was this
cultural monolith which arguably dominated their cultural imagination? On the surface, both Shakespeare and modernism would seem
distinct and relatively obvious literary categories – an author and a
broadly defined literary period. Shakespeare is Shakespeare and modernism, albeit complicated, is a knowable aesthetic event. My premise here,
however, is that neither represents an absolute historical reality, either
about authorship or literary period – the man Shakespeare, the moment
of modernism – and where we find these two fields intersecting in
late nineteenth and early twentieth-century England is precisely in the
narratives of their cultural construction. If Shakespeare was central to the
modernist project, he was so because, as a cultural formation in conflict
with its own self-constituting systems, he was demonstrative of modernity
and the subsequent crisis of modernism.

The remarkable history of Shakespeare from the seventeenth century to
our own has been mostly predicated upon the assumption that Shakespeare
represents a single imaginative consciousness, an assumption complicated
by the well-known absence of Shakespeare's holograph manuscripts.
What we have instead are, to begin, numerous extant printed texts of
the plays in Quarto and Folio versions, ascribed to Shakespeare, but each
with varying and still highly debated claims to single authorship. In
addition to these are the extant printed narrative poems and sonnets
whose authority is generally better, but which are constrained by the
conventions of courtly poetry and, as the creative expressions of their
author, are mostly undervalued in relation to the plays. Finally, a series of
holograph signatures and a final will not in his own hand, as well as some

genealogical and financial records, represent in total remarkably little to connect us directly and unproblematically to the man Shakespeare. Perhaps as a result of this relative absence, the majority of Shakespeare commentary through history has been, to greater and lesser extents, concerned with issues of literary, dramatic and textual authority, even up to but not always or unconditionally in our own contemporary critical paradigm. The ever-present heretical theories regarding the authorship of the plays, from the Baconians to the Oxfordians, among numerous others, may seem like pedantic attempts throughout history to exploit this absence, but what they are at least evidence to is the vulnerability to which the unification of these texts as the authentic expressions of Shakespeare has always been subject. Despite the obviousness of Shakespeare's genius, maintaining the apparent unity of his authorship has required significant intellectual energy and discursive output.

These observations are now commonplace as much contemporary criticism has exposed the problematic bias of an authorship which the various disciplines of editing, criticism, biography and performance have imposed on the texts. We might read the whole history of Shakespeare's reception as an operation of an author function, the immaterial author an implicit objective in the pursuit of the authoritative text, the ideal performance, the historical truth or the organizing theme. This is a totalizing account which necessitates much qualification, but the point has been commonly noted that the search for or representation of an elusive textual meaning is always discreetly related, even when intentional fallacies are denounced, to the always-absent author in any given literary field.[1] This is not unique to Shakespeare. The history of Shakespeare's reception, however, is exceptional: the concept of a single, powerful, unifying imagination otherwise obviating the heterogeneity of numerous texts and cultural situations has become a major dialectical framework, the increasingly formidable reputation of Shakespeare as the foremost representative of a literary canon contrasting with a growing diversity of interpretive and performative possibilities. This is no less apparent in the modernist paradigm when various new adumbrations of Shakespeare study – biographical criticism, scientific bibliography, Elizabethan antiquarianism, historicism, and a burgeoning academicism – sought to delimit Shakespeare's authorship by allegorizing the concept of a unified canon, projecting various structural systems – psychological, sexual, thematic, historical – upon the texts. Modern textual strategies, developments concomitant with the progressive expansion and diversification of modern industrial society, simultaneously generated and contained the various canonically disintegrating impulses against which they sought to defend the unity of Shakespeare.

Moving through history from the early modern to the post-modern, we learn that successive generations have reinvented Shakespeare in the image of their own cultures, a process which suggests the universal adaptability and dynamism of the canon through modernity, but which actually functions to reify the unity of modernity itself in the face of an inexorably forward-moving, diversifying modernization.[2] Shakespeare, not of an age but for all time, becomes representative of unique and diverse cultural situations because his canon serves as corollary to the teleology of modernity upon whose trajectory these cultures are seen, or see themselves, to develop. Given the relatively unstable unity of the canon, is it merely ironic or self-fulfilling that Shakespeare should occupy a central position in this allegory, an exemplary author who embodies the development of humanist ideology within modernity while always containing the possibility for his own de-centring and diversification? If modernism represents a crisis of modernity, a moment containing the distinct possibilities offered by a similar dialectical negotiation between a unifying, collective modernity and its potentially frightening, potentially emancipating, alternative, then Shakespeare, we are surprised to discover, was also a modernist.

Of course, like Shakespeare, the concept of an authentic or knowable modernism, based as it is upon the assumption of modernity as a historical situation, is hydra-headed. Modernism has witnessed innumerable differing formalist accounts of its chronological and geographic boundaries, defining characteristics and principal representatives. The constant redefinition and re-conceptualization of modernism is indicative of the *telos* of modernity itself: the constant revolutionizing, the always-impending newness implicit in the temporality of the word 'modern' producing ever-new divisions, definitions and theorizations for its own conceptual framework.[3] In its essence, though, like the concept of 'renaissance', 'modernity' suggests a chronological periodicity based on a dialectical structure of rupture and continuity, both discontinuous (modern, new) and continuous (developed from, improving upon). The modern generates, on the one hand, a sense of breaking with the past, from a prior order to a modern one. For modern*ism*, that break emerges out of a triangulated relationship with its 'modern' correlates: where modern*ity* is the historical situation, its own break occurring somewhere in the sixteenth century (though possibly earlier, possibly later), modern*ization* refers to the forward-moving process of modernity, and modernity's -*ism*, an aesthetic field expressive of the reaction to that process in its later, more fully developed stage. Modernism is thus conceived as a reaction-formation, a rupture in late modernity, a collective expression of angst and futility precipitated by the disenfranchising, dehumanizing forward-movement of modernization. On the other hand, modernism retains the positive ethos of the modern, the sense of continuity with the past combined with the libidinal charge of the new, the utopian possibilities implied by innovation and progress, by the teleology of modernity.

The modernist narrative shares a chronological and ideological framework with the Marxist narrative which has become, not surprisingly, one of the most powerful interpretive models for modernism (as, by the same token, 'modernist' has become a characteristic label for many early Marxist writers). Whereas modernity marks the transition from feudal to capitalist society in the Marxist narrative, modernization designates the process of economic development in industrial capitalism. The precedent here is Karl Marx himself who, with Friedrich Engels in *The Manifesto of the Communist Party*, described the constant revolutionizing of the means of production inherent in bourgeois society, and the concomitant uncertainty and agitation which it produces, the uninterrupted disturbance of all social relations.[4] Modernism becomes a condition of capitalism, an expression of the uncertainty and dissociation produced within, and a movement of resistance to, bourgeois society. As an aesthetic reaction-formation, modernism resists the social forces which would degrade the artwork to a market commodity.[5] In its anti-bourgeois orientation, modernism insists upon art's aesthetic autonomy, resorting to the humanistic valuation of art as fetish, a *l'art pour l'art*, for its own sake, separated from the economic conditions of its production.[6] Marxism thus articulates an engagement with modernity which is expressive of the modernist experience and which, increasingly through the twentieth century, has become its enabling discourse.

Though modernity as an epistemological category predates Marx, the central revelation that modernity, reduced to its determining economic factors, equals capitalism makes modernism a form of capitalist critique, a philosophical/aesthetic resistance to bourgeois society. At the same time, modernism expresses the same inner dynamic of modernization, the perpetual innovation – in the famous dictum of Ezra Pound, the need to 'make it new'. At times, therefore, modernism shares the emancipatory potential of Marxism, embracing the liberating spirit of a popular consciousness. Whereas capitalism, we might argue, represents a fairly objective condition of history, the Marxist narrative interprets that condition as the struggle between an enslaving economic system and the utopian future of the proletariat. The modernist narrative produces a similar dialectic of oppression and emancipation through its aestheticization of life. Not simply a reaction-formation, modernism also offers an aesthetic alternative, an emancipatory art which embraces the possibilities of modernity, the future technologies and machineries, and the liberating spirit of revolution echoed in real political movements and revolutions. This alternative would resonate in avant-garde movements such as expressionism and futurism. As a rupture within modernism, the avant-garde would turn against the idea of aesthetic autonomy, insisting upon art's social praxis, an insistence which would lead to the avant-garde's identification with real political and social movements such as fascism.[7] With its emphasis on the artist and the artwork as autonomous – an insistence which simultaneously reasserts the very categories of bourgeois thinking, the valuation of the self descended from the Enlightenment – to which it also revolts, modernist artworks would also express a contradictory self-denial, a regression from modernity. Writers roughly contemporary with Marx such as Nietzsche and Freud would harness a shared resistance to 'false consciousness', valorising the primitive and pre-rational experience by positing a division between the rational conscious and pre-rational subconscious. Both of their writings would reverberate through narratives of literary modernity in the twentieth century.

Within the framework of these narratives – *l'art pour l'art*, the work of art in the age of mechanical reproduction, romantic anti-capitalism, the will to power, modern psychopathology – modernism becomes an expression of both the positive and negative possibilities of modernity, as well as a crisis within the very categories of modernity itself. If the works of writers from Marx, Benjamin and Lukács to Nietzsche and Freud help to characterize modernism in the context of roughly contemporaneous social and aesthetic theory, we also find their vocabularies echoed in the narratives of Shakespeare's cultural construction throughout this same period. The resistance to bourgeois commercialism, the fear of a mass culture hastened by class dissolution and industrial mechanization, the prescriptive demands for revolutionary forms of theatre and writing, the anticipation and wonder engendered by scientific discoveries, medical technologies and psychological theories, the emancipatory potential of art – these are the issues that were central to the artists, writers, theatre practitioners, literary commentators, biographers, academics and enthusiasts for whom Shakespeare was a subject. Or rather, what we might say is that Shakespeare proved a central and largely inevitable subject for those modernists who, in constructing their cultural narratives, were trying to understand and relate their own contemporary experience. Shakespeare as a cultural category becomes one of the focal points for modernism because he contains all the positive and negative, conflicting possibilities of modernity.

Shakespeare and Modernism is a study of Shakespeare as a narrative system read and written within the meta-narrative of modernism.[8] My purpose here is neither to define modernism according to its engagement with Shakespeare nor to demonstrate how close modernists came to the historical truth about Shakespeare. Rather, my purpose is to explore how artists and writers in late nineteenth and early twentieth-century England engaged with the cultural traditions of Shakespeare as a means of defining and relating what they understood to be their own distinct historical experience. The methodological focus employed here builds upon a critical perspective which has been developed through recent works by Terence Hawkes, Hugh Grady and Richard Halpern in their seminal studies of this field.[9] The highlighting of narrative systems, however, marks an important, if only subtle, distinction between this and previous studies. Modernism is viewed here as a highly plastic narrative trope, an explanatory system rather than an actual historical phenomenon with distinct chronological boundaries, a beginning and end, a formal aesthetic or representative and non-representative figures.[10] This is not to deny the use of the term – modernist artists, modernist artworks, modernism as literary period – but to recognize that the construction of modernism is contingent upon, as noted earlier, the assumption of modernity as our own historical situation.

This de-emphasis on modernism's formal aesthetic boundaries would seem to suggest an evasion of the project implied by the title of the book, the defining of a single modernism and its reception of Shakespeare. The methodology arguably courts a relativism that comes from viewing modernism as, rather than a series of recoverable truths, a complex system of 'stories' determined by and always read within the present. The first purpose for my emphasizing narrative, however, is to recognize and make explicit the embeddedness of Marxist cultural critique within modernism as a critical formation, articulated within its anti-bourgeois and utopian dimensions, but also within modernism constructed as a cultural category post modernism. Indeed, the often insurmountable complexities of modernist discussion would seem to result in part from a dialectic, unresolved in Marx, initiated by the central division between base, or mode of production, and superstructure, encompassing, among other things, cultural production. Simply put, culture might be seen either as determined by the base, prescribed by the economic conditions of production, or as an autonomous or semi-autonomous critical sphere capable of fomenting the class revolution which reorders the relations of economic production. The Marxist revelation that all forms of production in society depend upon and are predetermined by the organization of class systems (carefully modified by Althusser to answer the charge of a 'vulgar' Marxist determinism with ideology critique) provides the central tenet of materialist criticism. In my view, the materialist perspective radically undermines reductive formalist accounts of modernism which underplay or ignore the ideologies of class and gender which are everywhere manifest in modernism. The methodology used here therefore employs a materialist emphasis on class and gender systems and the economic or material dimension of cultural activity, with specific consideration given to the social and political transformations of the period: in particular, the increasing industrialization, mechanization and urbanization of society; the growth of a middle-class and forms of mass cultural production; the increased advocacy of the Suffrage movement and transforming gender relationships; and the emergent totalitarian ideologies of Europe.

The limitations of a closed 'stucturalist' approach to cultural production, however, are now widely recognized, the main objection arising from the totalizing emphasis on economic or ideological determinism at the expense of art's autonomy status, a status upon which modernism would seem to insist. To echo the Marxist maxim, we make our own destinies, though not in the conditions of our choosing, and the ambiguity about the role of culture in the utopian future of the proletariat, again unresolved in Marx, is precisely what has given rise to diverse Marxist-influenced aesthetic theories in the twentieth century. Whereas discourse analysis enables the historicist reading of modernity from renaissance self-fashioning to contemporary gender studies, Marxist aesthetics engage more explicitly with a critique of industrial capitalism which privileges an aesthetic or critical sphere as the binary opposite of an increasingly commercial, uncritical mass culture, particularly in the later phases of industrial capitalism. This idea has provided the framework for cultural theorists from Walter Benjamin to Theodor Adorno and Jürgen Habermas – that increasingly commercial and mass-produced forms of cultural production in late nineteenth and twentieth-century capitalist society, and the simultaneous growth of a mass-audience dominated by the values of a bourgeois middle-class seeking ever-new products to consume, have produced and will continue to produce a necessary cultural deterioration.[11] Marxist aesthetic theory continues to provide the basis for much contemporary discussion of modernism.

Hugh Grady, for example, when attempting to characterize an aesthetic which is singular and autonomous – the modernist Shakespeare – privileges modernism as 'a carrier of anti-instrumental values and practices' by, rather deftly, combining Thomas Kuhn's scientific concept 'paradigm' with the aesthetic theory of the Frankfurt school, most notably that of Horkheimer and Adorno.[12] As he suggests, an historically aware aestheticism is a 'desirable approach to art in an era of colonizing and levelling ideologies and practices which threaten to absorb everything resistant to a life of pure commodity-exchange'.[13] To a degree, his study relies upon Horkheimer and Adorno's emphasis on cultural dialectics, the Enlightenment insistence upon rational order and instrumental reason turned into an autonomous system of discourse, increasingly secular and rationalized, and increasingly at odds with its originally emancipatory impulse. The result is a professionalized literary criticism developing in the early twentieth century which Grady describes in terms of a dialectical negotiation between social inscription and individual psychic fantasy in criticism's engagement with art. *The Modernist Shakespeare* is largely restricted to the discussion of institutionalized academic criticism's engagement with literary high art, a discussion which goes far to demonstrating modernism as a formal aesthetic paradigm functioning in the triangulated relationship of modernity/ization/ism. Both Terence Hawkes and Richard Halpern adopt a broader materialist emphasis on diverse heterogeneous cultural practices, an emphasis which arguably comes at the expense of not crediting modernism's utopian dimension.[14] Halpern, perhaps, achieves a more dialectic approach by adopting a double focus on 'allegory and on the economic'.[15] His use of the term 'historical allegory', which he defines as the relation between history and allegorical processes, applied to each of his five 'allegorical mappings' arguably coincides with my own use of 'narrative' here, though the terms serve different ends. But adopting the economic focus of the Marxist framework produces, as he notes, a 'recognizably "modernist" approach to modernism, with both the strengths and weaknesses that this focus entails'.[16]

One of those weaknesses is the negative valuation of bourgeois culture and the necessary elitism it produces, especially as entrenched within the literary academy, and particularly entrenched in its distinction of high modernism. Moving from discussions of modernism to post-modernism, the question of an aesthetic sphere functioning in a reified capitalism becomes more dialectic, the post-modern embracing its own commodity status in a process of complex, self-reflexive commentary which would seem otherwise antithetical to modernism. Still, attempts to define modernism largely cling to one of modernism's primary discourses, incorporating, anticipating, dramatizing or effacing its insistence upon the autonomy status of art in bourgeois society. This insistence inevitably privileges modernism as the antithesis to an increasingly degraded bourgeois culture. My purpose here, then, is to adopt a kind of critical distance, however paradoxical, which will allow us to read Marxist debate as, rather than providing an unresolved narrative which explains modernism, a set of narrative strategies endemic within modernism. The paradox comes from adopting an economic or materialist focus which credits the utopian possibilities and energies harnessed within modernism – that is to say, taking a 'modernist' approach to modernism – but which is undermined by the endless deferral of narrative to a stable, identifiable history. Narrative, however, allows us to think in terms of the historicity of the concepts and categories themselves which have made our conceptualization and understanding of modernism possible.[17]

A second purpose for de-emphasizing the formal boundaries of modernism in this study is to give a greater emphasis to the nineteenth-century proto-modernist cultures which shape the diverse, heterogeneous encounters with Shakespeare in the modernist period. Working somewhat against the grain of received chronologies of the period, modernism is thus viewed here as a kind of socio-cultural matrix, with important connections to and continuities with pre-modernist figures such as Nietzsche, Freud, Wilde and Shaw. The idea of a modernist matrix with more fluid chronological, geographic and epistemological boundaries has been proposed and used to great effect by Sanford Schwartz who, like Grady after him, develops his argument from a reading of Kuhn's *The Structure of Scientific Principles.*[18] Kuhn's concept of the 'paradigm' serves to conceptualize the notion of a break or rupture which is central to the ideation of modernism, a modernism which is both socially determined, but which, as an aesthetic–critical paradigm, is also a locus of anti-institutional values and utopian vision. For much the same purpose as mine here, Grady explains his use of Kuhn's paradigm as a 'model for the dynamics of shared cultural activities' which combine to produce modernism, a modernism which, importantly, might be seen to be coextensive with prior and subsequent paradigms and which is articulated in a series of major and minor breaks in an intersubjective sphere.[19] As this work emphasizes throughout, modernists were not the first to react to the processes of modernization and the boundary lines are indistinct, if not somewhat arbitrary, but what unites this range of responses to the global processes of modernization in an aesthetic–critical paradigm is, however broadly, their articulation of a simultaneous sense of break and continuity with the modern. On the one hand, modernists articulated a sense of epistemic rupture with the teleology of modernity; in particular, the ideologies of rational discourse, autonomous self-hood and industrial/technological development, developing from the mid-nineteenth century and increasingly vocal in the early twentieth century. On the other hand, they shared a utopian vision of communal and individual psychic fantasy which would solidify into a formal aestheticism, one which harnessed the possibilities offered by the 'new'.

One of the narrative frameworks which thus runs through the whole book is Marxist ideology contemporary with modernism, especially Benjamin, Lukács and, in England, that of the Fabian Society. The groundwork for this discussion is laid in chapter 1 in T. S. Eliot's social criticism. His collected commentary on English culture, particularly that on the theatre, anticipates the development of anti-bourgeois rhetoric in the twentieth-century Marxist critiques of mass culture through his implicit equation of bourgeois commercialism with the increasing massification of society and its attendant deterioration of culture. Chapter 3 develops this current by reading the shift from the nineteenth-century actor-manager system, in conjunction with the campaigns for national and repertory theatres, in the context of Benjamin's consideration of the work of art in the age of mechanical reproduction. In particular, this chapter considers the recurrence of Shakespeare in the theatrical tracts of the period, Shakespeare's cultural authority at the intersection of issues of class, new modes of mechanical reproduction, aesthetic value and the traditional theatre institution as a producer of art. Chapter 3 also addresses a persistent problematic of European modernism: the point where the utopian dimension of an anti-bourgeois aesthetic idealism becomes political idealism, aligning itself with contemporary political movements to produce, for example, a fascist art. At the centre of this discussion are the remarkable productions of Shakespeare at Stratford-upon-Avon by Russian-born theatre director Theodore Komisarjevsky between 1932 and 1939.

While anti-bourgeois discourse provides a major context for reading modernity, chapter 1 begins by exploring George Bernard Shaw's repeated denunciations of Shakespeare alongside, rather than his Fabian socialism, his appropriation and popularization of Nietzschean currents in English culture. Nietzsche thus provides a second narrative framework for the discussion, and in particular, his two texts which might be seen to have defined and cultivated a modernist aesthetic ideology in England, *The Birth of Tragedy* and *Thus Spoke Zarathustra*.[20] Shaw's popularization of Nietzsche, in particular, would serve to strengthen Nietzsche's association of Shakespeare, despite Shaw's own denunciations, with a cult of artistic genius, thus transforming the romantic idealization of Shakespeare to which Shaw was so adamantly opposed into a kind of modernist fetishization. By comparison, Eliot's use of historical allegory in his criticism and poetry also demonstrates the degree to which modernism perpetuated a primitivism broadly comparable to, if not derivative of, to some degree, Nietzsche's neo-classicism. Both Shaw and Eliot would therefore help to cultivate and would harness the ideological force of Nietzsche in twentieth-century England to write their own art into a narrative of modernity.

The third framework is provided by yet another German writer who might be seen to have emerged out of a similar resistance to the bourgeois ideology of the Enlightenment. Not unlike Marx and Nietzsche, Freud's disavowal of human autonomy – people not as free agents acting entirely upon their own will, but conditioned by social forces which compel them to behave in certain ways and to believe certain lies – underlies his extensive discussion of the unconscious.[21] Specifically for this argument, though, Freud, like Nietzsche, defined an ideology of aesthetic production in reaction to the nineteenth-century conception of the self; that is, creative output as intimately related to the psychosexual life of the artist, a relationship demonstrated for Freud by, among others, Shakespeare. The main tenets of Freudian psychoaesthetic production would be anticipated by and absorbed within the early twentieth-century reception of Shakespeare in England. And as with Nietzsche, this produced a specifically sexualized and gendered figuration of the modern artist. Both Freud and Nietzsche provide the primary framework for chapter 2 which begins with a discussion of the network of biographical relationships linking Shaw, Frank Harris and Oscar Wilde and their respective Shakespeare fictions, and which culminates in a discussion of the central library episode of James Joyce's *Ulysses*.

By contrasting Harris' biographical criticism with the simultaneous development of Freudian psychoanalytic interpretation of Shakespeare, chapter 2 demonstrates how writers such as Harris would inscribe phallocentric models of writing in their engagement with Shakespeare. The corollary between sex and writing in chapter 2 necessitates discussion of the fourth and perhaps most powerful narrative at work in modernism, the patriarchal narrative. *Ulysses* in particular, even while the text cleverly dramatizes the complex relationship between historical literary narrative and authorship in its critical engagement with Shakespeare's *Hamlet*, foregrounds the implicit phallocentrism of appropriating Shakespeare as a model for authorship. Chapter 5 attempts to redress the arguably inevitable patriarchal focus of the previous four chapters by turning to the writing of Virginia Woolf. By way of conclusion, this final chapter explores the complexities of discussing the female artist or writer in relation to modernism. The first half of the chapter considers Woolf writing within the context of a male literary tradition, and in particular, her writing in two texts in which Shakespeare appears as the central idealized literary imagination, *A Room of One's Own* and *Orlando*. To what degree these two texts can be both feminist and modernist is considered against the pattern of archetypal construction within which they both participate. The second half of the chapter then turns to Woolf's *Freshwater*, a play based on the life of Ellen Terry, Woolf's only extant play and a play which explores and dramatizes the possibility of a positively valued female artist like Terry.

Narrative also suggests an emphasis on writing cultures and there is an undeniable privileging of text throughout this work. Chapter 3, for example, although focused primarily on theatrical culture in England between the wars, gives primary emphasis to the written word – theatre reviews and descriptions of performances in newspapers, books on theatre reform and aesthetic philosophy, and the comments and perspectives of theatre practitioners recorded in their biographies. Theatre studies have long since grappled with the contradictions produced by the theatre between material culture and the immediateness and ethereality of performance, as well as by the transition of performance from present to past, its textualization in history. These contradictions were immanent in the early twentieth century: the modernist engagement with Shakespeare repeatedly dramatized the conflict between material real and immaterial ideal. Chapter 4 explores this conflict in detail by isolating a single year, 1923, as a critical juncture in the history of Shakespeare's texts. At a time when the different spheres of Shakespeare production were being dramatically transformed by various new practices – New Bibliography, New Criticism, New Stagecraft, New Drama – what we find in 1923 are different cultural practices engaged with representing the text intersecting at the idea of performance.

The scope of the material contained within the following five chapters is clearly broad, but by no means comprehensive or exhaustive. Numerous important figures go largely unmentioned. Moreover, the organizational methodology of the book derives from a self-consciousness about narrative-making. By this token, the chapters seek to present the material, firstly, by crediting its intrinsic resistance to subordination to a narrative, one based, as it would have to be, on simplistic or reductive speculation; secondly, avoiding the teleology of modernity itself by, for example, arranging the material according to a chronology of development or by compartmental-izing the discussion into familiar categories; finally, by emphasizing plural-ity and changeability, Shakespeare and modernism as narrative systems always subject to the processes of interpretive perspective. This is not to deny the inevitability of narrative process, at work in my own writing. We *write* modernism, just as our modernist predecessors *wrote* Shakespeare, in a process of self-definition, in order to understand ourselves. The assump-tions to which this book is therefore happily committed are that modern-ism, even understood as a system of narratives, provides a valuable, necessary and satisfying framework for reading aesthetic practice in this period; and that the modernist engagement with Shakespeare, in all of its wonderful variety, was uniquely related to the collective imagination and aesthetic life of modernism.

CHAPTER I

The Shakespeare revolution

Writing in 1897 in a letter to Ellen Terry, the acclaimed Shakespearean actress of Henry Irving's Lyceum Theatre, George Bernard Shaw, her friend and correspondent, declared with his characteristic bombast the reason for his often vituperative criticism of Shakespeare and the importance of the 'New Drama' – both Ibsen's and his own – as a counterpoint to Shakespeare's hegemony: 'The theatre is my battering ram as much as the platform or the press: that is why I want to drag it to the front. My capers are part of a bigger design than you think: Shakespear, for instance, is to me one of the towers of the Bastille, and down he must come.'[1] The fact that Shaw was fighting an impossible battle, as Shakespeare's claim to cultural authority continued to increase through the late nineteenth century, was little deterrence to his own agenda, his mission to educate the English audience with the New Drama as his social instrument. And though his was a fairly solitary voice, his criticizing of Shakespeare would later be echoed by prominent writers such as T. S. Eliot. Earlier, in 1896, Shaw had written to Terry claiming that 'Shakespear is as dead *dramatic-ally* as a doornail'.[2] Whether or not he truly believed this particular claim, the source of his veracity was a strong disdain not only for Henry Irving's version of Shakespeare, and the kind of grand commercial productions staged by many of the contemporary actor-managers, but for what he termed 'bardolatry', the blind hero worship which placed Shakespeare above practical criticism. Shaw was, in contrast, a relentless and often astute critic of Shakespeare, well read and very familiar with Shakespeare criticism, a noted fan of Samuel Johnson, and, in his own way, an admirer of much of Shakespeare's writing.[3] He was also a very practical theatre critic, having made his reputation during the 1890s reviewing theatre for the *Saturday Review*. As an admirer of Terry, Shaw's derision of Shakespeare (and, in particular, Irving's Shakespeare) was part of his design to lure her from Lady Macbeth and Ophelia to Candida and Lady Cicely, the roles he was now writing, perhaps with her in mind, as he turned his primary attention from dramatic criticism to his own drama.[4] His vituperative rhetoric was also a peculiarity of his writing style, his deliberate overemphasis and, sometimes, insensitivity his necessary means to bring the point home: 'Omelettes are not made without breaking eggs', he warned Terry.[5]

The late 1890s were a turning point in Shaw's career and, to a degree, in the English theatre as well, especially insofar as his New Drama was an important feature of the changing theatrical landscape of the period. Shaw was an ardent advocate of theatrical reform, strongly denouncing the actor-manager system while supporting national and repertory theatre schemes. For Shaw, the English theatrical traditions, especially as they had descended through the eighteenth and nineteenth centuries to the mainstream theatres of London's West End, perpetuated the kind of romantic idealization in the theatre which made of Shakespeare an unqualified dramatic genius, and more, were now demonstrative of an uncritical sentimentalism. Instead, Shaw championed the drama of naturalism, housed in local repertory and state-subsidized theatres, a drama which advocated the stage as a vehicle for real social and political issues, especially issues of class and gender privilege. Although Shaw's own drama, plays such as *Man and Superman* and *Back to Methuselah*, would tend towards more abstract social philosophy, they would articulate clearly his anti-bourgeois position, as well as his idiosyncratic socialism. In claiming a break with the romantic traditions of the actor-manager theatre and rendering that break in the anti-capitalist language of early English socialism, while also embracing the liberating spirit of revolution made possible by a *new* drama, Shaw thus heralded the arrival of English theatrical modernism.

And here we find Shaw placing Shakespeare, as one of the towers of the Bastille to be brought down, at the centre of his revolution. The rhetoric of revolution in the cultural life of the late nineteenth century – the necessity to create a new drama and a new kind of theatre, to write a new literature, or to establish a new criticism – was in place before Shaw rose to prominence. The kind of aphorisms phrased so flamboyantly by Shaw would also resonate throughout the decades following the turn of the twentieth century, and in particular, in the interwar years when the social and political dimensions of those various calls for reformation and revolution in art would be greatly amplified by the actual social and political events of the period, the real revolutions and wars. But Shaw's anti-romantic platform, and especially, his desire to topple Shakespeare, articulated as elsewhere in his letters to Terry, signalled a turning point from the bardolatry of Shakespeare appreciation and production in the theatre he so vehemently denounced to the early twentieth-century Shakespeare revolution.[6] This ethos of revolution implied by the very idea of the modern – the dynamic of innovation and progress, the libidinal spirit of the new – which Shaw was embracing, would resonate in the spheres of production associated with Shakespeare, resulting in numerous 'new' adumbrations of cultural practice, from the New Stagecraft to the New Criticism and the New Bibliography. Even while he condemned bardolatry, by singling out Shakespeare as one of the towers of the Bastille, Shaw was articulating what he understood to be the central significance of Shakespeare in a period of paradigmatic transition; and as with T. S. Eliot, Shaw would articulate this opposition not only in the language of contemporary aesthetic theory, but also in the context of social transformation, the nineteenth-century traditions of theatrical and literary production and reception coming into conflict with the changing class and gender relations of modern industrialized society.

'ÜBER'-SHAKESPEARE

As a harbinger of a distinctly modern drama, part of Shaw's aim in denouncing Shakespeare was to dissociate his own drama from any sense of literary influence or inheritance. To emphasize their distance, Shaw would frequently make the comparison in his writing between his own superior ability and drama with that of the inferior Shakespeare: 'With the single exception of Homer', he wrote in one of his earlier and more famous theatre reviews for the *Saturday Review*, 'there is no eminent writer, not even Sir Walter Scott, whom I can despise so entirely as I despise Shakespeare when I measure my mind against his' (26 September 1896). In the same vein of his persistent comparisons with Shakespeare was Shaw's famous assertion, countering Ben Jonson in his dedication to the First Folio, that Shakespeare was 'for an afternoon, but not for all time'.[7] This kind of derision was characteristic of Shaw's theatre reviews, often locating the deficiencies of a given *theatrical* production (in the example above, Henry Irving's production of *Cymbeline* at the Lyceum Theatre in 1896 in which Ellen Terry played the role of Imogen) largely in the *writerly* dimension of Shakespeare's authorship. This derision also reflected Shaw's distinction between the sentimentalism of audience-pleasers such as *As You Like It* and *Much Ado About Nothing* and his own philosophical, moral drama, written not to please, but to educate his audiences. Not only were Shakespeare's dramas expressive of an

Elizabethan world view rather than contemporary social issues, more significantly, Shakespeare himself was a panderer to public taste in his comedies and a sentimentalizer in his tragedies. Between Shakespeare and Shaw lay an abyss: 'between the fashionable author who could see nothing in the world but personal aims and the tragedy of their disappointment or the comedy of their incongruity, and the field preacher who achieved virtue and courage by identifying himself with the purpose of the world as he understood it'.[8] But even Shaw knew that this kind of thinking ran counter to the more popular belief in what was seen to be Shakespeare's continued relevance. In contrast to his own colourful denunciations, belief in the essential modernity of Shakespeare was widespread and served to strengthen Shakespeare's central position in late nineteenth and early twentieth-century narratives of theatrical and literary culture.

This kind of idealization of Shakespeare has been most recently and perhaps most remarkably demonstrated by Harold Bloom who, by crediting Shakespeare with no less than the invention of the human, would seem to exemplify the sort of bardolatry against which Shaw was reacting.[9] In his well-known exploration of *The Anxiety of Influence*, Bloom asks: 'How do men become poets, or to adopt an older phrasing, how is the poetic character incarnated?'[10] In the following explanation, in which 'strong poets' succeed one another by overcoming the anxiety generated by their predecessors, Bloom appropriates Freud's Oedipal metaphor: 'Oedipus, blind, was on the path to oracular godhood, and the strong poets have followed him by transforming their blindness towards their precursors into the revisionary insights of their own work.'[11] In *The Interpretation of Dreams*, Freud rather famously discussed Shakespeare's Hamlet, whose psychology Freud regarded to be the epitome of the Oedipus complex.[12] Coincidentally, Bloom's literary lineage begins with Shakespeare as the first and greatest precursor. Given the Oedipal model, Shakespeare becomes the first in a male literary tradition, the first of a series of literary fathers in a tale of patricidal succession. Bloom also cites Nietzsche as one of his own primary influences. Here, he quotes *Twilight of the Idols*: 'Great men, like great ages, are explosives in which a tremendous force is stored up. . . Once the tension in the mass has become too great, then the most accidental stimulus suffices to summon into the world the "genius," the "deed," the great destiny.'[13] Citing Nietzsche's characterization of genius and great destinies emerging out of the potentially explosive turning point of a new age, Bloom places Shakespeare firmly at the centre of Nietzsche's allegory of modernity. Nietzsche's psychosexual language also seems anachronistic-ally Freudian, and the circularity of association between Shakespeare, Freud and Nietzsche in Bloom's study is almost certainly deliberate, a clever demonstration of a trans-historical influence at work.

Bloom's own allegorical model, however, perhaps one of the last real modernist narratives, neatly demonstrates the degree to which both Freud and Nietzsche were central in the early twentieth century to such narratives which constructed Shakespeare as the archetypal representative of a modern English canon. At the time of Shaw's writing in the late 1890s, however, more than a decade prior to Freud's first English translations, it was Nietzsche's writing in particular which offered the most compelling theories for a modern aesthetics, especially his concept of the *Übermensch*, as commonly appropriated by, among others, Shaw. Nietzsche's own coinage, though one based on a fairly standard model of German word formation and roughly translated as the 'Over-man', the *Übermensch* was popularized in England after early translations of his work first appeared in the late nineteenth and early twentieth centuries. In particular, *Thus Spoke Zarathustra*, which was the second of Nietzsche's texts to be translated into English in full by Alexander Tille in 1896, remained the most widely popular of his works. This was also the first text to be published in *The Complete Works of Friedrich Nietzsche* series, produced under the editorship of Oscar Levy between the years 1909 and 1913.[14] The model of the *Übermensch* proposed in that work, Nietzsche's call for the sublimation of the will to power and for the overcoming of an otherwise inevitable and inexorable nihilism, his answer to the cultural and moral dissolution of modern industrialized society, was much debated in periodicals such as A. R. Orage's *New Age*, and became notably influential in relation to discussions of Darwinism and eugenics.[15] In the broader public sphere, however, more read than Nietzsche's works in translation were literary and dramatic texts which appropriated Nietzsche, as well as vituperative condemnations of his aesthetic and moral philosophy. Particularly popular was the 1895 English translation of Max Nordau's *Entartung* (*Degeneration*) in which Nordau, a German Jew, denounced both Nietzsche and Wagner as anti-Semitic 'egomaniacs'.[16] A cogent allegorical figure in the public imagination of the period, the superman, which would become the more popular Nietzsche-inflected coinage in England after Shaw, was thus made popular less by actual engagement with Nietzsche's writing and more by its reworking in popular discourse, and particularly, in literary and dramatic interpretations and derivations. By the early twentieth century, the addition of '*Über-*' as a prefix, such as in Edward Gordon Craig's theoretical '*Über*-marionette' actor (*c.* 1907), would come to indicate anything of intellectual or physical superiority.

If the superman archetype as derived from *Thus Spoke Zarathustra* at the turn of the century represented a kind of culmination of Nietzschean philosophy as understood in wider English culture, among the community of artists and writers, however, what was arguably the more influential of his works was *The Birth of Tragedy*, whose first English translation appeared in 1909, with its distinction between Dionysian and Apollonian categories of art.[17] Within these two works are the primary Nietzschean currents which are echoed in many of the aesthetic discourses of the period: starting with *The Birth of Tragedy*, the distinction between the two reigning deities over polarized categories of art, Dionysus and Apollo, frenzied and chaotic truth versus false consciousness; add to this the psychological language which characterized Nietzsche's distinction; his sense of an emerging crisis or cultural turning point in civilization; and in *Thus Spoke Zarathustra*, his proclamation of the will to power.[18] For Nietzsche, or at least for Nietzsche broadly in these two works, art held a special redemptive power, for within the artist lay the potential for deliverance from a specifically modern nihilism, the potential for transition from the apprehension of truth and the descent into despair to the will to power.

Perhaps more than any other writer of the period, Shaw in particular helped to raise the currency of Nietzsche's first English translations after the turn of the century. When *Man and Superman* was first published (1903) and later performed (at the Royal Court Theatre, 1905), the controversy surrounding Shaw's take on the superman derivative and the publicity furore which followed echoed the controversy which Nietzsche's writing had initially precipitated in the late nineteenth century, particularly during the time of Nordau's *Degeneration*. Ever the willing nonconformist, Shaw seemed to be capitalizing on Nietzsche's notoriety, incorporating into his own writing, if not the theoretical depth of Nietzsche, at the least, the same kind of manifesto declarations (included in 'The Revolutionist's Handbook' which accompanies the play's text). Thus, not only does the epistle dedicatory to *Man and Superman* make reference to Nietzsche as one source of influence, the play comically includes Nietzsche as an offstage character in a farcical exchange, during the 'Don Juan in Hell' episode, an episode which reflects Shaw's and Nietzsche's shared atheism, as well as their fluctuating enthusiasm for Wagner:

THE STATUE And who the deuce is the Superman?

THE DEVIL Oh, the latest fashion among the Life Force fanatics. Did you not meet in Heaven, among the new arrivals, that German Polish madman? What was his name? Nietzsche?

THE STATUE Never heard of him.

THE DEVIL Well, he came here first, before he recovered his wits. I had some hopes for him; but he was a confirmed Life Force worshipper. It was he who raked up the Superman, who is as old as Prometheus; and the 20th century will run after this newest of the old crazes when it gets tired of the world, the flesh, and your humble servant.[19]

As elsewhere, Shaw was here keen to note that his own superman idea derived in the main from other writers. Making formal acknowledgement to the authors upon whose works Shaw modelled his artist-philosopher superman, the epistle dedicatory to *Man and Superman* dismissively cites Nietzsche along with Goethe, Shelley, Schopenhauer, Wagner, Ibsen, Morris, and Tolstoy as 'among the writers whose peculiar sense of the world I recognize as more or less akin to my own'.[20] Shaw associated his own superman model with a transcendental ideal which he saw himself as reworking and rewriting. Accordingly, he concluded: 'The vogue for the Superman did not begin with Nietzsche, nor will it end with his vogue.'[21] Shaw was an enthusiast of both Ibsen and Wagner, but also well-read in pre-Nietzsche German philosophy, especially Schopenhauer. In fact, while many of his contemporaries regarded Shaw as a chief Nietzschean in England, he was, at best, only an admirer who never really engaged with Nietzsche's works with anything approaching a theoretical rigour.[22] In his 1896 review of Tille's first English translation, *The Case of Wagner*, Shaw in fact denounced Nietzsche as 'simply awful': 'his epigrams are written', Shaw claimed, 'with phosphorous on brimstone' (*Saturday Review*, 11 April 1896).

Nevertheless, Shaw found in Nietzsche some common ground, particularly his scathing criticism of the bourgeois value system. What Shaw admired most was Nietzsche's 'transvaluation of values', his criticism of 'morality and idealism. . . his way of getting underneath moral precepts which are so unquestionable to us that common decency seems to compel unhesitating assent to them, and upsetting them with a scornful laugh' (*Saturday Review*, 11 April 1896). He may have had a very different writing style, but Shaw was equally scornful of English moral precepts and, like Nietzsche, was keen to upset them with his own satiric humour. After later reading the first English translation of *Thus Spoke Zarathustra*, Shaw would begin to think about appropriating the *Übermensch* towards his own ends. Shaw's superman, however, was significantly different. To begin with, although Nietzsche was resolutely undemocratic, Shaw never parted with the idiosyncratic socialism of the Fabian Society to which he belonged, and so his superman reflected the Fabians' select minority of cultural 'experts' who would extend their own tastes and values to a broader mass audience.[23] Relatively unique to Shaw at that time, however, was this fierce opposition to Shakespeare. Although Nietzsche revered tradition, championing in particular the classical and renaissance periods, Shaw was committed to his anti-traditional platform.

For Nietzsche, even though Shakespeare had suffered the reflective morality of the German romantics, Shakespeare's writing, especially in *Hamlet*, reflected his own modern nihilism. Allusions to Shakespeare's plays are a central feature throughout Nietzsche's writing, but particularly in *The Birth of Tragedy*, Shakespeare would seem to have exemplified the kind of ideal artist figure who could mediate true understanding into art. Indeed, Shakespeare had thematized this problem in *Hamlet*. Again, the central premise of *The Birth of Tragedy* is Nietzsche's often impenetrable distinction between two principles of artistic productivity, the Apollonian and the Dionysian, and their ideal union in Greek tragedy. In his description of the Dionysian, however, which Nietzsche finally privileges above the Apollonian, he invokes Hamlet: 'Both have looked deeply into the true nature of things, they have *understood* and are now loath to act. . . What, both in the case of Hamlet and of Dionysiac man, overbalances any motive leading to action, is not reflection but understanding, the apprehension of truth and its terror.'[24] Forming a central demonstrative example in *The Birth of Tragedy*, *Hamlet* expresses an acutely modern nihilism which Shakespeare could overcome by translating experience into art. Art, which mediates Dionysian understanding into Apollonian consciousness, becomes the medium which makes modern existence bearable: 'Then, in this supreme jeopardy of the will', writes Nietzsche about the artist, 'art, that sorceress expert in healing, approaches him; only she can turn his fits of nausea into imaginations with which it is possible to live'.[25] By placing *Hamlet* at the centre of this allegory of the birth of tragedy, Shakespeare becomes the kind of Dionysian ideal in whom resides the potential for redemption from a specifically modern nihilism.

Freud as well chose *Hamlet* in *The Interpretation of Dreams* because he found Shakespeare's play to be a suitably representative text of the post-feudal modern epoch of civilization, an age of secular repression in the emotional life of mankind.[26] Both Nietzsche and Freud were transforming nineteenth-century humanist idealizations of Shakespeare, especially vis-à-vis German romanticism, the readings of Goethe and the translations of Wilhelm Schlegel and Ludwig von Tieck. Whereas the romantics characterized Shakespeare as Hamlet, an introspective idealist – in the words of Goethe which Freud would quote, as 'sicklied o'er with the pale cast of thought' – Freud would re-characterize Shakespeare's writing in the language of a nascent psychoanalysis, probing the 'deepest layer of impulses in the mind of the creative writer' to reveal the conflict between conscious and unconscious impulses.[27] Nietzsche had earlier produced a similar reaction to nineteenth-century sentimentality, also harnessing the language of psychology to distinguish between true- and false-consciousness (or Dionysian and Apollonian), though for Nietzsche, it was the artist and not the therapist who achieved this understanding. But in *The Interpretation of Dreams*, the assumption of Shakespeare's genius remains otherwise unexamined: the inclusion of Shakespeare as a demonstrative example of modern psychopathology was justified, as in the case of Sophocles' *Oedipus Rex* from which the complex name derived, by its exemplification of primeval dream-material which had 'as its content the distressing disturbance of a child's relation to his parents owing to the first stirrings of sexuality'.[28] For Nietzsche, in contrast, Shakespeare's writing was central to his own *because* Shakespeare was an exemplar of his cult of artistic genius. Developing out of German aesthetic philosophy, particularly from notions of genius as developed by Kant and Hegel, Nietzsche's genius would emerge as fiercely individualized rather than universalized, not a representative of the modern epoch of civilization, but one who resisted and reacted to it, who prescribed his own rules not to exemplify them to others, but to achieve his own ends.[29] This would appear to be the sense in which Harold Bloom cites Nietzsche (great men as explosives) to qualify his Oedipal metaphor.

At the same time that Nietzsche's cult of genius was slowly being absorbed and appropriated through artists such as Shaw in the emerging aesthetic ideology of modernism, Shakespeare's status as the foremost representative of an English literary canon continued to rise, his lionization to the status of a cultural superman whose writing epitomized an essential modernity becoming a familiar trope. Although Nietzsche's association of Shakespeare's *Hamlet* with Dionysian vision in *The Birth of Tragedy* did not appear in English translation until 1909, in 1896, the Danish critic Georg Brandes, in his immense volume on Shakespeare, would write of *Hamlet*: 'Hamlet belongs to the future, to the modern age. He embodies the lofty and reflective spirit, standing isolated, with its severely exalted ideals, in corrupt or worthless surroundings, forced to conceal its inmost nature, yet everywhere arousing hostility.'[30] Brandes' description of Hamlet is clearly inflected with Nietzsche's reading of Goethe; and, interestingly, Brandes is the only secondary author to be mentioned by Freud in his reading of *Hamlet* in those passages from *The Interpretation of Dreams*.[31] Drawing from the 1898 English translation of Brandes' work, writers from A. C. Bradley to Frank Harris, Ernest Jones and even James Joyce would continue to explore the idea of Shakespeare's psychology as read within, especially, *Hamlet*. More broadly pervasive, however, in literary and theatrical discussions of Shakespeare was the articulation of a kind of Nietzschean emphasis on Shakespeare as an archetypal artist whose art demonstrated an immediacy and modern relevance. In his 1907 contribution to the Men of Letters series, for example, Walter Raleigh would begin by suggesting that: 'Every age has its own difficulties in the appreciation of Shakespeare. The age in which he lived was too near to see him truly.'[32] By 1907, however, Shakespeare had come into his own as an English man of letters: 'he has been separated from his fellows, and recognised for what he is: perhaps the greatest poet of all time'.[33] As a writer in the early twentieth century exemplifying a nineteenth-century style of literary appreciation, Raleigh's evaluation of Shakespeare was clearly in the vein of what Shaw disparagingly labelled bardolatry. But if Raleigh's idealization descended from English romanticism, his emphasis on Shakespeare as an unparalleled artistic genius not fully appreciated until the early twentieth century, despite a universalizing and romanticizing impulse, also resonated with the model of the superman as descended from Nietzsche.[34]

Interestingly, it's in the preface to *Man and Superman*, after crediting Nietzsche as, among others, setting the precedent for his own model, that Shaw makes the distinction between Shakespeare and his ideal artist-philosopher. In a characteristic denigration, which also happens to include Charles Dickens, Shaw writes: 'they have no constructive ideas; they regard those who have them as dangerous fanatics; in all their fictions there is no leading thought or inspiration for which any man could conceivably risk the spoiling of his hat in the shower, much less his life'.[35] For Shaw, Shakespeare was simply bewildered by the world, by the 'great stage of fools', and so his dramas failed to serve Shaw's larger purpose. Moreover, Shakespeare in the late nineteenth century was irrevocably bourgeois, fixed too securely to the romantics. The antithesis between the outdated Shakespeare and the modern Ibsen, for example, was comparable to that between the mellifluous melodies of the popular Mendelssohn, whose incidental music habitually accompanied productions of *A Midsummer Night's Dream* on the Victorian stage, and the demanding intensity of Wagner (who would later become for Nietzsche a bourgeois romantic). What Shaw shared with Nietzsche was an opposition to bourgeois institutions and art, but where he parted from Nietzsche, as from so many of his contemporaries in England, was his refusal to assign a special significance to Shakespeare.

However much he admired Shakespeare's writing as a fellow dramatist, Shaw's ideological opposition to the bard of the nineteenth century necessitated Shakespeare's exclusion from the modern canon and theatre institution which Shaw envisioned. Thus, in his comments to Ellen Terry, he employed the metaphor of political revolution to differentiate his modern drama from that of Shakespeare. And yet, Shaw's own role in the popularization of a twentieth-century cult of artistic genius would also serve to strengthen the Nietzschean identification of Shakespeare with the superman artist-philosopher of an explosive new age in wider English culture. This association, which reworked the very same romantic emphases on Shakespeare's expressive individuality and artistic genius to which Shaw was so adamantly opposed, would be taken up by the inheritors to the nineteenth-century traditions of Shakespeare appreciation and theatrical production. Despite his opposition to Shakespeare, his sense of a revolution in which Shakespeare would be replaced by a new different drama, Shaw's own aesthetic philosophy would help to disengage Shakespeare from the nineteenth century and prepare for his entrance into the twentieth century.

T. S. ELIOT AND HIS PROBLEMS

In 1923, in one of his many book reviews published in magazines such as the American *Dial*, T. S. Eliot heralded the importance of James Joyce's *Ulysses*. First published in 1922 in full book form by the Shakespeare and Company bookshop of Paris, Joyce's gargantuan work of fiction was banned from publication in America until 1934 for violating anti-obscenity laws. Earlier serial publication of the first few chapters in another American literary journal, the *Little Review*, and in England, in the *Egoist*, had stirred enough controversy to make the whole volume nearly impossible to publish. Tantalizing an audience that would not see a legitimate American edition until early 1934, Eliot enthusiastically endorsed the idea of a mythical correlative structuring the narrative into thematically corresponding episodes, ascribing to the unorthodox narrative style the significance of a scientific discovery. Manipulating a continuous parallel between contemporaneity and antiquity exemplified an ideal method of ordering the modern world through classical allegory into art: 'It is simply a way of controlling', he suggested, 'of ordering, of giving a shape and a significance to the immense panorama of futility and anarchy which is contemporary history.'[36] Contemporary history must have seemed indeed an age of futile and anarchic destruction and disorder for Eliot, writing from the perspective of a wearied and disillusioned postwar Europe as *Dial*'s London correspondent. In the aftermath of the First World War, images of bodily dismemberment, lost youth, death and decay became recurring motifs securely fixed in the post-war literary imagination; and certainly in the case of Eliot, ageing, death and disorder were thematic obsessions for many of his poetic characters, from the anxieties of Prufrock and Sweeney to the dismay and resignation of Gerontion. This was an age decidedly fractured from the romantic idealism of the eighteenth and nineteenth centuries. 'The age demanded an image / Of its accelerated grimace', wrote Ezra Pound in 1919, in the second section of his episodic poem 'Hugh Selwyn Mauberly', the description of an incarnate, demanding periodization generating an overwhelming sense of moment.[37] For Eliot, Joyce's book met the demands of this moment, his praise for Joyce's mythical method consequently emblematizing *Ulysses* as a distinctly contemporary expression: 'I hold this book to be the most important expression which the present age has found; it is a book to which we are all indebted, and from which none of us can escape.'[38] For Eliot, *Ulysses* was a pioneer of a modern classicism, providing a structuring mythical analogue. However, *Ulysses* was also seen to express this same overwhelming sense of moment, of breaking with the traditions of the immediate past and of giving shape and significance to contemporary history.

If Shaw's writing harnessed in aggressive language the positive ethos of modernity, the spirit of revolution and progress, to disengage the New Drama from any sense of literary inheritance, in his own aesthetic philosophy, Eliot engaged more explicitly with the narrative of modernity to define his writing and the writing of select contemporaries. Although he never applied the term 'modernist' to his own acts of literary creation and interpretation, it would be difficult to deny the overwhelming self-consciousness of moment in Eliot's praise for Joyce, the sense in which he identifies *Ulysses* as the distinctive expression of a present age. The age demanded an image; and so throughout modernist artworks and aesthetic discourse reverberates this sense of a demanding periodicity answered by the works themselves. Unlike Shaw, though, Eliot's sense of a modern art, as expressed in his praise for Joyce, was based on a dialectical relationship to past literary history. This same sense of historical dialecticism – a sense of historical awareness or historicity, a continuity with the past, combined with a sense of modernity, of breaking with the immediate past – characterizes most of Eliot's writing, from his literary criticism and social theory to his poetry and drama. This awareness of history, Eliot's repeated attempts in his writing to define and understand his own historical moment by rewriting a version of the literary past, is also what defines his work as modernist.

Shaw and Eliot would seem an odd couple for comparison, Shaw, one of the foremost representatives of an explicitly realist drama in England, and Eliot, one of the foremost representatives of literary high modernism. If Shaw and Eliot differed in their characterization of modern art, Eliot was also unsympathetic to the overtly politicized language of Shaw's plays which he saw as representing a dilute philosophical rhetoric. In one of his few passing comments on Shaw in 1920, Eliot denounced his social theory as popularization: 'the moment an idea has been transferred from its pure state in order that it may become comprehensible to the inferior intelligence', he wrote, referring to the plays of both Shaw and Maeterlinck, 'it has lost contact with art'.[39] Eliot's few negative comments on Shaw would help to generate an antithesis between Shaw's naturalism and his own interest in the French-derived symbolist movement which would echo the more vociferous rivalry between Shaw and the theatrical designer and artist Edward Gordon Craig. This was only one manifestation of the broader *l'art pour l'art* debate – art as social instrument versus art for its own sake – which would continue through American and European modernist and avant-garde movements in the first half of the twentieth century. For Eliot, the problem with Shaw's 'comedy of ideas' was that the presentation of thought was not balanced with an emotional stimulus, the idea-emotion; without the appeal to a higher aesthetic ideal, Shaw's drama was too closely identifiable with the quotidian reality of its bourgeois audience to be called literary art. Considering the possibility of a poetic or verse drama in a formless age, Eliot thus lamented the absence of proper aesthetic form on the contemporary stage. Without entirely disposing of Shaw, he concluded: 'I do not find that any drama which "embodies a philosophy" of the author's (like *Faust*) or which illustrates any social theory (like Shaw's) can possibly fulfil the requirements—though a place might be left for Shaw if not for Goethe.'[40]

There is an underlying question in the comparison of Shaw to Eliot here, a question partly articulated in the naturalist/symbolist antithesis, about whether, or to what degree, Shaw's aesthetic philosophy can be seen to anticipate or is coterminous with Eliot's modernism. Much of Victorian culture was defined by its reaction to modernization, but did not undertake the radical revolution in aesthetic form which constituted modernism, a revolution advocated by Shaw in his drama of social philosophy, but perhaps only fully realized with the aesthetic innovations of the later Eliot and his contemporaries. Indeed, the comparison of Shaw to Eliot is almost impossible to articulate outside of the naturalist/ symbolist antithesis, and in particular, Eliot's own denigrations of artistic realism as demonstrative of the humanist traditions of rationality and personality in reaction to which he situated his own aesthetic ideologies. To exclude Shaw from modernism is to buy into Eliot's version of it. The question of Shaw as anticipating Eliot's modernism, however, can also be addressed, I would argue, partly by turning to their shared appropriation of the broadly Nietzschean cult of artistic genius and, particularly in the case of Eliot, Nietzsche's neo-classicist framing of modernity, and partly in the context of their shared double-thinking about Shakespeare: on the one hand, both Shaw and Eliot shared an essential admiration for Shakespeare's dramatic ability, particularly as an Elizabethan dramatist working within his own historical conditions, which would become, in the case of Eliot, a desire to connect contemporary literature directly to the poetic sensibilities of the renaissance; on the other hand, both held a greater disdain for the romanticized Shakespeare of the eighteenth and nineteenth centuries, and the equation of that Shakespeare with an increasingly commercialized mass culture against which both Shaw and Eliot would set their own prescriptions for cultural reform.

While both Shaw and Eliot had long and diverse careers, Shaw remained more consistent in his aesthetic philosophy, even in its wording. Phrases and comments recur in different places over many years. Eliot's writing, by comparison, is marked by different stages in his career: his early period as a poet newly arrived and establishing a reputation for himself in England, a period marked by the publication of his first and successful collection of poetry, *The Love Song of J. Alfred Prufrock and Other Poems* (1917), and his first collection of literary theory and criticism, *The Sacred Wood* (1920); the period of the 1920s during what has come to be known as high modernism in Anglo-Irish literature, marked by the publication of 'The Waste Land' (1922), a period in which he also developed his interest in Elizabethan drama and wrote as the London correspondent for the *Dial* (1921–2); and finally, his turn to Anglo-Catholicism in the later stages of his career, the publication of his poetic swan-song *Four Quartets* (1944), and the period of his drama. Those principal currents of his aesthetic ideology, however, expressed most vibrantly in the 1920s, can be seen across his whole career: his idea of the artist's historical sense and his definition of a literary tradition as the basis for a new kind of poetic sensibility and literary criticism; his expression of a contemporary crisis precipitated by the dehumanizing forces of progressive modernization in his poetry; and, particularly in his social commentary on English society for the *Dial*, his articulation of a class rhetoric which would characterize the crisis of modernity as the multiplication of nineteenth-century bourgeois culture in the growing mass culture of early twentieth-century England.

Perhaps Eliot's most characteristic explanation of the artist's historical sense occurs in the 1919 essay on 'Tradition and the Individual Talent'. In words which are among his most well-known and most enigmatic, Eliot here defined the artist's historical sense in the same cryptic language of dialecticism, as a perception 'not only of the pastness of the past, but of its presence': 'The historical sense which is the sense of the timeless as well as of the temporal and of the timeless and of the temporal together, is what makes a writer traditional.'[41] Eliot's tradition was not inherited, but achieved through great labour, and involved rather than mere rejection or appreciation of the past, a kind of presentist historicism, a readjustment of the past through the lens of contemporary literary sensibility. The poet's mind was, for Eliot, a receptacle 'for seizing and storing up numberless feelings, phrases, images, which remain there until all the particles which can unite to form a new compound are present together'. This utilitarian approach to history, the seizing and storing up of cultural bric-a-brac, far from demonstrating an academic pedantry, was the appeal of Joyce's book. This same density of allusion was simultaneously bringing Eliot fame as the author of the fragmentary poem 'The Waste Land', published again in the *Dial* upon the insistence of its European editor, Pound. In praising *Ulysses*, Eliot was in fact promoting his own literary technique.

Included among the numerous particles of literary texts and contemporary English culture scattered throughout the five episodes of 'The Waste Land' are several references to Shakespeare and his contemporaries. One of the last lines of the poem, taken from Thomas Kyd's *The Spanish*

Tragedy, is framed by the poem's narrator, however, not as allusion, but as a scrap of history: 'These fragments I have shored against my ruins / Why then Ile fit you. Heironymo's mad againe.'[42] Like Nietzsche's Zarathustra, this narrative figure represents the individual consciousness battling absorption into a dispiriting and consuming chaos, the consciousness through whom the eddying fragments of history are reordered into a modern, mystical, metaphysical art. First published in 1922, that epochal moment which also witnessed the first publication of *Ulysses*, the poem belongs to an impressive body of early writing, both poetic and critical, which propelled Eliot to an early literary fame. Moreover, 'The Waste Land' is commonly regarded as the quintessential expression of modernist anxiety. W. B. Yeats' widening gyre, Wallace Stevens' consuming whirlpool, Wyndham Lewis' exploding vortex; these images all seem to communicate the same angst expressed in the image of the waste land. As coinciding symbolic expressions, they represent the individual in conflict with the demanding and unsympathetic forces of an unrelenting modernization.

This same anxiety is expressed, perhaps more lucidly, in Eliot's prose writing. Eerily predicting the implications of early twentieth-century technology, Eliot anticipated Aldous Huxley's *Brave New World* and George Orwell's *Nineteen Eighty-Four* when he stated:

When every theatre has been replaced by 100 cinemas, when every musical instrument has been replaced by 100 gramophones, when every horse has been replaced by 100 cheap motorcars, when electrical ingenuity has made it possible for every child to hear his bedtime stories from a loudspeaker, when applied science has done everything possible with the materials on this earth to make life as interesting as possible, it will not be surprising if the population of the entire civilized world rapidly follows the fate of the Melanesians.[43]

The Melanesians, we are informed earlier, were a native community of the Melanesian archipelago who, because of the imposition of progressive forces of civilization upon them, had been deprived of all interest in life. The example of the Melanesians articulated in prose what Eliot also expressed thematically in his poetry, his perception of an urgent contemporary crisis precipitated by the inexorable course of modernization – the relentless forward-movement of industrial development, the invention of new technologies, and the introduction of modes of mass communication and media, the whole teleology of modern progress. The immense panorama of futility and anarchy, Eliot's description of the present age in his review of *Ulysses*, was thus corollary to modernity.

The patterning of allusion in 'The Waste Land' is thematically demonstrative of Eliot's narrative of modernity, the prominence of classical motifs, medieval folklore and renaissance drama contrasted with trivial snippets of contemporary culture, imagined gossip and English pub life. For Eliot, the products of modernity in the aesthetic field – the deterioration of artistic conventions into verisimilitude or realism, and of the descent of the sublime into sentimentality – had their beginnings in the Elizabethan period in the transition from feudal to renaissance art, and had led to a complete dissociation of sensibility at some point in the seventeenth century. This theory was developed most prominently in two well-known essays, 'Four Elizabethan Dramatists', first published in 1924, and 'The Metaphysical Poets', published earlier in 1921.[44] The poets of the seventeenth century, successors to the dramatists of the sixteenth, who were successors to the medieval and classical traditions, demonstrated a development of sensibility, an ability to synthesize feeling and thought in poetic expression. The complete dissociation of this sensibility occurred with the appearance of Milton and Dryden. Echoing his criticism of Shaw, he described the first effect of this dissociation as the refinement of a poetic language which was consequently incapable of mediating abstract feeling into art, a process in fact already begun in the Elizabethan age. The second effect occurred in the 'sentimental age' with the reflective traditions of the romantics. Eliot's repeated attacks on the personality of the artist elsewhere in his early literary criticism typified his rejection of the intellectual and humanist traditions of English Puritanism and the philosophy of the Enlightenment, with their shared emphases on rationality, individuality and progressive order, while also demonstrating his rejection of romantic sentimentalism and personal reflection. The task of the modern poet, reacting to the progressive developments of modernization, was thus to retrieve a refined sensibility, a task which, given the variety and complexity of contemporary civilization, required a 'more comprehensive, more allusive, more indirect' forcing or dislocation of language into meaning, 'a method curiously similar', he argued, 'to that of the "metaphysical poets"'.[45] Incising and extracting the better part of three centuries of literary history, Eliot would rewrite literary tradition to connect the poetry of the early twentieth century directly to that of the early seventeenth century.

While the narrator of 'The Waste Land' invokes fragments of renaissance texts to contrast with the tedious reality of contemporary existence, also included in this cacophony are numerous echoes of eastern religious mysticism. Eliot's example of the Melanesians similarly reflected his

interest in early twentieth-century anthropology and what were understood to be primitive cultures. Especially in the late nineteenth century,
the growth of an increasingly academic social anthropology reflected the
widespread interest in non-Western cultures which were seen as previous
to Western civilization along an evolutionary path and were, therefore,
demonstrations of the instinctual and non-rational mental functions
repressed in post-Enlightenment bourgeois European culture. In particular, Eliot was drawn to the studies of French anthropologists Lucien
Lévy-Bruhl and, later, Émile Durkheim.[46] Modernist primitivism, which
combined an interest in the more sophisticated early twentieth-century
anthropological studies of primarily southeast Asian pre-industrial cultures with the classicist studies of Cambridge academics such as Jane
Harrison and Gilbert Murray, Greek drama similarly 'primitive' in its
ritualistic origins, was thus an attempt to demonstrate the sociological
development of modern western culture and to romanticize its pre-
industrial phase.[47] So too for Eliot, the Melanesians represented the loss
of a ritualistic pre-industrial primitivism.

In a 1923 article for *Nation and Athenaeum*, in which he reviewed a
recent study of the Fool in *King Lear*, Eliot described the origins of the
drama as similarly primitive and ritualistic by drawing upon his reading
of Aristotle's *Poetics*, the drama an imitation by means of rhythm, a
'ritual, consisting of a set of repeated movements. . . essentially a dance'.[48]
Richard Halpern has recently demonstrated how Eliot here situated the
Elizabethan drama in a primitivist allegory, the Elizabethan drama demonstrative of this ritualistic rhythm, a position which would culminate
in his denigration of twentieth-century dramatic realism: 'It is the
rhythm, so utterly absent from modern drama, either verse or prose',
writes Eliot, 'and which interpreters of Shakespeare do their best to
suppress, which makes Massine and Charlie Chaplin the great actors
that they are, and which makes the juggling of Rastelli more cathartic
than a performance of "A Doll's House".'[49] Halpern notes that Eliot
would repeat this position in his later 'Four Elizabethan Dramatists', an
essay which also served as introduction to his 1934 volume *Elizabethan
Essays* and which was partly formed as a polemical response to William
Archer's 1923 *The Old Drama and the New*. For Archer, the Elizabethan
dramatists lived in a 'barbarous age, profoundly unconscious of its barbarism', and produced 'savage satires' and 'cynical tales of debauchery'
which, though they contained moments of humanitarian feeling, were
'obscured by dense clouds of puerility, vulgarity and barbarism'.[50] In
contrast to the 'primitive' qualities of the Elizabethans stood England's

New Drama, a principal representative of which was Shaw, though Archer's praise for Shaw was not unreserved. As Halpern notes, both Archer and Eliot were anthropologizing the Elizabethans, each for different purposes. But Archer was adopting a typically Shavian opinion of the renaissance as the unprivileged binary opposite of late nineteenth and early twentieth-century dramatic realism, though for Archer with the notable exception of Shakespeare. For Eliot, by comparison, the problem of the renaissance drama was precisely its engagement with modernity in the post-feudal period, the Elizabethans as equally disoriented as the Melanesians by the progressive forces of civilization (and perhaps here, Archer's 'lesser Elizabethan dramatists', for Eliot, excelled above Shakespeare by their relative primitivism).[51] Eliot's own primitivist narrative of the Elizabethan drama, written largely in response to Archer, not only provided the context for his few scattered criticisms of Shaw, but served as the principal rationale for the naturalist/symbolist antithesis which largely defined his modernist aesthetics.

While Eliot's primitivism was clearly conditioned by early twentieth-century ethnography and English neo-classicism, what I would like to emphasize is the undeniable resonance in 'The Beating of a Drum', as elsewhere in those essays of the 1920s, between Eliot's sense of art's ritualistic origins and the aesthetic theory of *The Birth of Tragedy*, Nietzsche's differentiation between Apollonian order and Dionysian dream state. If Shaw shared with Nietzsche an abstract opposition to bourgeois institutions of art and the Nietzschean cult of genius as exemplified in the diluted ideology of the superman, Eliot's own aesthetic theory would seem to have reiterated Nietzsche's sense of an emerging crisis in the genealogy of modern civilization, and his proclamation of the will to power. Eliot was not openly committed to Nietzsche's aesthetic theory, though he would appear to have known enough of Nietzsche in 1927 to denounce Shaw's idea of Nietzsche, 'whatever that is', as nothing like the real Nietzsche.[52] Still, Nietzsche's writing sets the pattern for Eliot's own literary imagination: his desire to regress from modernity, to rewrite the history of literary tradition and to connect with pre-industrial culture, all of which Nietzsche does in *The Birth of Tragedy*. Eliot's artist recovers and embraces the frenzied Dionysian spirit, the primitive rhythms and rituals which echoed through the Elizabethan drama. In so doing, the artist transcends the post-Enlightenment emphasis on individual rationality, what he described in 'Tradition and the Individual Talent' as the artist's personality. At the same time, however, the psychological dimension of Nietzsche's writing suggests a specifically individual or personal dimension which culminates in the valuation of the highly individuated artist figure and the utopian dimension of the artist's will to power. So too we find Eliot allegorizing modernity in a typically Nietzschean framework of cultural deterioration in his poetry and, in his essays on literature and literary criticism, attempting to identify his own art according to the self-imposed criteria of a modern paradigm, to be both new and significant, and to transform his work into an archetypally modern art.

As noted earlier, Shakespeare's writing served as a central literary example of Nietzsche's Dionysian ideal in *The Birth of Tragedy*. Interestingly, in this same 1927 essay on 'Shakespeare and the Stoicism of Seneca' in which he disparaged Shaw's understanding of Nietzsche, Eliot also made, if only briefly, the connection between Shakespeare, Nietzsche and aesthetic ideology. Here, he described their shared stoicism as 'the refuge for the individual in an indifferent or hostile world too big for him'.[53] First published in 1927, this essay represents one of his few sustained commentaries on Shakespeare, although the essay contains little of Shakespeare beyond the connection with Seneca, instead enmeshing the discussion with references to Chapman, Marlowe, and Dante.[54] The essay does begin, however, by mocking some contemporary examples of unconventional Shakespeare criticism and, noting the limitations of human understanding and literary criticism, the tendency of such criticism to draw Shakespeare in the image of its own political or social interpretive criteria: 'If they do not give us the real Shakespeare – if there is one – they at least give us several up-to-date Shakespeares.'[55] Eliot also admitted here his own high estimation of Shakespeare's greatness as poet and dramatist: 'And I would say that my only qualification for venturing to talk about him is', he wrote in a moment which reminds the reader of Shaw's own self-comparisons with Shakespeare, 'that I am *not* under the delusion that Shakespeare in the least resembles myself, either as I am or as I should like to imagine myself.'[56] But despite the veiled denigrations of his contemporaries and the distracting scope of his discussion, this essay offers, amidst references to both Shaw and Nietzsche, a significant ideological positioning of Shakespeare. Here we find Eliot's own Shakespeare placed, not in the renaissance, but in a modernist setting (an indifferent or hostile world), and demonstrative of a Nietzschean resistance to modernity (the individual seeking refuge), Shakespeare an early precursor in a transcendental literary tradition of Senecan stoicism.

Eliot's most remembered comments on Shakespeare, however, far from suggesting an idealization of Shakespeare in the vein of Nietzsche's

Übermensch, are famous for their disparaging criticism of *Hamlet*. First published in the *Athenaeum* in 1919, his essay 'Hamlet and his Problems', a review of recent book publications by J. M. Robertson and E. E. Stoll, is also known to contain the description of that elusive critical construct, the objective correlative.[57] This essay forms part of *The Sacred Wood*, published in 1920, Eliot's first collection of critical essays examining both the appreciation and the writing of drama and poetry. Eight years later, Eliot would come to disdain the stylistic faults of the volume and the tiresome 'pontifical solemnity' of his prescriptive tone.[58] Still, these essays, including 'Tradition and the Individual Talent' and 'The Possibility of a Poetic Drama', are among the most didactic and compelling of his essays on literature and literary criticism, and, as noted earlier, outline the basic tenets of an aesthetic ideology to which Eliot would return, in modified versions, throughout the 1920s. In speaking of Hamlet and his 'problems', Eliot was imitating Robertson and Stoll by parodying the kind of character criticism which tried to explain the cause of Hamlet's delay. For such sentimental idealists as Goethe and Coleridge, the character Hamlet had an especial temptation: 'These minds often find in Hamlet a vicarious existence for their own artistic realization.'[59] For Eliot, by comparison, the problems of *Hamlet* were inherent in Shakespeare's construction of the play, and were, therefore, aesthetic rather than thematic.

Beyond the allegory of literary tradition and the modern artist, what further links the essays of *The Sacred Wood* is their shared goal of defining standardized terms for the discussion of literary texts. Concepts like the 'historical sense' and the 'objective correlative' repudiated the intensely personal and subjective interpretations characteristic of eighteenth- and nineteenth-century (post-dissociation) critics in favour of recognizable and seemingly objective, though problematically obscure, principles for literary criticism. In a characteristic moment, Eliot argued: 'the work of art cannot be interpreted; there is nothing to interpret; we can only criticize it according to standards, in comparison to other works of art'.[60] In the case of *Hamlet*, the inherent problems of the play's construction were due primarily to the absence of an appropriate and objective formula of expression. Like his tradition and the artist's historical sense, the objective correlative represented a universalized formula for art's expression. In the absence of such a correlative, Shakespeare proved incapable of mediating the abstract experience of the work into an appropriately expressive structure: '*Hamlet*, like the sonnets', he wrote, 'is full of some stuff that the writer could not drag to light, contemplate, or manipulate into art.'[61] While both Nietzsche and Freud transformed the romantic introspective Hamlet by harnessing the language of psychology to distinguish between Shakespeare's conscious and sub- or false-conscious fields of aesthetic imagination, by comparison, Eliot would instead problematize not only the romantic interpretations of *Hamlet*, but also Shakespeare's writing, by invoking the same distinctions, the 'stuff' which Shakespeare could not drag to light.

The appeal of both Robertson and Stoll to Eliot lay in what appeared to be their scientific methodology, their claim to evaluating rather than interpreting the work. Robertson was a journalist, liberal free-thinker and Member of Parliament between 1906 and 1918, as well as a private literary scholar inculcated with the principles of metrical analysis and scientism of the New Shakespere Society. Among the volumes of critical analysis which were ever-multiplying through the late nineteenth century, studies in attribution and biographical speculation were numerous. Literary societies such as the New Shakespere Society, founded in 1874 by the mathematician F. J. Furnivall, combined a traditional humanist insistence upon Shakespeare's genius with a characteristically Victorian belief in the principles of modernity, the values of scientific progress and development, as advertised by their newness. In what would become a remarkably sustained attempt to 'decode' the authorship of what he deemed were Shakespeare's lesser plays and passages, Robertson would complete his five-volume analysis of the Shakespeare canon in 1930.[62] Rather than on principles of scientific analysis, however, Robertson would rely more and more upon his own preconceived ideal of Shakespeare's literary quality, a point noted by E. K. Chambers in his 1924 British Academy Shakespeare Lecture in which he famously denounced Robertson's works as studies in canonical 'disintegration'.[63]

In 1919, however, Eliot praised both Robertson and Stoll for 'moving in the other direction' of romantic idealization in favour of an historical and intellectually rigorous criticism. That Eliot would pit his own modern criteria for literary criticism against romantic interpreters Goethe and Coleridge by invoking the works of Robertson and Stoll is not without some irony given their equally idealistic belief in Shakespeare's greatness. More important, however, was their clear disavowal of a critical tradition of emblematizing the character Hamlet. By disintegrating the canonical status of *Hamlet*, disintegrationist critics such as Robertson threatened to dislodge the play from the cultural centrality it had achieved in the nineteenth century. From literary appreciation, cultural appropriation, and topical allusion to theatrical production and review, no

other play in the canon rivalled the critical response and cultural identification which *Hamlet* inspired through the nineteenth century; Hamlet,
read as Shakespeare's literary doppelganger and the ideal representation
of character in art, would reverberate from romanticism through to
psychoanalysis.[64] In 1911, Eliot's J. Alfred Prufrock, rejecting such romanticized identities, declared, 'No! I am not Prince Hamlet, nor was meant
to be.'[65] Prufrock denies any similarity to Hamlet with a sense of disappointment and rejection, instead aligning himself with the comical
Polonius,

> Deferential, glad to be of use,
> Politic, cautious, and meticulous;
> Full of high sentence, but a bit obtuse;
> At times, indeed, almost ridiculous –
> Almost, at times, the Fool.

This disavowal of identification with Hamlet, however, is difficult to read
without a sense of irony given Eliot's later criticism of the play's romantic
interpreters. Similarly, in 1919, the disintegrationist theories of *Hamlet*
proved an especial temptation for Eliot since, by repudiating the romanticizing of both the character and the play's author, he was able to contrast
the romantic tradition against his own aesthetic criteria for modern art.

Eliot's disdain for the nineteenth century's obsession with Shakespeare
explains in part his desire to promote the drama of Shakespeare's contemporaries and the poetry of the 'metaphysicals'. At some points in those
essays of the 1920s, Shakespeare appears, in the company of his much
underrated contemporaries, in the guise of renaissance artist, his writing
demonstrative of a poetic sensibility essential to the modern artist. At
other points, Shakespeare appears in the guise of a post-renaissance
romantic whose artistic failings are demonstrative of the dissociation of
sensibility circa Milton and Dryden, and by that token, is thus excluded
from the privileged status enjoyed by his true contemporaries. As with
Shaw, though by a different logic, Eliot's anti-romantic allegory of literary
tradition required a similar toppling of Shakespeare. Unlike Shaw, Eliot
preferred aestheticism to political propaganda, and despite a general
conservatism which would become more conspicuous in his Catholic
years, he was not openly associated with political or social ideologists
such as the Fabians.[66] Nor, unlike Pound, would the urgency and
declamatory authoritarianism of his writing lead to overt associations
with or idealizations of contemporary political movements such as
fascism, thus sparing his post-war reputation. Eliot's essays on literature

and literary criticism, and especially the essays of *The Sacred Wood*, are
starkly apolitical. He would probably have recoiled from the rhetoric
of revolution which Shaw readily embraced to describe the conflict
between old and new, with its suggestion of generational class conflict.
Elsewhere in his writing, however, in particular, in his 'London Letters'
written for the *Dial* between 1921 and 1922 as London correspondent,
Eliot would equate the bourgeois culture of the nineteenth century, to
which the romantic Shakespeare was firmly connected, with an emerging
mass culture in the twentieth century. These letters, therefore, situate
his otherwise apolitical literary essays in a decisively politicized context;
as in the case of Shaw, in the context of a crisis of modernity rendered
in the language of a conflict between nineteenth-century aesthetic traditions and the changing class and gender relations of twentieth-century
England.

What distinguishes the 'London Letters' from the essays of, for
example, *The Sacred Wood*, is their socially oriented discussion of contemporary theatre and art. Although the distinction is somewhat arbitrary
since most of the articles in *The Sacred Wood* began their life as book
reviews and articles published for similar magazines, the 'London Letters',
read collectively, communicate a sustained diatribe against an 'insurgent
middle-class' which Eliot feared had achieved economic, political and
ideological hegemony.[67] Thus, the middle classes (the threat was multiple) are disparaged throughout the letters for lacking in individuals
(a position which contrasts sharply with Eliot's repeated demand that
the artist forego personality), for being morally corrupt, for instilling
listless apathy with respect to the arts, and for reducing other classes to
a similar state of protoplasm.[68] Rather than represent a coherent class
discourse, however, the anxieties expressed in the letters would appear to
suggest a fear of the growing massification of culture, or mass culture,
which Eliot equated with middle-class culture. Accordingly, his images of
middle-class art are drawn in the terms of indiscriminate consumption
and mass media; the cheap and rapid-breeding cinema, the lifeless revue,
gramophones, telephones, and London's large, stagnant theatres such
as His Majesty's. Read within the context of these letters, the individual
talent of *The Sacred Wood*, striving to reconnect with a pre-industrial
spirit of art, is threatened by the undifferentiated bolus of mass-culture
society.

While the letters consistently indict the middle classes for levelling
hierarchy and blurring distinction, by comparison, they commend the
lower classes for precisely the opposite reason, for maintaining social

distinction. The most remarkable example of such praise occurs in the 'London Letter' which is better remembered as Eliot's eulogy for the music-hall entertainer Marie Lloyd. This is the same letter which also contains Eliot's reference to the social psychologist W. H. R. Rivers' *Essays on the Depopulation of Melanesia.* The death of Lloyd, who was 'the expressive figure of the lower classes', signalled the death of the music-hall, and the simultaneous encroachment upon the lower-class of middle-class entertainments such as to be found in the cinema.[69] The example of the Melanesians invoked at the end of the letter is offered as an analogy to the situation of the lower-class, the Melanesians' loss of all interest in life as the product of progressive technological civilization mirroring the absorption of the formerly vibrant lower-class within the apathetic middle-class, and the dissolution of a distinct social class system. Eliot's praise for Marie Lloyd and the music-hall experience demonstrated, here as elsewhere, his genuine interest in and sense of group association with an idealized working-class culture – remember Eliot's praise for Massine, Chaplin and Rastelli as expressive of the ritualistic beating of the drum – with contrasts directly with the dislocation and anxiety experienced by the isolated individual in his poetry.[70] The fact that Marie Lloyd happens to be a female artist who is commended for her personality as expressive of the lower classes, however, would also seem to contrast with Eliot's demand for the artist's impersonality in *The Sacred Wood* essays. By comparison with his outspoken praise for Lloyd, Eliot's literary essays appear silently committed to a text-based aristocracy of male art.[71]

The significance of Eliot's description of class culture in the 'London Letters' to his literary essays lies in that equation between the middle-class and the growing massification of industrial society. These letters provide the formula in which the crisis of modernization is characterized as social equalization, the growing mass-consumption culture abetting the ever-increasing numbers of the middle-class. Whereas the 'London Letters' articulate a discretely gendered class discourse as reaction to the complex social reorganization of the period, Eliot's literary essays actively engaged with the regulation of a redefined literary art. Attempting to regulate the production and reception of art according to standardized aesthetic forms, constructs such as a transhistorical sense of tradition rejected the teleology of industrial development, renewing apparatuses of cultural legitimation made redundant in a modernized society; and accordingly, Eliot's writing would later serve as an important feature of professional academic literary criticism, his aesthetic constructs recurring in the criticism of academics such as G. Wilson Knight and Northrop Frye.[72] By insisting upon the primitive origins of literature and its aesthetic autonomy, Eliot's literary art transcended material social transformations of early twentieth-century English society such as the rise of middle-class affluence, the increasing advocacy of the Suffrage movement culminating in the 1918 Representation of the People Act, and the liberalization of education which followed the Education Act of 1870. These social phenomena all demanded new systems of regulation and standardization to accommodate the entrance of formerly excluded groups into an increasingly massified and commercial culture industry.

If his literary essays and poetry can be seen to rehearse a typically Nietzschean allegory of art and modernity, when read against his 'London Letters' they also anticipate the development of both late nineteenth and early twentieth-century anti-bourgeois rhetoric, such as that of Nietzsche and Shaw, in twentieth-century Marxist critiques of mass culture. The idea that the increasingly commercial, mass-produced work of art in industrial capitalism, and the resulting growth of a mass culture audience inculcated with the values of a liberal bourgeois middle-class, equals a necessary deterioration of culture, has been a central tenet of Marxist cultural critique; from Walter Benjamin, who described this process as the 'bourgeoisification' of the artwork, to Jürgen Habermas, who would later describe the transition from a culture-debating to a culture-consuming public.[73] While Eliot's literary essays functioned to redefine literary art as aesthetically autonomous, in his scattered social commentary, Eliot articulated his vision of a bourgeois commercial culture which threatened to multiply and expand with the increasing development of technology and the application of that technology to mass media. For Eliot, the commercial dimension of art posed the greatest challenge to the artist, and necessitated his insistence upon its autonomy. Although it necessarily existed within the system of commercial enterprise and thus served ends beyond itself, the work of art, Eliot argued, was 'not required to be aware of these ends, and indeed performs its function, whatever that may be, according to various theories of value, much better by indifference to them'.[74] In the case of both Shaw and Eliot, their prescriptions for a modern art would engage with the libidinal spirit of the modern while pitting the artwork against the increasingly commercial culture industry of modern industrialized society.

As with Shaw, Eliot's disdain for the growth of bourgeois culture and the attendant commercialization of art would resonate in his contempt for the mainstream theatres of London's West End. With a rhetorical vigour, he strongly denounced the penchant for grand and expensive pictorial spectacle which dominated production, lamenting, 'England sits in her weeds: eleven theatres are on the point of closing, as the public will no longer pay the prices required by the cost'.[75] Indeed, the problem with contemporary Shakespeare was largely theatrical, the modern productions of the plays mired by stagnant conventions, strained through the nineteenth century and dwarfed to the dimensions of histrionic non-entities such as Sir Johnston Forbes-Robertson and Sir Frank Benson.[76] Whereas Shaw would champion the drama of naturalism to counter the hegemony of bourgeois productions of Shakespeare in the theatre, Eliot would turn to the productions of non-Shakespearean renaissance drama by private subscription companies such as the Phoenix Society, whose namesake bird symbolized their project of dramatic revival, writing several reviews through the 1920s. By the mid-1920s, he would also begin to think about his own dramatic writing. In an introduction for an edition of the dramatic poem *Savonarola* edited by his mother Charlotte Eliot, Eliot outlined his programme for a new type of drama predicated upon, once again, the primitive rhythms of art: 'The next form of drama will have to be a verse drama but in new verse forms. Perhaps the conditions of modern life (think how large a part is now played in our sensory life by the internal combustion engine!) have altered our perception of rhythms.'[77] As elsewhere, the possibility of a poetic drama represented the synthesis of thought and emotion in a structured verse form, a form which, unlike the pseudo-philosophical dramas of Shaw, would be 'capable of greater variation and of expressing more varied types of society, than any other'.[78] Such an ideal drama, however, would have to be a closet drama, to be read or declaimed rather than acted, far removed from the exigencies of commercial production and the whims of producers and actors.

The problem with the contemporary drama, therefore, was not solely one of a dissociation of literary sensibility or an absence of poetic form, as his criticism of Shaw would suggest, but also a problem of artistic control in a socially conditioned, increasingly commercial theatre. If only briefly employing the language of rebellion characteristic of Shaw, Eliot would thus claim in 1924: 'I rebel against most performances of Shakespeare's plays because I want a direct relationship between the work of art and myself.'[79] In contrast to Shaw's New Drama revolution, Eliot's own aesthetic prescriptions engaged with the allegory of modernity by appealing to historical continuity, by rewriting literary tradition and defining the modern artist's historical sense, and by envisioning a modern literary art which necessarily contrasted with and excluded Shaw. What these two writers shared, however, was a desire to disconnect modern literature and theatrical practice from the nineteenth century, from the idealizing and romanticizing tendencies of literary appreciation and theatrical production, and from association with what they understood to be the bourgeois commercialism of an increasingly massified culture industry. If they failed to topple Shakespeare in the early twentieth century, what they helped to do was disengage Shakespeare from the nineteenth century and to prepare him for the anti-commercial academic and national theatre cultures of the twentieth century.

CHAPTER 2

Sex, lies and historical fictions

In the preface to *Shakespeare and his Love*, a play written over a period of years and, though still not yet produced, finally published in 1910, Frank Harris accused George Bernard Shaw of plagiarizing his Shakespeare theories. Set in the late sixteenth century, at a critical juncture in Shakespeare's sonnet period, the play dramatizes Harris' theory: that Shakespeare's writing was inspired by his friendship with the young Lord William Herbert who, in the play, acts on behalf of Shakespeare to court the object of Shakespeare's infatuation, Mary Fitton, a lady of Queen Elizabeth's court. Herbert subsequently betrays Shakespeare through his own affair with Fitton. The Earl of Pembroke after the death of his father in 1601, a patron of Shakespeare's company and, with his brother, Philip, dedicatee of the First Folio of 1623, Herbert was, in Harris' theory, the mysterious 'onlie begetter of these insuing sonnets Mr W. H.', as the inscription on the title page of the 1609 Quarto edition reads. Herbert was, therefore, also the youth to whom sonnets 1 to 126 are addressed, a youth of wealth, beauty and status. Fitton, on the other hand, was the mysterious 'dark lady', supposed inspiration for the extremes of passion and bitterness expressed in the later grouping of sonnets, 127 to 152. Historically, Fitton was the centre of a court disgrace involving an affair with William Herbert, also in 1601, which is the primary evidence supporting their association.[1] *Shakespeare and his Love* dramatizes this supposedly triangular affair between Shakespeare, Fitton and Herbert, in the five-act structure, according to Harris, of a Shakespearean history.

The Pembroke–Fitton theory is also the subject of Shaw's play, *The Dark Lady of the Sonnets*, written and performed in 1910 and first published in English in 1914 with a preface by Shaw. Having read the announcement in the *Observer* (13 November 1910) that Shaw's play was to be produced by the National Shakespeare Memorial Committee, and having also read the accompanying interview drafted by Shaw which publicized the Pembroke–Fitton theory, Harris was incensed and refused either to see or read the play: 'it looks as if he had annexed my theory bodily so far as he can understand it', complained Harris, 'and the characters to boot'.[2] Unfamiliar with Shaw's play, Harris was, therefore, unaware that this very short work, a comic *pièce d'occasion*, was written as a platform for promoting the National Theatre cause for a single fund-raising event.[3] In the 1914 preface to the play, Shaw actually denied the viability of the Pembroke–Fitton theory altogether: his play was origin-ally to have been written by Edith Lyttleton, who devised the plot which Shaw then adopted.[4] Indeed, Mary Fitton is only a minor character in his play: one midsummer night, the young Shakespeare steals into the gardens of Whitehall to meet his mistress, and finds instead Queen Elizabeth, disguised by a cloak and the dark. Without an original thought of his own and with an extremely poor memory, Shaw's Shakespeare scribbles on his tablets the Queen's musical phrases – 'All the perfumes of Arabia will not whiten this Tudor hand', 'Sir, you are overbold. Season your admiration for a while' – for later use.[5] The dark lady is quickly supplanted by the cloaked lady as the object of Shakespeare's desire, and so, *The Dark Lady of the Sonnets*, far from endorsing the Fitton theory, ironically reflects the fictive Shakespeare's obsession with the pale virgin Queen. While Shakespeare's fickle infatuations serve as a comic back-drop to Shaw's plea for a National Theatre, nevertheless, the advertise-ment of the play and Harris' resulting indignation propelled Harris finally to publish his own, entirely earnest, dramatization of Shakespeare's supposed affair with Fitton.

Apologizing for the literary and academic tone of his writing, Harris wrote in his preface to *Shakespeare and his Love*: 'It seemed to me that no one had the right to treat the life-story, the soul-tragedy of a Shakespeare as the mere stuff of a play.'[6] Harris could introduce his play with such an apology because, not only was he not primarily a dramatist, he had treated the subject of Shakespeare's supposed sexual biography in a longer critical volume, *The Man Shakespeare and His Tragic Life Story*, published one year prior in 1909.[7] Adapted and extended from a popu-lar series of articles written in 1898 for the *Saturday Review*, for which Harris was also the editor and owner at the time, *The Man Shakespeare* explored the triangular relationship dramatized in *Shakespeare and his Love*, supplying numerous examples of internal textual 'evidence' – quotations and character profiles derived from Harris' reading of Shakespeare. For Harris, all of Shakespeare's writing, and especially the plays (as opposed to the sonnets), could be interpreted according to Shakespeare's biography. Indeed, in the absence of solid biographical facts about Shakespeare, the plays were the historical texts which revealed episodes in Shakespeare's life otherwise undocumented: 'it is possible from Shakespeare's writing', argued Harris 'to establish beyond doubt the main features of his character and the chief incidents of his life'.[8] More importantly, these episodes concerned, almost single-mindedly, Shakespeare's sexual misfortunes: the first, being wooed and then wounded by an older woman, his estranged wife Anne Hathaway, was allegorized in *Venus and Adonis*; the second, and more significant, betrayal by Fitton, was repeatedly dramatized throughout his later plays. While the entire canon, written over the course of Shakespeare's life, could be interpreted broadly according to a biographical chronology, for Harris, it was Shakespeare's *Hamlet*, written in the period immediately following his affair with and betrayal by Fitton, which was his greatest and most self-revealing drama. In particular, Hamlet the character was the archetype of Shakespeare's own personality: 'with many necessary limitations', Harris proposed, 'Hamlet is indeed a revelation of some of the most characteristic traits of Shakespeare.'[9] Insofar as Hamlet was Shakespeare, Shakespeare therefore painted Hamlet over and over again, 'as Macbeth and Jaques, Angelo, Orsino, Lear, Posthumus, Prospero and other heroes'.[10] While Harris' theories about Shakespeare's sexual biography were the impetus for his dramatic exploration in *Shakespeare and his Love*, they had been explained at great length one year prior in *The Man Shakespeare*: 'The play', explained Harris in his preface, 'therefore, as a play is full of faults.'[11] As a dramatic exploration of and companion piece to the theories of *The Man Shakespeare*, the play was faulted not by its fictive elaboration of biographical theory, but by its strict adherence to academic facts about Shakespeare's life demonstrated by Harris' internal evidence.

Born in western Ireland in 1855 and educated in America, Harris was a highly literate, though notoriously boorish, London socialite, writer, editor and speculator. Extremely well read, fluent in French and German, and with a palate for expensive wine and food, Harris would often entertain London's literary elite in fine restaurants; but with his penchant for making inflammatory declarations, his explicit discussions of sex, and his booming bass voice, he also had several detractors. Shaw called Harris a buccaneer, describing him as 'a man of splendid visions, unreasonable expectations, fierce appetites which he was unable to relate to anything except to romantic literature, and especially to the impetuous rhetoric of Shakespeare'.[12] Oscar Wilde also summarized the scope of Harris' social influence: 'Frank Harris has been received in all the great houses – once!'[13]

Harris achieved modest critical success with his 1895 collection, *Elder Conklin and Other Stories*, as well as the 1901 *Montes the Matador and Other Stories*, and in 1899, he wrote and produced the play *Mr and Mrs Daventry*, based on a plot bought from Oscar Wilde, for a profitable long run.[14] As well as writing fiction and the occasional drama, Harris edited numerous newspapers and magazines, including the *Evening News*, *Fortnightly Review*, *Saturday Review*, *Vanity Fair*, and *Pearson's*. Between 1915 and 1927, Harris also published a series of biographical exposés he titled *Contemporary Portraits*, which were based on his personal meetings with and intimate knowledge of contemporary artists and literary figures, among them, Carlyle, Whistler, Browning, Swinburne, Guy de Maupassant and Anatole France.[15]

Titillation, prudery, even outrage and disgust, were not uncommon reactions to the publication of his portraits. In 1922, Harris began publishing his five-volume autobiography, *My Life and Loves*, which was scandalous in its description of his numerous sexual encounters.[16] The language and graphic details Harris used to describe these encounters remain explicit even by contemporary standards. A sex enthusiast, Harris was deliberate in his intention to shock the English out of the priggish snobbery, moral decorum and reverence for tradition which he saw as stifling the development of culture and art. The volumes, however, whose sales were initially blocked in England, had the rather adverse affect of isolating Harris from influential friends and literary associates, while booksellers and publishers dropped his other works out of circulation.[17] But in 1909, his full-length study of Shakespeare, which applied the same sexual emphasis to his biographical criticism of Shakespeare, was something of a sensation, eliciting enthusiastic acclaim. The *Saturday Review*, albeit not without a certain bias, praised *The Man Shakespeare* as 'a brilliant and fascinating tour de force. As a book concerned with the greatest poetry, we assign to it critical merit of the first order. . . we predict for it a permanent importance' (20 November 1909). In America, where it was simultaneously released, the *New York Times* claimed: 'This is the book for which we have waited a lifetime' (6 November 1909). The American *Independent* also proclaimed it a 'remarkable book, ingeniously conceived, and based on a comprehensive knowledge of the bard's works' (18 November 1909). Not all reviews were positive, but those which criticized *The Man Shakespeare* were equally extreme in their denunciations. The *Spectator*, for example, slated Harris: 'his theory is totally unrelated to fact, and he brings in support of it no evidence which a competent historian could accept' (13 December 1909). That Harris' study could generate such contradictory reactions testifies to the sense of sensation, perhaps even scandal, which surrounded its publication.

In the 1914 preface to *The Dark Lady of the Sonnets*, Shaw would also praise Harris as a critic with a 'range of sympathy and understanding' and *The Man Shakespeare* as one of the best books of its generation on Shakespeare.[18] Shaw acknowledged his debt to Harris despite the controversy which the latter had attempted to stir during the publication of *Shakespeare and his Love*. However, though he defended the serious quality of Harris' play compared to his own 'brief trifle', Shaw correctly credited the late nineteenth-century editor of the sonnets, Thomas Tyler, who first propounded the Pembroke–Fitton theory in an 1886 photofacsimile edition of the Quarto, and later developed that theory in his 1890 typeset edition.[19] The association of 'W. H.' with Pembroke was not original to Tyler, having been first suggested in the early nineteenth century.[20] The association of Fitton with the dark lady, however, represented Tyler's original contribution to the Victorian fascination with Shakespeare's biography. Indeed, both the substance of Harris' theories, as well as his methodology, descended in a direct line from late nineteenth-century sonnet study. Tyler, for example, similarly argued in his longer introduction in the 1890 edition that Shakespeare's writing was biographical, his dramas 'a many-coloured veil, concealing, or but imperfectly and intermittently disclosing, the soul of the artificer'; though Tyler, unlike Harris, still accorded a special significance to the sonnets, in which 'we come nearer to that august presence, and attain a more continuous, if not unrestricted, view'.[21] Arthur Acheson also argued in his 1903 *Shakespeare and the Rival Poets* that Shakespeare, fired by the passion and intensity of his love for the dark lady (though in this case, not Fitton), 'produced in those years the marvelous rhapsodies of love in "Romeo and Juliet," "Love's Labour's Lost," and other of his love plays'.[22] Even the central role played by *Hamlet*, as argued by Harris, was not without precedent. In a rather remarkable work, *Shakespeare Self-Revealed*, published in 1904 under the initials J. M., the author proposed that Shakespeare took an active interest in publishing the second legitimate quarto of *Hamlet* because the play demonstrated a biographical picture which would be amplified in the sonnets: 'He constituted it that child of his mind which was to be in existence in order that the picture presented in the Sonnets might be of interest and might be believed.'[23]

In addition to the numerous single-volume editions of the sonnets which were appearing through the late nineteenth and early twentieth centuries, several studies of Shakespearean biography were also exploring the possible identities of W. H. and the dark lady. The late nineteenth and early twentieth centuries were witness to a brief proliferation in Shakespeare biographies which perhaps culminated with the volumes by Sydney Lee and F. J. Furnivall.[24] As with Lee and Furnivall, most sonnet enthusiasts favoured Henry Wriothesley, the Earl of Southampton, above Pembroke, though Tyler's identification of Fitton with the dark lady must have been briefly exciting. But by 1909, years after Lee's and Furnivall's conservative biographies, Tyler's theory had long been out of fashion, and so Harris could lay claim to the Pembroke–Fitton theory as his own with little notice. In his preface to *The Dark Lady of the Sonnets*, Shaw claimed to have been present at the birth of the theory, in the British Museum during the 1880s when both Tyler and Shaw were daily readers, and during which time they would engage in lengthy discussions about Shakespeare. This was the extent of Shaw's interest, so he claimed: to defend the work of Tyler which, pitifully, was the only progeny of a man 'of such astonishing and crushing ugliness', Shaw describing him as 'waistless, neckless, ankleless' and with a monstrous goiter on his chin.[25] Accordingly, Shaw complained that, 'when I, as a pious duty to Tyler's ghost, reminded the world that it was to Tyler we owed the Fitton theory, Frank Harris, who clearly had not a notion of what had first put Mary into his head, believed, I think, that I had invented Tyler expressly for his discomfiture'.[26] In this manner, Shaw's preface cleverly answered Harris' charge of plagiarism with a counter-charge of plagiarism, made all the worse by the pitiful figure of Tyler.

Shaw's interest in Shakespeare's biography, however, was limited. By portraying Shakespeare as an absentminded pillager of other people's phrases, prone to romantic infatuations and wistful declarations of his passion, Shaw was, unlike Harris, satirizing the tendency of nineteenth-century Shakespeare biographers and critics to romanticize and idealize Shakespeare the man. Although he admired much of Shakespeare's writing, for Shaw, Shakespeare was an Elizabethan whose dramas failed to reflect the social conditions of modern society. Satirizing Shakespeare was one way to promote the 'New Drama' which Shaw championed, particularly the drama of naturalists such as Ibsen and Chekhov, not to mention his own few plays. That cultural monolith, Shakespeare, insofar as he represented the nineteenth-century traditions of the actor-manager theatre and the romantic idealizations of literary appreciation, was a primary obstacle to the achievement of his envisioned National Theatre and drama. What Shaw therefore admired about Harris' Shakespeare criticism was the forthrightness and disregard for decorum with which

Harris exposed the elements of Shakespeare's biography otherwise dis-tasteful to Edwardian society. Of Harris' 1909 *The Man Shakespeare*, Shaw wrote of his great delight to see the literary world of London discomfited by the warm critical reception of such a provocative and unconventional interpretation: 'There is a precise realism and an unsmiling, measured, determined sincerity which gives a strange dignity to the work of one whose fixed practice and ungovernable impulse it is to kick conventional dignity whenever he sees it.'[27] Shaw's praise for Harris as a buccaneer and the 'utter contrary' of fastidious refinement, delicacy of taste, correct-ness of manner and tone, high academic distinction and literary repu-tation were of the highest order.[28] Despite Harris' own claim that his Fitton theory was 'so contrary to tradition . . . and so contemptuous of authority', a true 'discovery', the theory itself was not without nineteenth-century precedent.[29] But for Shaw, the value of *The Man Shakespeare* was its clear disavowal of the conventional dignity associated with Shakespeare:

For, after all, what is the secret of the hopeless failure of the academic Bardolaters to give us a credible or even interesting Shakespear, and the easy triumph of Mr Harris in giving us both? Simply that Mr Harris has assumed that he was dealing with a man, while the others have assumed that they were writing about a god, and have therefore rejected every consideration of fact, tradition, or interpretation, that pointed to any human imperfection in their hero.[30]

Shaw did not write sustained literary criticism, and so he probably expected that Harris' books would outlive his own few musings related to Shakespeare which were scattered throughout the prefaces to his plays, in short pamphlets and in his theatre reviews.[31] Thus, in the 1914 preface to *The Dark Lady of the Sonnets*, Shaw promoted *Shakespeare and his Love* as the more serious work, 'both in size, intention, and quality'.[32] For Shaw, however, more important than Harris' actual theories were the effect they had on the established traditions of Shakespeare appreci-ation. Shaw, with the mere critical distance of four years, could suc-cinctly pinpoint the significance of Harris' Shakespeare criticism; that is, even while Harris developed, if not plagiarized, the impressionis-tic studies of nineteenth-century biographers and interpreters, the titil-lating suggestion of a sexually charged Shakespeare and Harris' disregard for conventional taste contributed to an entirely new biographical portrait of Shakespeare. *The Man Shakespeare* was, for Shaw, a revolu-tionary work of Shakespeare criticism. Like Shaw's own writing on the subject of Shakespeare, Harris' psychosexual fictions of Shakespeare,

both his critical volumes and his play, broke with the idealizing sentimentality of nineteenth-century literary appreciation and also anticipated a mode of textual reading which would culminate in the
psychoanalytic narrative of Shakespeare's authorship.

BIOGRAPHICAL CRITICISM

Writing in 1933, Carl Jung described the Victorian era in decidedly
derogatory language as 'a period of repression, a convulsive attempt to
keep artificially alive by moralizings, anaemic ideals framed in a bourgeois
setting'.[33] This, suggested Jung, was the historical matrix which preceded
Freud and which formed his groundwork, making a phenomenon like
Freudian psychoanalysis necessary. Once a disciple of Freud's fledgling
psychological medicine, Jung would move on to repudiate the basic
doctrines of Freudian psychoanalysis; in particular, Freud's theories of
sexual repression, and especially, the Oedipus complex, which is a central
premise of *The Interpretation of Dreams*. Rather than a herald of twentieth-century psychological medicine, Freud, argued Jung, was more correctly viewed as a reaction to the nineteenth century, 'as an exponent of
the *ressentiment* of the incoming century against the nineteenth, with its
allusions, its hypocrisy, its half-ignorance, its false, overwrought feelings,
its shallow morality, its artificial, sapless religiosity, and its lamentable
taste'.[34] It was precisely Freud's main thesis, Jung argued, the doctrine of
sexual repression, which was most clearly conditioned by its historical
context: the idea of the unconscious as the receptacle for repressed
infantile sexuality was drawn directly from and reacted to the Victorian
conception of human consciousness as idealistic, counterfeited personality
concealing a darker background, a subconscious plane which Freud
sought to expose and uncover in the language of sexual desire and fantasy. Though Jung disagreed strongly with the central emphasis which
Freudian psychoanalysis placed on the sexual instinct as the stimulus for
all complex psychic phenomena, nevertheless, the chief significance of
Freud's theories was in their historical context as a reaction to the mental
'pussyfooting' of Victorian psychology: 'Like Nietzsche, like the Great
War, so too Freud (and his literary replica, Joyce), is an answer to the
sickness of the nineteenth century.'[35]

This is also the historical matrix out of which Shaw and Harris emerged,
both of whom were prominent writers and artists who began their careers in the late Victorian period and whose primary works challenged the
moral precepts and bourgeois sensibilities of nineteenth-century England.

Not unlike Freud's Oedipal theories in *The Interpretation of Dreams*, the
biographical theories of *The Man Shakespeare* were derived from largely
impressionistic literary interpretations, and were almost absurd in their
persistent emphasis on the central importance of Shakespeare's thwarted
sexual desires. In one of the few critical condemnations, the *Spectator* would
argue of Harris: 'his theory is totally unrelated to fact, and he brings in
support of it no evidence which a competent historian could accept. . . The
book resembles more those scandalous memoirs which have a certain vogue
at the present time than a work of criticism' (18 December 1909). In 1911,
Harris published his second volume of Shakespeare criticism, *The Women
of Shakespeare's Plays*, drawn from his series of articles written for the
English Review between 1910 and 1911.[36] Though his second full volume
of Shakespeare criticism complemented the style of biographical portraiture of *The Man Shakespeare*, his theory that all of Shakespeare's female
characters either reflected a female projection of Shakespeare himself – he
had originally intended to call the volume *The Woman Shakespeare* – or
were portraits of the four women in Shakespeare's life – his mother, his
wife, his mistress or his daughter – proved too much for the critics. The
prestigious *Dial* magazine, for example, wrote: 'If Mr. Harris were not so
serious and evidently convinced by his own reasoning, we should be
disposed to think it all a deliberate hoax, perpetrated possibly with the
object of showing the Baconians how, with persistence enough, one can
read anything he pleases into the text of Shakespeare' (16 March 1913).
Widespread denunciations of *The Women of Shakespeare* as 'uninstructed'
(*Nation*, 26 December 1912) would work retroactively to mire critical
appreciation of *The Man Shakespeare*. In 1909, however, Harris' blend of
biography, criticism and personal reflection was briefly sensational, because, as Shaw would note, it broke radically from nineteenth-century
traditions of Shakespeare idolatry. The analogy initiated by Jung between
Freud, Nietzsche, Joyce and the First World War served to categorize their
texts in the context of a (violent) reactionary antipathy to a pathologized
nineteenth century, in a narrative of epistemic rupture with nineteenth-
century bourgeois ideology. Although Harris was a minor literary figure
and critic whose writing would fail to demonstrate any significant lon-
gevity, *The Man Shakespeare* was arguably demonstrative of a similar
reaction to nineteenth-century Shakespeare criticism.

In its first printing, *The Man Shakespeare*, with its remarkable suggestion of Shakespeare's personal tragedy, was an impressive and substantial volume; at more than 400 pages, significantly longer than Walter
Raleigh's biographical study, *Shakespeare*, published in 1907, and rivalling

in length A. C. Bradley's 1904 *Shakespearean Tragedy*.[37] Along with the few volumes written by, among others, Furnivall, Lee, Edward Dowden and J. M. Robertson, these two latter works were arguably the most significant of the few academic monographs published in the first decade of the twentieth century. Instead, the Shakespeare book market was dominated by single-volume editions of the plays, which contained long critical introductions after the fashion of the nineteenth-century Cambridge single-play edition series, reprints of seminal nineteenth-century essays and lectures by Coleridge, Hazlitt, and Johnson, and the less formal criticism and appreciation of Shakespeare enthusiasts and essayists like Harris.[38] These works were characteristic of a less formal and arguably more popular style of Shakespeare essay writing common in the late Victorian period, a style which blended literary reading and personal reflection in a first-person memoir and which typically claimed to have discovered, revealed or deciphered the truth hidden within. The titles of contemporary volumes such as *Shakespeare's True Life*, *The Problem of the Shakespeare Plays*, *Shakespeare Self-Revealed* and *The Shakespeare Enigma*, all similarly advertised their objective: to explain Shakespeare's writing in the sonnets and plays according to the secret or mystery of his life.[39] Harris' own style, while typical of the Victorian essayist, also echoed the anecdotal biography exemplified in his *Contemporary Portraits*. This perhaps explains the relative popularity of *The Man Shakespeare*, a work which tapped into popular contemporary modes of writing. For subject matter, however, Harris' immediate predecessors were more conservative academic biographers such as Lee, Furnivall, and Raleigh, and literary critics such as Bradley.

As many recent scholars have demonstrated, professional literary studies in English largely originated with Raleigh and Bradley.[40] Raleigh was the first Chair in English Literature at Oxford, elected to the post in 1904, after which time he published his 1907 *Shakespeare* for the English Men of Letters series, a work which helped to institutionalize the study of English in a national university curriculum.[41] Bradley was the Oxford Chair of Poetry between 1901 and 1905.[42] Both Bradley's *Shakespearean Tragedy* (1904) and *Oxford Lectures on Poetry* (1909) were, as the latter's title indicates, derived from lectures delivered at Oxford during this period, and both were formative texts largely synonymous with the emerging study of English.[43] If Raleigh's and Bradley's studies reflected an emerging academic professionalism in literary studies, by comparison, *The Man Shakespeare* was indicative of a still larger fluidity between academic and non-academic modes of writing in which the works and life of Shakespeare were of central interest. Harris conceived of his own work as rivalling all previous 'commentators' on Shakespeare, a designation which encompassed critics from Johnson to Goethe and Coleridge, and presumably, more recent authors about whom Harris remained otherwise silent: 'Without a single exception', he wrote, 'the commentators have all missed the man and his story.'[44] Bradley, in a note to his 1909 biographical essay on 'Shakespeare the Man' cited the articles Harris published in the *Saturday Review*.[45] Although in Bradley's estimation the larger book was of lesser merit, he praised Harris' articles for their valuable ideas which revealed ostensibly new information about Shakespeare's life and character. Recognizing their affinity and defending his own authority, Bradley claimed that he had arrived at his ideas about Shakespeare the man independently of Harris' articles. In contrast, Harris derided Bradley's work: 'he took almost my very words', he complained in his *Vanity Fair* column in 1907, 'on the subject of Shakespeare's personality and Hamlet'.[46] Harris was a socialite and a popular writer rather than an academic scholar like Bradley, and even though their styles of criticism were broadly comparable, Harris' volumes on Shakespeare failed to receive serious scholarly attention.[47] Harris was possibly defensive about his lack of academic authority, or perhaps his denunciations were merely expressions of the self-promotion and sense of personal discovery – a first-person engagement with the texts and insight into the man – which characterized non-academic, popular works of literary criticism in this period.

As with *The Man Shakespeare*, Bradley's two main volumes of Shakespeare criticism were products of the period in which they were written. Although he endeavoured to enrich 'dramatic appreciation' of the plays, his strictly literary treatment and his elaborate character studies descended directly from the styles of romantic essayists like Johnson, Coleridge and Hazlitt, and were broadly comparable to the late nineteenth-century studies of Swinburne and Dowden, all of whom receive significant critical attention in *Shakespearean Tragedy*. Yet the language and style of Bradley's criticism were more characteristic of a late nineteenth-century scientistic approach typified by the works of the New Shakespere society. Established in 1874 by Furnivall, who had first studied chemistry and mathematics, the society sought to enlighten the plays by 'a very close study of the metrical and phraseological peculiarities of Shakespeare'.[48] Bradley's character studies were similarly methodical and exhaustive, 'enriched by the products of analysis and analytic interpretation', cautiously conservative, yet self-assured and erudite in tone.[49]

In its first publication, *Shakespearean Tragedy* was praised in reviews for its academic workmanship (*Athenaeum*, 13 May 1905) and careful attention to detail. The *Academy* wrote: 'In our opinion a book like that which is before us is not much less essential for the complete comprehension of Shakespeare's tragedies than an atlas is for the fruitful study of geography' (18 March 1905). By comparison, the style of *The Man Shakespeare* was declamatory, self-aggrandizing, and ambitiously comprehensive rather than exhaustive (at roughly equal length, *Shakespearean Tragedy* considered four plays, whereas *The Man Shakespeare* undertook the entire canon). Despite mutual disavowals of one another, however, what the two authors shared was an interest in the psychological composition of Shakespeare's characters, their fully sketched character studies reflecting the psychological profiles of an emerging medical discipline in late nineteenth-century England.

Bradley also believed that from Shakespeare's dramatic writing, 'probable conjectures' about his character could be hypothesized, even intuited, that 'the most dramatic of writers must reveal in his writings something of himself', although he was more cautious than Harris about trusting to impressions which were otherwise 'utterly unprovable'.[50] Bradley's criticism was primarily concerned with literary reading rather than the kind of biographical criticism of Harris. For subject matter, *The Man Shakespeare*'s most immediate precedent was the study of Shakespeare by the Danish critic Georg Brandes, written in 1895 and first translated into in English in 1898, thus coinciding with Harris' articles in the *Saturday Review* (Harris cited Brandes in two of the articles, but the citation was written out when Harris revised the work for *The Man Shakespeare*).[51] For Brandes, as for Harris in his later work, *Hamlet* the play was Shakespeare's most autobiographical work and Hamlet the character the author's most personal self-portrait: 'It cost Shakespeare no effort to transform himself into Hamlet. On the contrary, in giving expression to Hamlet's spiritual life he was enabled quite naturally to pour forth all that during the recent years had filled his heart and seethed in his brain.'[52] But while for Harris the impetus for writing *Hamlet* was Shakespeare's bitter attachment to Mary Fitton, for Brandes, that impetus was the result of a sequence of events which also included the death of his father – in general, *Hamlet* was a reaction to the hypocrisies, disappointments and betrayals Shakespeare experienced in life.[53] Other prominent biographers from the period such as Lee and Furnivall, though similarly interested in the intimate details of Shakespeare's life, were, like Bradley, more cautious about the practice of reading into 'Shakespeare's dramatic utterances allusions to personal experience'.[54] For both Brandes and Harris, however, not only were personal experiences causally related to the thematic structure of the texts, they also served to reinforce theories about the chronological order of the canon according to Shakespeare's biography. Interestingly, Brandes' comments on *Hamlet* occur in a section titled 'The Psychology of Hamlet', a title which anticipates the psychologism of Bradley and Harris, and the direction in which biographical interpretation of the plays was pointing.

Freud's *The Interpretation of Dreams*, which contained his famous comments on the Oedipus complex in *Hamlet*, first appeared in German in 1900. Freud's commentary was limited to a footnote in the German original and expanded to a few paragraphs incorporated into the main text of the 1913 English translation. The Freudian reading, however, was developed at length in an essay for the *American Journal of Psychology* in 1910, one year after Harris' *The Man Shakespeare*, by Freud's main disciple and promoter in England, Ernest Jones.[55] This essay would be expanded over the course of Jones' career to culminate in 1949 in the seminal psychoanalytic study, *Hamlet and Oedipus*. The essay demonstrates how the main tenets of psychoanalysis as explicated in *The Interpretation of Dreams* would develop into an interpretive model for *Hamlet*. At the core is the distinction between the conscious and unconscious – the self-aware versus the obscure mental processes inaccessible to introspection – a distinction which is indicative of an epistemic break with the bourgeois ideology of the subject; in Jones' own words, 'man not as the smooth, self-acting agent he pretends to be, but as he really is, a creature only dimly conscious of the various influences that mould his thought and action'.[56] The psychoanalytic subject represses into the Freudian 'unconscious' desires that are in conflict with the dicta of the community or herd, with the corollary that, since the herd usually places the greatest restrictions on sexual instincts, these instincts are most often repressed.[57] Of these sexual instincts, the earliest are infantile, unconsciously directed by the child (boy) towards its mother, creating an attendant feeling of sexual jealousy directed towards the father, and a desire to 'kill' or make him disappear. This is the Oedipal conflict dramatized unconsciously by Shakespeare in *Hamlet*, the repressed childhood wish to kill the father and sleep with the mother. In Freud's interpretation, Claudius shows Hamlet the repressed wishes of his own childhood realized, and thus, the loathing which should drive Hamlet 'on to revenge is replaced in him by self-reproaches, by scruples of conscience, which remind him that he himself is literally no better than the sinner whom he is to punish'.[58]

In Jones' expansion of Freud, the realization that Claudius killed his father stimulates to unconscious activity in Hamlet's mind his repressed desire to take his father's place, and produces his tortured soliloquies whose stimulus is otherwise incomprehensible to his conscious mind. Gertrude's demonstrable affection for Hamlet evidences the excessive affections he must have received as a child and which subsequently produce in him extreme disgust for his mother, the misogyny of which is reflected in his treatment of Ophelia, as well as a resulting excessive guilt and an inclination towards femininity.

The principal division between 'conscious' and 'unconscious' thus explains the mystery of Hamlet's inaction, but also serves as the rationale for reading *Hamlet* biographically, a point which Jones explains by turning to Freud's description of creative process in *The Interpretation of Dreams*. The unconscious has no access to the conscious other than through dream-formation in the pre-conscious, or in the non-conscious dimension of fantasy. The processes of creative output therefore bear an intimate relation to the psychosexual life of the author: 'the creative output', writes Jones, 'is a sublimated manifestation of various thwarted and "repressed" wishes, of which the subject is no longer conscious'.[59] Although the character Hamlet enacts Freud's theories of infantile sexuality and psychological neurosis, the psychology which the text inevitably demonstrates for both Freud and Jones is that of Shakespeare: 'it can of course only be the poet's mind which confronts us in Hamlet'.[60] Harris' own theories about the psychosexual tensions reflected in *Hamlet* differed considerably from those of Freud, particularly in the absence of Shakespeare's mother and father. Still, the importance of the comparison with Freud here would appear to be that sexualized and gendered affiliation between text and author. For both Freud and Jones, the repressed sexual desires of the artist's unconscious mind were seen to shape and order the activity of writing, thus initiating an association between sexual pathology and writing which would echo throughout Freud's later work. In 1926, Freud would write: 'As soon as writing, which entails making a liquid flow out of a tube on to a piece of white paper, assumes the significance of copulation', it stops because it represents 'the performance of a forbidden sexual act'.[61] For Harris, in contrast, once Shakespeare's writing becomes a substitute for denied sexual desires, it becomes effusive. Still, his theory inscribes the kind of phallocentrism typical of Freudian psychoanalysis: the activity of writing/creating is portrayed as a male-gendered activity, a phallic wielding of the pen, representative of a forbidden sexual act. Inverting the typically romantic motif of woman as muse, *The Man Shakespeare* posits Shakespeare's sexual misfortunes, principally the supposed affair with Fitton, as the necessary problems for the creation of his literary masterpieces. The play becomes an encoded symbolic 'dream text' which, properly interpreted, reveals a repressed sexual desire and which explains a psychological neurosis, or, in the case of biographical criticism's pre-psychoanalytic language, the enigma, mystery or hidden tragedy of the author.

The Interpretation of Dreams was not published in English until 1913, and even though Harris read German, there is no evidence to suggest either that he read the original or that, if he did, it had any bearing on his own theories about *Hamlet*. Nor is there any evidence to suggest that Harris read Jones' 1910 essay. The appearance of Jones' article at roughly the same point in English literary culture, however, was no mere coincidence: the psychological dimension of an early twentieth-century strain of biographical criticism as typified by Harris anticipated, in its own antiquated late Victorian language, the principal tenets of psychoanalytic criticism, a criticism which similarly sought to explicate, as in the case of Jones' article, the 'mystery' of the texts.[62] As recent critics of Freud have demonstrated, Freud's explanatory modes and analogies were largely indebted to and characteristic of late Victorian literary culture and folk wisdom.[63] Moreover, his reading of Shakespeare descended from German romanticism: the translations which Freud read were those of Wilhelm Schlegel and Ludwig von Tieck, translations which enhanced the introspection and inwardness characteristic of Goethe's readings of Shakespeare.[64] Biographical criticism in England emerged in tandem to psychoanalysis in Germany, drawing equally from a romanticism shaped as much by Goethe as by Johnson and Coleridge, and both were also, as Jung noted, exponents of a *ressentiment* of the incoming century directed towards the psychopathologies of the nineteenth. Thus, Harris would write in the introduction to *The Man Shakespeare* that the twentieth century, 'with its X-rays that enable us to see through the skin and flesh of men. . . has brought a new spirit into the world. . . and with it a new and higher ideal of life and art, which must of necessity change and transform all the conditions of existence':

The faiths and convictions of twenty centuries are passing away and the forms and institutions of a hundred generations of men are dissolving before us like the baseless fabric of a dream. A new morality is already shaping itself in the spirit; a morality based not on guess-work and on fancies, but on ascertained laws of moral health; a scientific morality belonging not to statics, like the morality of the Jews, but to dynamics, and so fitting the nature of each individual person.[65]

At the centre of Harris' moral revolution stood Shakespeare, the Old-Man-of-the-Sea on the shoulders of the youth, 'an obsession to the critic, a weapon to the pedant, a nuisance to the man of genius'.[66] Harris envisioned his own criticism, conditioned by the technological developments of industrial society and written in a clinical language, as an exponent of a new scientific morality, a higher ideal of life and art, because its principal object was to problematize Shakespeare, to 'see through' the plays with x-ray vision to the tragic events (of a specifically sexual nature) which shaped Shakespeare's psychology and which would lead to his greatest dramatic achievements. Although Harris believed that Shakespeare was the most complex and passionate personality that ever lived, by giving expression to all that was common and vicious in him, Harris' intention was, as he noted, to 'get rid of Shakespeare': 'I want to liberate the English', he proclaimed, 'so far as I can from the tyranny of Shakespeare's greatness.'[67]

These last few statements must have been the ones which excited Shaw. Indeed, one wonders if Shaw read much beyond the introduction to *The Man Shakespeare*. And it must have been the failure of Harris' play, *Shakespeare and his Love*, to incite the same sense of social revolution, instead reinforcing the romantic characterization of Shakespeare which Shaw despised, the reflective and introspective Shakespeare of Goethe, rather than the neurotic Shakespeare of Harris' criticism: 'Frank conceives Shakespear to have been a broken-hearted, melancholy, enormously sentimental person', Shaw complained in his response to *Shakespeare and his Love*, 'whereas I am convinced that he was very like myself'.[68] Shaw would make the comparison between Shakespeare and himself elsewhere, a fact which Harris would scorn and with which he would disagree strongly in his unauthorized biography of Shaw, published in 1931.[69] In one of the more bizarre twists to this narrative, Shaw agreed, after Harris' death in 1930, to correct the proof-sheets for the publisher and to write a post-script to his own biography, even though he failed to agree with many of Harris' conclusions.[70] With a marvellous circularity, in a chapter on Shaw's sex-credo, Harris would also make the inevitable comparison with Shakespeare: 'While Mary Fitton was banished from London Shakespeare could write nothing but tragedies', Harris observed. 'As nothing like that happened in Shaw's life we can only get a text-booky, sexless type of play.'[71] That there was a defect in Shaw was evident, Harris surmised, and as that defect was apparently not physiological, it must have been psychological. Here, he deferred to the now well-established Freudian school: 'I must leave it to the psychoanalyst to run it to earth.'[72]

THE PORTRAIT OF MR OSCAR WILDE

Frank Harris' most significant biographical endeavour, however, was his two-volume *Oscar Wilde: His Life and Confessions*, first published in 1916.[73] Harris and Wilde had been close acquaintances, particularly during the period leading up to Wilde's trial and subsequent imprisonment. They had first met around 1884, both having frequented the luncheons and parties hosted in the drawing rooms of London's social elite. In *Life and Confessions*, Harris described his first impression of Wilde as 'oily and fat': 'fleshly indulgence and laziness. . . were written all over him'.[74] Despite initial physical impressions, Harris was immediately drawn to Wilde's agile and powerful mind, his 'extraordinary physical vivacity and geniality', and his superb talent for talking.[75] Their friendship developed and lasted until Wilde's death in 1900. Harris admired Wilde's wit, social ease and oral eloquence, as well as his taste for fine wines and food, and according to Harris, the two, while lunching or dining together, would often debate their favourite literary topics, among them, the works and life of Shakespeare. Their meetings became more frequent during the period leading up to and following Wilde's trial. Particularly during the years of his final exile on the continent, Wilde, no longer able to sustain his expensive lifestyle with the income from his diminishing literary output, would often beg Harris for small amounts of money to cover his hotel and dining bills.[76] In 1893, Wilde dedicated *An Ideal Husband*: 'To Frank Harris, a slight tribute to his power and distinction as an artist, his chivalry and nobility as a friend.'[77] A final controversy in 1899 and up until Wilde's death, however, regarding money which Wilde claimed he was owed for the production of *Mr and Mrs Daventry*, soured the last days of their friendship, and subsequently, fuelled the acrimony which surrounded the numerous editions of Harris' biography of Wilde.[78]

Although material from the two volumes on Wilde had appeared in England as a chapter in the first volume of *Contemporary Portraits*, Harris published his Wilde biography privately in America, possibly for fear of facing a libel suit as threatened by Alfred Douglas, and subsequently sold the volumes at varying prices.[79] Douglas was the young poet, Oxford dropout and protégé of Wilde, son of the Marquess of Queensberry who made the notorious accusation that Wilde was posing as a 'somdomite' and which led to the libel suit brought against him by Wilde in the first of Wilde's trials. Harris' Wilde biography received a second printing in 1918 which included a chapter by Shaw. The biography was published again in 1930, with an added forward written with Alfred Douglas in 1925, who was now seeking some income from his notorious association with Wilde. After Harris' death in 1930, Shaw revised and published the first English version in 1938 under the less provocative title, *Oscar Wilde* (apparently, Shaw undertook the project, as he did his own biography by Harris, out of goodwill, for the purpose of procuring some income for Nellie Harris who was left destitute after her husband's death). Like his contemporary portraits, Harris' descriptions of conversations and meetings with Wilde were praised for the intimate, and generally accurate, portrait which they painted, despite numerous factual errors. Harris held Wilde in extremely high regard, but his characteristically frank discussions of Wilde's sexual relations were seen to be exploitative of the controversy which peaked during the trials. Indeed, Harris' most vociferous opponent in this issue, the rival Wilde biographer, Robert Harborough Sherard, devoted an entire volume, *Frank Harris, George Bernard Shaw and Oscar Wilde*, to discrediting Harris' biography, as well as Shaw's support and praise for Harris.[80] But even Douglas – who discredited, then supported, and then later retracted his support for *Life and Confessions* – disparaged Sherard's view that Wilde's 'homosexual activities' were committed 'in periodical bouts of insanity engendered by syphilis'.[81] He rather admitted that 'many of the things related by Harris about Wilde. . . are perfectly true in essence, though Harris generally gets the details wrong'.[82] One criticism made by both Douglas and Sherard, and generally agreed upon by subsequent biographers of Wilde, is that Harris over-emphasized his role and importance during the trials. More generally, however, the fact that Harris' biography was published sixteen years after Wilde's death suggested that the lengthy dialogues between Harris and Wilde contained in the volumes were more likely fictive elaborations drawn from Harris' ageing memories of Wilde. Though based on a genuine relationship with Wilde, his biography was more an historical fiction not unlike *Shakespeare and his Love*, imagined dialogues animating his memories and theories.

Incidentally, in the late 1880s, Wilde had also written his own narrative concerning Shakespeare's sonnets, *The Portrait of Mr W. H.*, which also explored the idea of literary theorization. According to Harris, Wilde and he were often together during this period. While he was writing *The Portrait of Mr W. H.*, Wilde had supposedly discussed his sonnet theories with Harris, a plausible possibility as Wilde's later letters to Harris, which frequently mention Harris' Shakespeare articles of the late 1890s, testify to their shared interest.[83] In fact, Wilde had initially submitted the first manuscript to the *Fortnightly Review*, which Harris was editing at the time, expecting Harris to accept it. After the manuscript was rejected by an assistant while Harris was out of town, however, Wilde then submitted the story to *Blackwood's Magazine*, where it was published in 1889. Following the success of its initial publication, Wilde revised and greatly expanded the work, seeking to publish it as a separate volume. The expanded version was lost in 1895 after the auction of Wilde's books and manuscripts, only to resurface in America in 1920, where it was published the following year.[84]

In *Life and Confessions*, Harris wrote that he had advised Wilde not to publish the story because of its suggestions about Shakespeare's 'abnormal vice': '"The Portrait of Mr W. H." did Oscar incalculable injury', wrote Harris. 'It gave his enemies for the first time the very weapon they wanted, and they used it unscrupulously and untiringly with the fierce delight of hatred.'[85] Though there is little evidence to support Harris' claim that significant controversy regarding Wilde's sexuality resulted from its publication, the 1889 version did emerge in the first trial. While being cross-examined about passages from *The Picture of Dorian Gray* regarding the nature of an artist's affection for a young male, Wilde attributed the idea to Shakespeare's sonnets. When asked by the counsel for Queensberry, 'I believe you have written an article to show that Shakespeare's sonnets were suggestive of unnatural vice?' Wilde responded: 'On the contrary, I have written an article to show that they are not. I objected to such a perversion being put upon Shakespeare.'[86] The double meaning of Wilde's response, both denying the suggestion in the story of criminal behaviour and, conversely, suggesting that the idea of love between men was not a perversion, mirrored the slippery evasion of male–male sexual love in his fiction of Shakespeare.[87] Wilde's linguistic sidestepping, however, could not prevent the ambiguous homoerotic suggestions of his writing – in *The Portrait of Mr W. H.*, in *The Picture of Dorian Gray*, and in his incriminating letters to Douglas – being interpreted by the reading public as unambiguously demonstrative of Wilde's own criminal behaviour, the point made by Harris in his Wilde biography.

Wilde's narrative reveals the identity of W. H. to be Willie Hughes, an actor from Shakespeare's company whose youth and beauty Shakespeare celebrated in the language of a Platonic male love, filtered through the tones of the late Victorian, effete – though not explicitly homosexual – aesthete.[88] Unlike Harris' *Shakespeare and his Love*, however, *The Portrait of Mr W. H.*, rather than endorse a specific sonnet theory, instead thematizes the problematic practices of literary theorization. The story

reworks a more obscure nineteenth-century hypothesis about a young
man named Willie Hughes who was thought to have been an actor during
Shakespeare's day, a theory based not on historical record, but, once
again, on internal evidence derived from the sonnets, particularly the
sequence of sonnets which play on the words 'will' and 'hues'.[89] At the
centre of Wilde's story, however, is a literary forgery, the eponymous
portrait commissioned by the story's character, Cyril Graham, to prove
the truth of his theory. Graham, a beautiful and effeminate young actor
known for his portrayals of Shakespeare's female characters, devises his
sonnet theory about Willie Hughes which he then relates to his friend,
Erskine. To prove to the unconvinced Erskine the truth of his theory,
Graham produces the forgery which he claims to have found nailed to
the side of an old chest bought at a farmhouse in Warwickshire. When
Erskine discovers the fact of the forgery and confronts Graham, Graham
commits suicide as a demonstration of his belief in the theory. This story-
within-the-story actually emerges during a conversation about literary
forgeries between Erskine and Wilde's unnamed narrator. Hearing the
story, the narrator becomes convinced of the theory's truth and proceeds
to develop and elaborate the theory through his own research. In a letter
to Erskine, the narrator relays his discoveries, but, oddly, loses his conviction in the theory after sending the letter. Erskine, now convinced, writes
the narrator from France with his intention to commit suicide, again, to
prove to the narrator his belief in the theory. When the narrator rushes to
France to stop Erskine, however, he arrives too late only to learn that
Erskine had in fact died of consumption rather than suicide.

For Cyril Graham, when the truth of his theory could no longer be
demonstrated by his forgery, the most he could prove was his own belief,
which he chose to do with his suicide, after which his role in the theory
would become narrative. Erskine's death becomes a further layer of the
narrative, though his failure to produce a believable suicide is perhaps
what leaves the narrator finally unconvinced of the theory's truth. Left
with the portrait which he hangs in his library, the narrator ponders,
with an almost wishful desire to believe: 'But sometimes, when I look
at it, I think that there is really a great deal to be said for the Willie
Hughes theory of Shakespeare's Sonnets.'[90] Death, as a demonstration of
belief, is a substitute for an elusive proof – the truth about Shakespeare
which resides within the text, but just out of reach – and like that proof,
itself almost impossible to believe: 'To die for one's theological beliefs
is the worst use a man can make of his life,' the narrator opines, 'but to
die for a literary theory! It seemed impossible' (224). The title of Wilde's

own narrative is ironically self-referential because the portrait of the title is a forgery, or fiction, and because the narrative allegorizes the processes by which biographical events become narrativized. The only 'truth' about Shakespeare to which we can turn, but ultimately not believe, the story seems to suggest, is to be found in the paradoxical and inevitable conjunction of history with fiction.

Wilde had been dead for nearly ten years when *Shakespeare and his Love* was finally published. In 1898, he had read articles by Harris containing the Shakespeare theories which would be developed in *The Man Shakespeare*, in issues of the *Saturday Review* which Harris sent to Wilde in France.[91] The first published version of *The Portrait of Mr W. H.* in 1889 predated Harris' first published work on Shakespeare by several years. Still, it's not impossible to imagine that the conversation between Erskine and the narrator, over coffee and cigarettes sitting in the library after dining, were not unlike those between Wilde and Harris in the late 1880s and when, according to Harris, they would discuss Shakespeare. Whether Wilde's story enacts Harris' enthusiasm and conviction for literary theories about Shakespeare and Wilde's more sceptical reservation, like his Willie Hughes theory, rests in the balance between textual interpretation and historical truth. Indeed, Wilde's thematizing of historical narrativization brilliantly characterizes Harris' own psychosexual fictions of Shakespeare, if not of Wilde as well, as literary forgeries; that is, as idealized representations of his literary theories based, as are those of Cyril Graham, on internal evidence derived from readings of Shakespeare; but finally, forgeries, which purport to demonstrate the truth of his theories in the absence of hard evidence, except for the fact of their fiction – historical fictions which substitute for an always elusive historical truth.

Wilde died in 1900, though not for his theory about Shakespeare, and so he was unable to comment on the numerous fictions Harris would create in his biography of Wilde; unlike Shaw, in whose case Harris' own death made Shaw's commentary on his own biography possible. And yet, interestingly, despite those numerous fictive elaborations, Shaw would praise Harris' *Oscar Wilde* as the 'very best literary portrait of Wilde in existence'.[92] Shaw was acquainted with Wilde from about 1879, though they met on only a handful of occasions.[93] Wilde's career had largely peaked in the period when Shaw was only beginning to make a name for himself in the literary and social circles of London. In 1894, Frank Harris, well established in London society and significantly wealthy, bought the struggling weekly the *Saturday Review* and revived its reputation by putting together a formidable team of writers and columnists including

H. G. Wells as chief reviewer of novels, and with regular contributions from Matthew Arnold, John Davidson, and Swinburne, paying them generously.[94] Harris asked Shaw, who had been writing as music critic for the *World*, to act as dramatic columnist, a move which largely propelled Shaw to success. The notoriously sharp-tongued G. B. S. was known for his often scathing denunciations of Shakespeare and the traditions of the actor-manager theatre, and his relentless promotion of Ibsen and the New Drama. After 1910, Harris' social standing declined as he isolated himself from London society and slowly squandered his fortune on poor speculations. During the same period, Shaw's literary reputation continued its ascent. As Harris had acted as a reluctant patron to Wilde during Wilde's final years, so too, Shaw, though reluctant to meet Harris in person, periodically aided Harris' literary career with prefaces, essays and letters which he allowed Harris to publish.[95]

Harris provides the primary biographical association between Wilde and Shaw, his respective biographies enmeshing biographical fact and historical fiction in a wonderfully triangular network of narrative portraiture. Shaw's description of Harris' Wilde biography as a 'literary' portrait also characterizes their three respective fictionalizations of Shakespeare. Admittedly, the differences between these three works of fiction, two very dissimilar plays and a short story turned novella, are stark. Harris' *Shakespeare and his Love* contains none of the complexity, irony and narrative layering which distance Wilde from his own writing: where *The Portrait of W. H.*, though offering equally compelling internal evidence, remains finally detached from the Willie Hughes theory, *Shakespeare and his Love* is an almost propagandic advertisement of Harris' critical theories. Of Harris' preface to *Shakespeare and his Love*, the *Times Literary Supplement* complained: 'He has yet to offer his justification for making a play (which is a work of art of one kind) out of matter which is clearly more suitable for a biography – let us say for the same author's "The Man Shakespeare," which is a work of art of quite another kind' ('Another Play About Shakespeare', 1 December 1910). If Wilde's story problematizes the kind of literary portraiture characteristic of Harris' writing, Shaw's *The Dark Lady of the Sonnets* is a blatant parody of literary speculation about Shakespeare's character prevalent in the late nineteenth century. Shaw's Shakespeare is a wistful romantic, a literary plagiarist, a buffoon, a self-portrait, a caricature – anything but a serious statement after the fashion of nineteenth-century Shakespeare biographers. Even as a short comic piece, though, *The Dark Lady of the Sonnets* is characterized by strong and serious naturalist impulses; satiric, anti-idealizing, and centred around the promotion of a genuine social cause, the establishment of a state-subsidized repertory system.

A second major difference between these three works is their treatment of Shakespeare's sexuality. Thematically, all three works share an interest in the sexual dimension of Shakespeare's biography, albeit muted in Wilde's story. *The Portrait of Mr W. H.* articulates a subtly deferred, though readily interpretable, homoerotic subtext which is, arguably, its primary objective. Harris, virile heterosexual and notorious womanizer, denounced the possibility of Shakespeare's sexual inversion emphatically, both in his biography of Wilde and in his longer work of biographical criticism, *The Man Shakespeare*. In the preface to *The Dark Lady of the Sonnets*, Shaw would also agree with Harris' defence of Shakespeare's 'normal' sexual constitution: 'The language of the sonnets addressed to Pembroke', wrote Shaw, 'extravagant as it now seems, is the language of compliment and fashion, transfigured no doubt by Shakesepear's verbal magic . . ., but still unmistakeable for anything else than the expression of a friendship delicate enough to be wounded, and a manly loyalty deep enough to be outraged.'[96]

Despite their differences, however, as a broadly conceived genre of historical fiction, these three works characterize a literary/critical paradigm bridging nineteenth-century Shakespeare appreciation and early twentieth-century academic criticism. To begin with, all three of these authors were, though educated and highly literate, not academic. As writers of fiction, drama, prose and biography, they received wide audiences for their work, especially Wilde and Shaw. Harris, however, in particular, typified the late Victorian popular writer exploiting different genres. *The Man Shakespeare* blended the style of anecdotal biography exemplified in his *Contemporary Portraits* with informal literary criticism. His play, though based upon the same theories developed in his two full volumes of criticism, developed tangentially out of a tradition of narrative and dramatic writing for which Shakespeare's supposed biography served as subject, a genre which exploited more popular modes such as the serial journal, the novel and novelette, and, most prominently in the early twentieth century, the drama. The proliferation of plays which dramatized fictive episodes in Shakespeare's life, such as his love affairs, his friendships or his escapades as a deer poacher in Stratford, ran from the mid-nineteenth century well into the twentieth century.[97] *The Man Shakespeare* and *Shakespeare and his Love* developed from and cross-fertilized modes of writing which were non-academic and popular

and which shared a preoccupation with Shakespeare's biographical portraiture. The fictions of Wilde and Shaw also embraced this tradition of
historical fiction which drew both energy and subject matter from the late
Victorian style of essay writing typified by Harris.

While the Shakespeare fictions of Wilde and Shaw would become
minor works in the canons of these central literary figures, Harris'
Shakespeare and his Love, like the numerous lesser-known plays about
Shakespeare from this period, would be mostly forgotten. Still, all
three texts broke from the idealizing tendencies of nineteenth-century
Shakespeare appreciation, in different ways and degrees, but all partly
by developing an interest in and exploiting the sexual dimension of
Shakespeare's life. More importantly, this sexual dimension was predicated upon a specific mode of textual interpretation developing parallel
to Freudian psychoanalysis: the plays and poems were not simply biographical portraits of the author vis-à-vis Victorian Shakespeare biography, but more specifically, were conduits for the sexual energies
redirected from Shakespeare's personal life. For Wilde, the sonnets were
vehicles for an unarticulated sexual desire, 'the love that dare not speak
its name', the 'strange worship' of W. H. (again unnamed) in the sonnets,
equally unarticulated in *The Portrait of Mr W. H.*, but substituted by the
narrative itself in an endless deferral: 'Who was that young man of
Shakespeare's day', asks Erskine, 'who . . . was addressed by him in terms
of such passionate adoration that we can but wonder at the strange
worship, and are almost afraid to turn the key that unlocks the mystery
of the poet's heart?' (198). The story thus represents a series of literary
forgeries, or forged sexualities, there to be read and interpreted, but, like
the historical fiction in which they are embedded, not to be believed
(at least not in a criminal court). For Harris, Shakespeare's betrayal by
Mary Fitton was the central defining episode of his life which led to his
greatest dramatic creations. In his theory, Fitton becomes an inverted
muse, Shakespeare's sexual frustration and disappointment the necessary problems for his art. For both Wilde and Harris, writing thus
becomes a substitute for a forbidden sexual act. Even for Shaw in his
short comedy, Shakespeare derives a kind of sexual pleasure from the
Queen's phrases which he incorporates, word for word, into his own text:
Shakespeare's muse, who scorns his advances, actually writes for him,
countering the claims to his brilliance. In all three texts, sexual encounters
and desires are not the sources of literary inspiration, but are rather
thwarted and then transmuted into a substitutive text.

In Freudian fashion, Shakespeare's plays and poems become reposi-
tories for the psychosexual tensions experienced in his life, richly coded
texts which are deciphered according to Shakespeare's diverted and repressed sexual desires. If Wilde maintained some distance from this
biographical criticism by thematizing the problems of narrative process,
as did Shaw with his own satiric sense of humour, both in contrast to
Harris and his entirely earnest attempt to solve Shakespeare's mystery, this
is no doubt testimony to their superior critical capacities and literary
talents. Three very different fictions and three very different authors
notwithstanding, these three texts are demonstrative of a psychosexual
model of authorship which would resonate through the twentieth century. This allegory would resurface in 1922, in the 'Scylla and Charybdis'
episode of James Joyce's *Ulysses*. And of course, if the echoes are not
obvious already, the psychosexual model would resonate, most recently
and resoundingly, in *Shakespeare in Love*, the 1999 film scripted by Tom
Stoppard and Marc Norman. Joseph Fiennes' Shakespeare, after relaying
his sexual frustrations about his wife to Antony Sher's anachronistic
Freud-like therapist, falls in love with Gwyneth Paltrow's Viola De
Lesseps, an Elizabethan lady otherwise beyond Shakespeare's social
reach and already betrothed to a gentleman of the court. As they lie on
the bed, enjoying the sexual pleasure which will finally be forbidden them,
Shakespeare writes the drama, albeit not *Hamlet*, which mirrors their own
eventual fates as tragic lovers.

HAMLET, SHAKESPEARE AND STEPHEN. JOYCE.

In the central library episode of James Joyce's *Ulysses*, when Stephen
Dedalus is expounding his theory about the biographical relationship
between Shakespeare and *Hamlet*, a troubling equation of identity – 'I,
I and I. I.' (182) – emerges as one of the expressions within his private
interior plane.[98] This equation occurs during a sequence of interior
comments provoked by Stephen's debt to George Russell, or A. E., one
of the auditors initially present in the National Library of Dublin reading
room where Stephen delivers his theory. Stephen subsequently conceives
of two possible selves, physical and spiritual, as represented by the two
pairs of 'I's. Divided by a conjunction, one pair of 'I's is separated by a
comma, the other pair differentiated by a full stop. Stephen imagines
himself within these two conflicting categories of identity: 'Wait. Five

months. Molecules all change. I am other I now' (182). And then, later:
'entelechy, form of forms, am I by memory because under ever-changing
forms' (182). The first type of identity is a transformational exterior form,
a physical self which is manifestly transformed over time. 'I' remains fully
and materially separated from previous incarnations of itself. The bodily
Stephen that was given a pound by A. E. would be physically discon-
nected to the present Stephen: 'Other I got pound' (182). The second
category of identity, in contrast, is constant and unchanging, entelechy or
the soul which creates and orders all incarnations of material form. In this
category, the self is constituted by memory, composed of as well as
prefiguring the successive transformations, the comma serving equally
important functions of distinguishing and conjoining stages in the trans-
figuration of the 'I'. Though continuous in memory, as a spiritual or
metaphysical identity, this self would also transcend the material obliga-
tions of Stephen's debt. The sequence then concludes with a pun which
reaffirms his debt: 'A. E. I. O. U.' (182).

    If the dialectical opposition between physical and metaphysical selves
fails to define Stephen's identity, this dialecticism also fails to account for
the complex relationship between textual activity and authorial identity
as posed a few lines earlier in his Shakespeare theory. Stephen's equation
of identity – 'I, I and I. I.' – might also be interpreted, however, according
to the more literal value of the punctuation. In contrast to the propor-
tional division of the self into conflicting identities, in the alternative
reading, the three 'I's of the first sentence might be seen as merging into
one final 'I' of the second, a fusion which immediately evokes the idea of
the holy Trinity.[99] Perhaps this triangular configuration reflects the
tensions between religious, colonial and secular discourses as organized
within Stephen's own psychosocial consciousness, the religious and nationalist indoctrination of his childhood (father) versus his own secular
consciousness (son) and his desire for a kind of metaphysical transcend-
ence in his art (holy ghost). But the trinity of father/son/ghost is also an
emphatic image against which resonates Stephen's recent narrative description of Shakespeare performing his own role of King Hamlet's ghost
on the stage of the Globe. With rhetorical virtuoso, Stephen describes the
scene of Shakespeare playing the ghost to Richard Burbage's Hamlet on
an afternoon in 1602, leading him to question:

Is it possible that that player Shakespeare, a ghost by absence, and in the vesture
of buried Denmark, a ghost by death, speaking his own words to his own son's
name (had Hamnet Shakespeare lived he would have been prince Hamlet's twin)

is it possible, I want to know, or probable that he did not draw or foresee the logical conclusion of those premises: you are the dispossessed son: I am the murdered father: your mother is the guilty queen, Ann Shakespeare, born Hathaway? (181)

Here as well, the self, afflicted by conscience as is Hamlet, is haunted by the ghost of memory, by the image of the father, and also by the image of the author, Shakespeare, who inheres within the ghostly form. In this second interpretation, the idea of representations of the self duly acquires an increased resonance: 'As we, or mother Dana, weave and unweave our bodies', Stephen says in a later moment, 'from day to day, their molecules shuttled to and fro, so does the artist weave and unweave his image' (186). Self-representation in art becomes the vehicle which serves to unify physical and metaphysical identities: 'In the intense instant of imagination, when the mind, Shelley says, is a fading coal that which I was is that which I am and that which in possibility I may come to be' (186). The metaphor of filial connection, the author as fathering the text, and the suggestion of ghostly or unconscious textual presences, also introduces a specifically Freudian dimension to the psychological style of Joyce's narrative. Whereas the first interpretation of 'I' provides a compact dialectical framework between physical and metaphysical selves, the idea of a consubstantial or composite aesthetic identity thus confronts us with a confusing plurality of biographical associations and familial metaphors uniting Hamlet, Shakespeare, Stephen and, finally, Joyce himself. The reader is left to wonder: what separates Joyce from his own text, comma or full-stop?

Ulysses is a famously difficult work of literature – cryptic, highly allusive, unyielding to interpretation – which is also its attraction: self-consciously imbued, perhaps, by what Roland Barthes has identified as *jouissance*, a pleasure principle derived from the text that is bound to the transparency of language and meaning, *Ulysses* seems at once both to offer and to deflect interpretive strategies, Stephen's scepticism for his own theory warning the reader about the perils of prolonged interpretation.[100] *Ulysses* is also often said to be a highly autobiographical work, drawing on the Dublin of Joyce's youth, a further, more elaborate, portrait of the artist as a young man. The suggestion of an autobiographical dimension to Joyce's writing would seem substantiated by his apparent interest in the relationship between artists and their fictions, particularly as thematized in this episode, dubbed 'Scylla and Charybdis' in Joyce's notes. Reworking the biographical criticism of figures contemporary with the setting of the book such as Brandes and Harris, Stephen creates his own psychosexual fiction to disconnect Shakespeare from the nineteenth-century interpretive models to which the episode gives narrative identity. But while his biographical exploration, exploiting the rich figurative language of Freudian psychoanalysis, serves as corollary to his own psychoaesthetic experience, rather than corroborating his supposed identification with Joyce, Stephen's Shakespeare theory serves as allegory for a model of literary authorship, one predicated upon an aesthetic ideology indicative of contemporary primitivist/modernist narratives.

Joyce composed *Ulysses* over a period of several years spanning the First World War up to the publication of the full text in 1922. The 'Scylla and Charybdis' episode was initially composed some time between 1915 and its publication in serial form in 1919, when Joyce was living in neutral Zurich.[101] The episode is set, however, in 1904 Dublin. The historical setting of the novel, Dublin prior to Irish Independence, makes it tempting to read Joyce's engagement with Shakespeare in *Ulysses* as developing out of or in reaction to colonial and Irish nationalist discourse. Primarily, however, Stephen's Shakespeare theory, like those of contemporary Irish ex-patriots Wilde, Harris and Shaw, emerges out of the intersection between Anglo-Irish romanticism, late nineteenth-century aestheticism, and the European intellectual avant-garde.[102] The classical parallel is the 'Scylla and Charybdis' episode of Homer's *Odyssey*, when Odysseus, leaving Circe's island, must choose between two routes; either to navigate the ferocious dread whirlpool Charybdis, or to confront the six-headed monster Scylla. Odysseus chooses the latter, knowing that he will lose six of his men. Though he is usually associated with Telemachus, the journey here is Stephen's as he enters the National Library of Dublin at around two in the afternoon to navigate his theory of Shakespeare through the dangerous territory of the Library reading room. Within the Homeric framework, the twin dangers Scylla and Charybdis are represented here in contemporary neo-classicist discourse by the opposing ideologies of Aristotle and Plato, both of which feature prominently in the episode. The opposition is presented as one of Aristotelian form versus the Platonic world of ideas: 'Art', notes George Russell, responding to Stephen's biographical theory, 'has to reveal to us ideas, formless spiritual essences' (177), an aestheticism which Stephen counters by trying to demonstrate how biographical facts ground the text in history.

The neo-classical context, particularly as descended through Nietzschean aesthetics, arguably provides a framework for Stephen's Shakespeare theory. Primarily, however, the main characters articulate the predominant critical practices of nineteenth-century Shakespeare studies with which Stephen engages in intellectual combat. The chief librarian, Thomas Lyster, who epitomizes the archaeological encounter with romanticism, begins the episode by invoking Goethe's often quoted remarks on *Hamlet* in *Wilhelm Meister*: 'A hesitating soul taking arms against a sea of troubles, torn by conflicting doubts, as one sees in real life . . . The beautiful ineffectual dreamer who comes to grief against hard facts' (176). Stephen is largely dismissive of both Lyster, who wanders in and out of the discussion, and the assistant librarian, Richard Best, whose interest in contemporary and European literature is faddish. Best introduces French aestheticism to the discussion through Mallarmé, while his misrepresentation of Wilde's *The Portrait of Mr W. H.* parodies Wilde's own affected disinterest in the sexual dimension of Shakespeare's biography. By comparison, George Russell, who, uninterested in Stephen's biographical speculation, leaves in the middle of the episode, reflects a more serious interest in contemporary aestheticism, particularly as epitomized within Irish nationalist literature: 'All these questions are purely academic', he says with regard to Hamlet's biographical resemblances, 'Clergymen's discussions of the historicity of Jesus' (177). Stephen's primary opponent in the episode, however, is John Eglinton, the other assistant librarian and editor of Irish literary magazine *Dana* in which, we discover, Stephen longs to publish his theory. Eglinton gives narrative voice to contemporary conservative scholarship, the neo-classicism of writers such as Walter Pater and Arthur Symons, and the academism of late nineteenth-century Shakespeare scholars such as Edward Dowden and Sydney Lee. Plato to Stephen's Aristotle, Eglinton's tone is mildly reproachful when he responds to Stephen's theory with the rejoinder, 'The bard's fellowcountrymen . . . are rather tired perhaps of our brilliancies of theorising' (190).[103] Stephen's own brilliancy of theorizing, by comparison with the other participants in the discussion, embraces a more modern approach to reading Shakespeare: Stephen offers a version of literary history which, though perpetuating the romantic emphases on individual autonomy and rationality as typified by the nineteenth-century reading of *Hamlet*, seeks to disengage literary culture from the nineteenth century by rewriting Shakespeare's authorship of *Hamlet* within an anti-idealizing allegory, and in particular, by emphasizing the sexual dimension of his authorship.

Joyce's desire to disengage literary and theatrical culture from the nineteenth century had been in evidence from his earliest writing, particularly in critical essays which are nearly contemporary with the setting of the book, the period of Joyce's early adulthood when he was seeking, like Stephen, to establish his reputation as a literary writer and commentator. His first formal publication, at eighteen years of age, was a review of Ibsen's *When We Dead Awaken* for the *Fortnightly Review*. Joyce had read Shaw's 1891 essay on the *Quintessence of Ibsenism*. His own review echoes Shaw's enthusiasm for Ibsen's modern style, Ibsen's presentation of, in the young Joyce's words, 'average lives in their uncompromising truth': 'But the naked drama – either the perception of a great truth, or the opening up of a great question, or a great conflict which is almost independent of the conflicting actors, and has been and is of far-reaching importance – this is what primarily rivets our attention.'[104] This would resonate in the themes of his own fiction, no less in *Ulysses* with its continuous parallel between Homeric heroic ideal and the everyday in 1904 Dublin. An address on 'Drama and Life' which Joyce gave earlier in the same year to the Literary and Historical Society while a student at University College also champions a 'New School' of drama, and articulates a similar sense of the drama's social power: 'drama is strife, evolution, movement in whatever way unfolded'.[105] Instead of advocating the drama as social instrument, however, the essay appeals to the more abstract ideal of truth, making the important distinction between contemporary aestheticism and a characteristically Shavian art-philosophy: 'Beauty is the swerga of the aesthete; but truth has a more ascertainable and more real dominion. Art is true to itself when it deals with truth.'[106] Interestingly, this earlier essay also roots the drama in 'the historical cult of Dionysus, who, god of fruitage, joyfulness and earliest art, offered in his life-story a practical groundplan for the erection of a tragic and a comic theatre'.[107] This connection must have been made at some point in Joyce's studies, and possibly derives from a reading of Nietzsche (perhaps in French translation), or possibly of Shaw (there is passing praise for Wagner) or Max Nordau, though more likely, the connection derives from readings of Walter Pater and Arthur Symons who had explored the same connections with the cult of Dionysus.[108] More significantly, however, both of Joyce's essays privilege dramatic form. 'Drama and Life' distinguishes literature from drama as occupying the realm of accidental manners and humours, whereas drama is the expression of the underlying laws and the principle of truth. The distinction is demonstrative of the allegory within which the essay rewrites literary history, a history of perpetual decline from classical drama to contemporary literature. Anticipating Eliot's dissociation of sensibility, the essay identifies the renaissance as a point of critical decline, 'for it was the power of the Shakespearean clique', writes Joyce, 'that dealt the deathblow to the already dying drama'.[109] Not unlike Shaw, the young Joyce reserved some praise for Shakespeare's literary talents, but the final comment on Shakespeare's dramas reduces them to 'literature in dialogue'.[110] Thus, Joyce's early essays employ the trope of reading literary history and the teleology of modern development antithetically, seeking to recuperate a Dionysian spirit of art.

Shakespeare clearly plays a more positive role in *Ulysses*, which suggests, if there is any currency to maintaining the biographical parallel, that Stephen resembles not Joyce in 1904, but Joyce in the period of the episode's composition in the late 1910s. The earliest indication that Joyce's opinion of Shakespeare underwent a significant development was when, prior to the war and his move to Zurich when he and his family lived in Trieste, he was asked to give a series of lectures on English literature at the *Università Popolare* between 1912 and 1913. Although the lectures themselves are lost, the surviving autograph notes which Joyce made give some indication as to the source material he used for the lectures, and which would also be integral to Stephen's discussion in *Ulysses*.[111] The notes indicate that Joyce had developed an archaeological interest in Shakespeare, relating the composition of the plays to documented historical information about Elizabethan culture and theatrical practice, as well as an interest in biographical speculation and criticism.[112] The lecture notes make particular use of John Dover Wilson's 1911 compilation of Elizabethan prose *Life in Shakespeare's England* and the 1911 edition of Brandes' biography, two volumes he is known to have purchased for his own personal library.[113]

In approaching 'Scylla and Charybdis', Joyce would also draw on Brandes' biography, as well as on Sydney Lee's 1898 biography. Of the seventeen names associated with Shakespeare mentioned in the 'Scylla and Charybdis' episode, Brandes and Lee provide most of what are ostensibly facts about Shakespeare's life as narrated by Stephen.[114] The style of Stephen's exposition, however, resembles both Brandes' biographical criticism and, more particularly, Frank Harris' *The Man Shakespeare*. Both Brandes and Harris are featured in the text: Stephen introduces Brandes briefly in relation to the story of 'another Ulysses, Pericles, Prince of Tyre' (187) to support his belief in Shakespeare's authorship of the play; Harris' *Saturday Review* articles are praised moments later by John Eglinton (188). As noted earlier, Brandes' reading of *Hamlet* is inflected with Nietzsche's reading of Goethe: he writes, 'Hamlet belongs to the future, to the modern age. He embodies the lofty and reflective spirit, standing isolated, with its severely exalted ideals, in corrupt or worthless surroundings, forced to conceal its inmost nature, yet everywhere arousing hostility.'[115] Brandes is cited by both Freud in *The Interpretation of Dreams* and Harris in the *Saturday Review* articles which formed the basis of *The Man Shakespeare*. For all of these writers, *Hamlet* reflected a psychology which was illustrative of the modern psychosocial experience. Thus, Harris writes, 'Hamlet, in his intellectual unrest, morbid brooding, cynical self-analysis and dislike of bloodshed, is much more typical of the nineteenth or twentieth century than of the sixteenth.'[116] While Joyce's early essays locate Shakespeare at the origin of the drama's decline in the early modern period, championing instead an Ibsenite modernism, the Trieste notes look forward to Stephen's collaboration with Shakespeare in *Ulysses*, his theory drawing on biographical criticism to relocate Shakespeare's authorship in the modern and to disengage literary culture from the nineteenth century.

Stephen's theory is an almost banal appropriation of Harris' extremity, his belief that Shakespeare himself was the model not for Hamlet but for Hamlet's father exemplifying a further literalizing of biographical criticism. Stephen explains: 'If you hold that he, a greying man with two marriageable daughters, with thirtyfive years of life . . . is the beardless undergraduate from Wittemberg then you must hold that his seventy-year old mother is the lustful queen. No' (198). Despite his variation from the more common association of Shakespeare with Hamlet, the correspondence is still clear. As with Harris, for Stephen as well, the motif of the failed or defeated lover provides the impetus for the play: Shakespeare, as Stephen suggests, seduced in a cornfield by a woman eight years older than himself, was forced into an unwanted marriage with Anne Hathaway. Moreover, Stephen holds that the humiliation of this mistake was further compounded by Shakespeare's two usurping, adulterous brothers who 'came after William the conquered' (203). Anne's supposed misconduct with Shakespeare's brothers is evidenced by and consequently accounts for the prominence of the names Richard and Edmond among Shakespeare's treacherous characters elsewhere in the canon. Attempting to rationalize Shakespeare's marriage to Anne Hathaway, John Eglinton responds, 'The world believes that Shakespeare made a mistake . . . and got out of it as quickly and as best he could' (182). But 'mistake' is not the choice of words Stephen uses to describe Shakespeare's seduction and cuckolding: 'A man of genius makes no mistakes. His errors are volitional and are the portals of discovery' (182). This idea of Shakespeare's volitional error being a portal of discovery through which the entire canon of his work originates, as with *The Man Shakespeare*, inverts the romantic motif of woman as muse.

Following the example of Harris by assigning a central symbolic significance to *Venus and Adonis*, Stephen elaborates upon the nature of this conflict: 'No later undoing will undo the first undoing. The tusk of the boar has wounded him there where love lies ableeding. If the shrew is worsted yet there remains to her woman's invisible weapon' (188). This metaphoric transition from boar's tusk to woman's invisible weapon suggests a gender inversion of sexual imagery, the invisible female phallus as violently penetrating, which perhaps implies the female muse as a penetrating influence. But while the allegory is drawn from Shakespeare, the suggestion of the dangerous potential of the absent female phallus is overwhelmingly Freudian, strongly reminiscent of what Freud describes as the female's penis envy and her castration complex: in the pre-Oedipal phase, before she recognizes the fact of her castration, the female imagines the clitoris to be a kind of penis, a psychical projection which, if retained throughout post-pubescent sexual development, potentially leads to psychosexual neurosis.[117] Freud's name is not explicitly mentioned in the episode, and there is only one passing reference to 'the new Viennese school' (197). As Freud's English translations post-dated the 1904 setting, textual references and allusions would have been potentially anachronistic. Stephen's interpretation of *Hamlet* also derives quite obviously from Harris, whose own psychological criticism developed independently of European psychoanalysis. Still, the Freudian resonances in Stephen's biographical reading are undeniable, which suggests that Joyce circa 1918 exploited the advantage of historical retrospect to rewrite biographical criticism circa 1904 by drawing upon the richly figurative lexicon of psychoanalysis.[118]

The currency of psychoanalysis in Anglo-Irish culture was greatly accelerated by the 1913 English translation of *The Interpretation of Dreams*, though by the time of the episode's composition, Joyce was living in Zurich and also fluent in German. Like most writers and intellectuals, Joyce must have been reasonably familiar with the main tenets of psychoanalysis during the period when he was composing 'Scylla and Charybdis'.[119] Four psychoanalytic works were among the extensive collection of his personal library in Zurich, which also included the volume by Brandes and other books on Shakespeare by Lee, William Hazlitt and Walter Raleigh. These and other volumes – including those of his contemporaries Shaw, Ibsen, Yeats and Wilde – reflect the broad European range of his reading. But the psychoanalytic texts, in particular, provided Joyce with further substantiation of his already well-established belief in the psychological and sexual dimension of literary writing.[120] In addition to the German versions of Freud's 1910 pamphlet on Leonardo da Vinci and the 1917 *The Psychopathology of Everyday Life*, Joyce had purchased for his personal library a German translation of Ernest Jones' 1910 essay on *Hamlet*.[121] In Jones' Freudian interpretation, Hamlet's repressed sexual jealousy is stirred to unconscious activity by Claudius, who shows him his own wishful fantasy to kill his father. Moreover, *Hamlet* is expressive of Shakespeare's own unconscious desires: the repressed sexual instincts of Shakespeare's unconscious mind bear a direct relation to the processes of his conscious creativity. The correlation between Stephen's biographical interpretation and the Freudian narrative is not immediate, differing most obviously in the locus of sexual jealousy, Shakespeare's wife rather than his mother. But Joyce's reading of Jones inarguably pervades the text, if only in the metaphoric possibilities offered by the Freudian narrative.[122] Stephen similarly identifies a triangular relationship of sexual jealousy in *Hamlet* between father, mother and son, and literally dramatizes the play's biographical connection to Shakespeare by evoking the common supposition that Shakespeare was the actor of King Hamlet's ghost. By further developing the equation between artistic creativity and the psychosexual life of the author, Stephen's Shakespeare theory underscores the correspondence between biographical criticism and the Freudian narrative, the activity of writing portrayed as a male-gendered activity which requires a female-gendered 'portal of discovery', the symbolic significance of which is less than subtle.

While the mythical correlative of *Ulysses* is supplied by Homer rather than Sophocles, there are strong echoes of the Oedipus complex. Stephen first notes that *Hamlet* was written in a period following the death of Shakespeare's father, a point made by Brandes and reiterated from Brandes by both Freud and Harris. Describing the relationship between fathers and sons, Stephen says: 'The son unborn mars beauty: born, he brings pain, divides affection, increases care. He is a male: his growth is his father's decline, his youth his father's envy, his friend his father's enemy' (199). In the Freudian narrative, the father is a sexual rival and the son is the destined successor, in the position of an enemy and impatient 'to become ruler himself through his own father's death'.[123] The power of the father is phallocentric because patriarchal as well as sexual: Oedipus kills his father and sleeps with his mother. In normal sexual development, the only way the son can overcome the powerful repression of his childhood Oedipal desires is to take his father's place by becoming himself a father. In Stephen's rather Freudian interpretation of Shakespeare's biography, Shakespeare's guilt and anger, which resulted from the indiscretions of his wife, are seen to provide the creative energy with which he could write *Hamlet* and claim the patriarchal authority of authorship. Thus, in writing *Hamlet*, 'he was not the father of his own son merely but, being no more a son, he was and felt himself the father of all his race' (199). In his discussion of *Hamlet*, Stephen identifies sexual jealousy as the stimulus for conscious creativity and allegorizes that process in the framework of the Freudian family romance.

That Hamlet never succeeds his father is, in the Freudian narrative, indicative of the overly strong bond between mother and son, and the intense repression to which Hamlet's infantile sexual desires have been subjected. In general, the result of such maternal influence, notes Jones, are intense feelings of shame and guilt, the manifestation of a feminine character in the male subject, or even, when combined with other factors, homosexuality.[124] Stephen, too, wishes to become, like Shakespeare, the father of his own race, though he is inhibited by excessive feelings of guilt and remorse, 'agenbite of inwit' (198), brought on by his mother's death. In the episode, the threat of homosexual desire encroaches upon his private interior plane in the repeated occurrence of that Wildean phrase, the 'Love that dare not speak its name' (194). This anxiety is intensified by the foppish Richard Best, 'blond ephebe. Tame essence of Wilde' (190). For Stephen, there would appear to be an equation in his own mind between masculine virility and creative potency, and Best epitomizes the opposite, the intellectually vacant and effeminate aesthete. Consequently, the image of the successful Best, 'tall, young, mild, light' (178), with his empty notebook 'new, large, clean, bright (178) . . . his private papers in the original' (186), and his repetitive use of 'don't you know?', goad Stephen into self-loathing for his own feelings of intellectual impotency. In contrast to Best is the masculine and virile Buck Mulligan who enters midway through the episode, provoking Stephen to remark to himself, 'Hast thou found me, O mine enemy' (189). Mulligan, foil to Stephen's artist, repeatedly aggravates homophobic anxiety by suggesting the threat of homosexual desire. Thus, he says to Stephen when Leopold Bloom passes them on the library's portico towards the end of the episode: 'Did you see his eye? He looked upon you to lust after you' (209). While for Freud homosexuality, or sexual inversion, is symptomatic of the failure of the subject to overcome his repressed infantile sexual desire and succeed the father, for Stephen, the threat of homosexual desire is equated with his own creative impotency, reminding him of the patriarchal destiny of authorship which he is being denied.

The degree of Joyce's interest in psychoanalysis has been the subject of considerable debate, especially with regard to the psychological dimension of the narrative style. The numerous, and remarkably unconventional, narrative techniques employed throughout *Ulysses* might be seen to give narrative identity to the gradations of conscious activity between conscious and unconscious. In 'Scylla and Charybdis', the narrative is authorial third person, but Stephen's perspective is privileged, the reader privy to Stephen's interior commentary. The narrative effect is to filter the objective events through Stephen's perspective and narrativize his interior thought-processes, the narrative events punctuated with sequences of Stephen's related thoughts, apparent feelings of conscience, and dreamlike images. As in the earlier 'Proteus' episode where the reader is treated to what might be called a sustained 'stream-of-consciousness' (though the fluidity of 'stream' fails to capture the sense of abandonment to rational control which characterizes the psychical narrative here), the thought-organization suggests origination in various levels of conscious, preconscious, subconscious and unconscious activity.[125] The narrative expression of the unconscious reaches a climax in the highly hallucinatory 'Circe' episode, where Stephen confronts the ghost of his dead mother. This episode also contains a dream-image which unites the Freudian family romance with Shakespeare's authorship:

(*Stephen and Bloom gaze in the mirror. The face of William Shakespeare, beardless, appears there, rigid in facial paralysis, crowned by the reflection of the reindeer antlered hatrack in the hall.*) (528)

The image offers a triangular configuration between father (Bloom), son (Stephen) and spiritual author (Shakespeare). And yet, the mirror reflects a paralyzed face, effeminate (beardless) and cuckolded (crowned with horns). In this final reflection of the unconscious, Joyce withholds from Stephen Freud's destined patriarchal succession.

The autobiographical dimension of Joyce's writing might also be seen to depend upon the Freudian parallel between dream text and literary text, creative output as representative of the author's psychosexual life. But while *Ulysses* exploits the metaphoric possibilities offered by the psychoanalytic narrative to animate Stephen's psychoaesthetic experience, rather than corroborate the autobiographical association with Joyce, Stephen's Shakespeare theory ultimately writes a model of authorship which, though drawing upon the metaphoric possibilities, is finally distinct from the Freudian narrative. Stephen is not a universalized representative of modern psychopathology, nor is he a mere autobiographical reflection of the author. Rather, Stephen is Joyce's highly individuated artist-figure. This figure, which is developed along a trajectory from the character's first appearance in *Stephen Hero* to *A Portrait of the Artist as a Young Man* to, finally, *Ulysses*, represents Joyce's continuing dialogue with the aesthetic and psychical ideologies of authorship.[126] In addition to the psychoanalytic works, Joyce had also purchased several volumes of English and German aesthetic theory and philosophy before 1918, including the 1909 English translation of Nietzsche's *The Birth of Tragedy*.[127] While the immediate sources for the 'Scylla and Charybdis' episode are the biographical studies contemporary with the 1904 setting, Joyce's reading during the period reflected the broad influence of European aesthetic ideology on Anglo-Irish literary modernism and, again, in particular, of Nietzsche's aesthetic theory in English translation. As with Nietzsche for whom romantic idealism provided the antithetical plane in which he could individuate his own consciousness, the idealized representations of Hamlet as espoused by his adversaries in the library are necessary because they make possible Stephen's own process of individuation.

Early in *Ulysses*, Buck Mulligan mocks Stephen's penchant for a rather Nietzschean egotism, declaring while preparing for his swim: 'I'm the *Uebermensch*. Toothless Kinch and I, the supermen . . . Thus spake Zarathustra' (22). Stephen's Hamlet is not democratized or universally representative, but rather highly individuated, an isolated figure within his surrounding environment; like Stephen, intensely subjective, critical, egotistical and spiritless; like Nietzsche, the modern tragic philosopher.[128] Stephen might be said to resemble, as Nietzsche suggests for Hamlet in *The Birth of Tragedy*, Dionysian man: 'Both have looked deeply into the true nature of things, they have *understood* and are now loath to act . . . What, both in the case of Hamlet and of Dionysiac man, overbalances any motive leading to action, is not reflection but understanding, the apprehension of truth and its terror.'[129] Contingency, the understanding of the truth which kills action, is what differentiates Stephen from the other participants in the discussion, his argument echoing Nietzsche's resistance to Platonic idealism. For Stephen, Hamlet is not an idealized representative of modern man; rather, he is the Dionysian spirit, the apprehender of truth, Zarathustra's *Übermensch* who resists absorption into a realm of Apollonian illusion and false consciousness. What makes Stephen and his construction of Hamlet acutely modern is not that they express the modern world in which they find themselves lost and isolated, but that they resist the temptation to illusion in this world, embracing their modern nihilism.

The peril of Dionysian consciousness, however, is this consuming nihilism which destroys the will to action; and even for Nietzsche, the resistance to modern existence was not solely one of a nihilistic will to death. The will of the artist replaces the will to action, art providing the necessary salvation: 'Then, in this supreme jeopardy of the will, art, that sorceress expert in healing, approaches him; only she can turn his fits of nausea into imaginations with which it is possible to live.'[130] The super-man for whom the will to death (the apprehension of truth) and the will to life (the will to power) coexist, and in whom resides the potential for redemption from a specifically modern nihilism, is the artist. The library episode of *Ulysses* thematizes a similar redemption from destruction through art, identifying the supremacy of the artist as demonstrated by Shakespeare.[131] Shakespeare is portrayed in Stephen's theory as an artist who achieves salvation by embracing the morbid conditions of his exist-ence, his sexual misfortunes and betrayals at the hands of his wife and brothers, or his volitional errors, and transforming them into art. Stephen essentially leads the reader to a typically Nietzschean conclusion, but typical not only for the way he denotes a similar relationship between identity and art, but also for the kind of identity for the artist which he inscribes. The artist is consubstantial rather than representative, 'all in all in all of us' (204). Just as the divine Trinity orders and merges all identity according to the image of the father, so too the artist engenders a patriarchal authority as the father of his race. Moreover, as the patriarchal metaphor would suggest, the artist is undeniably always male. For Nietzsche, art is the sorceress; female, acted upon, and life giving; the will to live. Art, not unlike Stephen's portal of discovery, is both the muse whom the artist penetrates and the portal through whom the artwork is born. Stephen's Shakespeare theory consequently essentializes the produc-tion of art as a male activity by coding it in the terms of patriarchal succession and male sexuality.

The essentializing power of Stephen's theory finally replaces the idea of *Hamlet* as representation – the iconic or emblematic capacity of the character to signify an aesthetic ideology or an archetypal psychology – and transforms it into a fetishized embodiment of the male artist. The play becomes no longer a demonstration of the mimetic capacity of art to represent life, but rather that life itself, animated by a male artistic spirit. This distinction might be understood by turning once again to

Nietzsche's delineation between the Apollonian and Dionysian, his dichotomous realms of structured artifice, the god of light and plastic powers who reigns 'over the fair illusion of our inner world of fantasy', versus the spirit which is seen to inhabit and animate that world, the god of rapture and physical intoxication.[132] The Apollonian realm is one of dream images, the symbolic significance of which betokens a level of reality underneath the dream images, not unlike Freud's unconscious. This reality underneath is the Dionysian truth, the immediate apprehension of which would precipitate a characteristically modern chaos, disorder and frenzied destruction. The artist is the channel through whom the Dionysian is ordered into Apollonian consciousness, making existence bearable. While the appeal of *Hamlet* for Stephen is on one level the capacity of the play to symbolize the process which creates art out of disorder, what Stephen rejects are the emblematic appropriations of Hamlet's character vis-à-vis nineteenth-century Shakespeare criticism. *Hamlet* the play is at once both Hamlet the character and Shakespeare the author, and Shakespeare comes to stand for the artistic tradition which emanates through rather than from *Hamlet*, and through to Stephen as artist, absorbing and synthesizing all of the appropriations into a single consubstantial face, the features of which are significantly male. Hamlet becomes that transcendental fetishistic spirit which is the modern artist.

As if deliberately satirizing the Nietzschean echo, John Eglinton responds to Stephen's theory in the library by returning the attention to woman: 'The will to live . . . for poor Ann, Will's widow, is the will to die' (197). This punning will to death would appear to be the same legacy which the text leaves for woman. Woman is the figure through whom the identity of the artist is given metaphorical, metaphysical birth, and she is the ghost, the dead mother, which haunts *Ulysses* from the margins into which she has been repressed. Woman is Stephen's dead mother who rises emaciated in the 'Circe' episode, crying, 'Repent, Stephen' (540). Woman is the nearly forgotten Anne Hathaway for whom Shakespeare famously bequeathed in his last will and testament his second-best bed. Here, in this final synthesizing image, his will, is the word which unites into one will all three wills; the artist (Will Shakespeare), his art (artistic will; will to power), and the inheritance left to forgotten woman (his last will and testament). The second-best bed, Shakespeare's last and greatest unsolved riddle, a final testimony to the impossibility of finally identifying the author, leads us to Joyce: what separates Stephen from Joyce? Is *Ulysses* an unconscious representation of the author? Is *Ulysses* one momentary, transfigural incarnation of his identity or does he provide the soul of the work, entelechy, form of forms? Or do all three of Hamlet, Shakespeare and Stephen merge into a single consubstantial authorial identity manifested finally in Joyce? These are the questions to which the text leads, but which, in the final analysis, refuses to answer. Perhaps this is the attraction of *Ulysses*, the idea of the second-best bed, Shakespeare's unsolved riddle, the inheritance which haunts the book; like the author, dissolving, splintering, shifting, re-emerging:

> Leftherhis
> Secondbest
> Leftherhis
> Bestabed
> Secabest
> Leftabed. (195)

CHAPTER 3

The theatre and a changing civilization

In 1911, the film producer William Barker persuaded the distinguished Shakespearean actor, Sir Herbert Beerbohm Tree, to commit several scenes from his current stage production of *Henry VIII* to film. The result, first shown in March of that year, was the most expensive and most successful Shakespeare film to be thus far endeavoured. Six weeks later, after a stipulated period, all twenty prints of the film were collected, counted and checked by Barker, unwound into a loose pile on a large iron sheet and, on a lot outside of Ealing Studio in London in front of a small gathering of spectators and the press, set alight. The twentieth century offered history numerous examples in which this kind of public demonstration, the almost ceremonial destruction of cultural artefacts, has been indicative of political turmoil or of intimidating displays made by authoritarian regimes. However, this was merely a publicity stunt, Barker having warned the public to see his film before it was quite literally too late. Moreover, this was a film from the earliest days of the medium. Not only were new reels appearing at a phenomenal rate, many advertising an advance in the technology of film production, there was little sense that films which had passed through the commercial cinema system needed to be preserved or that they contributed significantly, if at all, to art. Indeed, the sooner a film deteriorated from use or the sooner it became no longer marketable, the sooner another was required to take its place. At any rate, those who had missed the opportunity in the cinema could see Tree perform in the stage version upon which the film was based, still running at His Majesty's Theatre in London for at least a few more weeks.

As the film is completely lost, and the few accounts which remain are the brief descriptions culled from the trade journals of the period, discussion of the film's significance is necessarily limited. Those film historians who do not overlook the episode entirely tend to read Barker's film of *Henry VIII* in terms of its effect upon the cost of film production and distribution in England.[1] By 1911, American melodramas accounted for the majority of films being distributed in England, with English films accounting for roughly fifteen per cent of the market.[2] The system of distribution in which intermediary companies bought large quantities of cheap film prints to distribute to cinema houses for short runs favoured the large volume of inexpensive films being imported from America. Certainly, the cultural authority of Shakespeare contributed to the exclusivity of Barker's film, but as the American Vitagraph company had been consistently demonstrating since 1908, having produced ten Shakespeare films in that year alone, the murders, intrigues and romances of Shakespeare's plays provided as many thrills as the cinematic melodrama.[3] This type of fare was consistent with that of the English music halls whose audiences were primarily working-class. These audiences were also the primary spectators of early films, films often shown in the music halls themselves, interspersed with other forms of entertainment in variety shows. For these audiences, Shakespeare proved consistently popular material, and between the years 1908 and 1913, mostly American film companies produced no less than thirty-six Shakespeare film adaptations. What most significantly differentiated Barker's film from, for example, the Vitagraph films or, for that matter, from his own 1910 film version of *Hamlet*, was not so much the nature of the film itself, but the marketing apparatus and the terms of distribution which he dictated. While Barker himself remained responsible for the film's distribution in London, the rights to the provinces were granted to a single distribution company to which the film was rented, not sold. Only twenty prints of the film were made, ten for London and ten for the provinces, all of which were called in after a limited run of six weeks. Not only by these terms could the exhibitors justify higher ticket prices, but the prospect of an unprecedented limited run, in contrast to the seemingly unlimited stream of cheaply made mass-produced Shakespeare films coming mostly from America, proved a marketing success among a public anxious to see an 'exclusive' film.[4]

After the film's release, cinema house managers reportedly turned away large disappointed crowds. At the King's Hall in Shepherd's Bush, for example: 'Hundreds had to be turned away nightly, and the general impression of those fortunate to gain admission, was that it was the finest picture ever thrown on a screen.'[5] The success of the film, however, was not unwarranted, for Barker was a savvy producer. He augmented his announcement of the limited release with an unprecedented amount of pre-release publicity. Moreover, he engaged the well-known

Shakespearean Tree for the similarly unprecedented sum of £1000. When Barker produced his *Hamlet* in 1910, he used an entirely unknown cast, many of whom were not actors, and he shot the entire film in one day on location at his own private studio and grounds. Taking such expedient measures, he assured himself of a moderate financial success. When he came to produce *Henry VIII*, Barker again attempted his trademark single-day shoot, but his second Shakespeare film project was both financially and aesthetically quite different: a comparatively expensive media stunt which required the enormous task of organizing the immense cast and production team into the day's shoot.[6] Tree was not unaccustomed to such ambitious film projects. He had experimented with the medium before, and is credited with producing the first ever Shakespeare film, the recently discovered 1899 *King John*.[7] Tree had also recently produced a film of the opening storm scene from his stage production of *The Tempest* with the intention of incorporating the sequence into the stage version to go on tour. But for *Henry VIII*, Tree was engaged in what may be the earliest example of a headlining star whose marketability was seen to assure the success of the film. The *Kinematograph and Lantern Weekly* duly noted: 'That this film would be a great artistic triumph was a foregone conclusion, and the interest it will create, coupled with the great influence it will have on the uplifting movement, will, we are certain, more than come up to our anticipations.'[8] *Henry VIII* was made a commercially 'exclusive' film by the apparatus of distribution upon which Barker insisted, and by the high cost of production, but the credibility given the film by Tree acting Shakespeare assured Barker's *Henry VIII* was equally exclusive aesthetically.

Shortly after the run of the film, the stage version of *Henry VIII*, no longer commercially lucrative, was discontinued, the sets were decommissioned and the actors turned to new projects, the production ending as had the film when the prints were called in and destroyed. A few years later, Tree published his *Thoughts and After-Thoughts*, a broad collection of essays written over a period of years, which together offered a defence of his own theatrical style from the kind of changes being prescribed by more modernizing practitioners.[9] While the volume reproduced in full his earlier publication, *Henry VIII and His Court*, written in 1910 to coincide with his stage production, nowhere does the volume mention either the 1911 film or any of Tree's other film projects.[10] The omission reflects the manner in which Tree would seem to have viewed his various film projects – perhaps as entertaining experiments, but certainly outside of the scope of the art which he practised in the theatre. Even if

Tree had anticipated that the film would serve as record of his stage performance, from his perspective, the entire project was primarily intended to publicize and complement the stage run rather than pass as a filmic performance in its own right. Accordingly, the film was advertised during its release on a pamphlet distributed to the cinema houses as 'Scenes from Shakespeare's *King Henry VIII* As Given by Sir Herbert Tree at His Majesty's Theatre'. Although the five scenes selected were performed in the correct narrative order, regardless, the film was more or less composed of vignettes from the stage version, not as a coherent self-sustaining narrative. Moreover, the primary reason Barker gave before the release for his intention to withdraw the film was, especially should it prove unsatisfactory, to prevent the film from detracting from the stage production or interfering with ticket sales.[11] Barker was, by now, known for his ostentatious publicity tactics, and promise of the film's destruction perhaps elicited enough anticipation to generate a handful of witnesses at the event. Tree himself did not attend, but, in an ironic twist, the entire episode was filmed by a cameraman for the company and Tree was supposedly given a copy of this new film as a commemorative souvenir. Regardless, Tree was clearly not impressed enough to mention either the original or the commemorative film in his memoirs.

There must have been some sense of the potential for this film to preserve what had become a monumentally successful and important theatrical production, as well as some sense that the film was itself, as A. E. Taylor wrote for *Moving Picture World*, a 'great triumph of the kinematographer's art. The picture is without doubt the greatest that has even been attempted in the country, and I am almost tempted to say in any other.'[12] Nevertheless, both Barker and Tree's final attitude towards the entire project suggests that they viewed the film indifferently, or at least, as not important enough to necessitate preserving. Given the general lack of regard for film posterity among early twentieth-century producers and distributors, their disregard for the film's posterity is unsurprising. But why destroy the film so completely, wilfully and sys- tematically? To secure his financial success, Barker maintained control over and then recalled the prints of the film, but was the insistent finality of burning them publicly a necessary publicity stunt, especially after he had made his fortune?

Short of suggesting that the film's destruction was a deliberately polit- ical gesture, a conscious act of propaganda or protest, what I would like to suggest is a specifically politicized context for reading the whole episode, the film and its destruction as a site demonstrative of the various issues surrounding the reform of the theatre in early twentieth-century England. Indeed, what must be emphasized is how important the 1911 film of *Henry VIII* was itself, both aesthetically and economically, in relation to the early twentieth-century theatre and the theatrical production of Shakespeare. In 1911, this was the single most successful film of Shakespeare ever projected on screen, possibly the most successful film in England to the date, successful enough to rival the popularity of Tree's stage version of the play. Approximately 375,000 attended the stage version over the course of the run's 254 performances, by far Tree's most successful Shakespeare production at His Majesty's.[13] Given the absence of any records, the film's total audience is quite impossible to estimate with any claim to accuracy. But given the capacity of the newer 'picture palaces' around this time of between 1,000 and 2,000 patrons, and also of twenty prints during a six-week run, even with a cautious estimate of 200,000, the audience numbers for the film would have rivalled, if not exceeded, most contemporary Shakespeare runs in the theatre.[14] More importantly, however, Barker's publicity mechanism saw what was marketed as a culturally authoritative performance disseminated to an audience unprecedentedly diverse, both socially and geographically. The newer and larger cinema palaces – neither primarily bourgeois institutions like the mainstream London theatres, nor mere working-class venues of entertainment like the music halls – appealed to a broader and more fluid, urban middle-class. So Barker's film could exploit the cultural authority of Tree acting Shakespeare well beyond the more traditional scope of His Majesty's.

At the same time, the growth of broader, more democratized entertainment venues coupled with the sheer volume of films being produced was increasingly stigmatizing the film as a 'mass' or low medium. In America, the debate about high and low art, or about the representation of high art in a low medium, surrounded Shakespearean film adaptations such as those of the Vitagraph company, and finally led in the case of Vitagraph's *Julius Caesar* to the censorship of what were deemed, when taken out of the context of Shakespeare's rich language, overtly graphic and unnecessarily gratuitous depictions of violence and sexuality.[15] In England as well, as much as Shakespeare lent cultural authority to the film medium, silent and uncompromisingly visual compressions of the written text were seen as threatening to mitigate Shakespeare's art into a debased commercial commodity: 'A photograph, even a moving photograph', argued the popular dramatist John Drinkwater, 'may be an interesting thing, but it cannot be an artistically significant thing because in so far as it is anything, it is a literal reproduction of a natural object deprived of those dimensional aspects that make it susceptible to an art convention of the stage.'[16] For Drinkwater, film was merely commercial spectacle. Ironically, a similar criticism often made of Tree in the theatre was that his expensive and ornate productions threatened to reduce Shakespeare to commercial spectacle. Even though he was dismissive of his different film projects, the fact of Tree's participation in early film therefore represented a significant association between large-scale, mainstream theatre and cinema. Of the English Shakespeare films produced in the early years of the twentieth century, the majority featured older actor-managers like Tree and Frank Benson. Johnston Forbes-Robertson was sixty when he agreed to play Hamlet in the 1913 film produced by The Gaumont Company. Benson as well was in his fifties when his touring company was filmed performing a number of Shakespeare productions from 1911. This association between what was increasingly becoming an outmoded, older style of theatre and the growing cinema arguably provided a major impetus to theatrical reform in the period. That association represented the potential for an unlimited multiplication through 'mass' media like the cinema of a specifically bourgeois style of theatrical production typical of the actor-manager system.[17]

In other words, while the industrialization and urbanization of England in the late nineteenth century, the height of the actor-manager system, was increasingly problematizing theatrical production, the ever-increasing scale of West-end style productions necessitated an appeal to the broader, and subsequently, less critical tastes of a growing middle-class audience. The resulting crisis of the theatre in the early twentieth century was further heightened by the development of film technology, the emergence of a culture industry to meet the appeal of this new medium, and the subsequent reorganization of class cultures into a mass culture. And here we find the cultural authority of Shakespeare at the very intersection of these issues of class, new modes of mechanical reproduction, aesthetic value and the traditional theatre institution as a producer of art. In this sense, we might read the entire episode in the context of cultural revolution, the violence of the film's destruction as indicative of that revolutionizing of the entire apparatus of Shakespeare production, indicative of the potentially volatile relationship between Shakespeare as agent in the cultural enfranchisement of modern, urbanized mass society, and the traditional theatre institution as a producer of art.

SHAKESPEARE IN THE AGE OF MECHANICAL REPRODUCTION

In his 1924 publication *The Organised Theatre*, St John Ervine posed the question: how would a young Shakespeare, carrying a manuscript of *Hamlet* to a West End theatre in contemporary London, fare in attempting to make a living out of dramatic writing? Having derived the title for his book from Matthew Arnold's call in 1880 to 'organise the theatre', Ervine considered the problems which would greet a young genius in what he regarded to be an age of confusion in theatrical production.[18] As the first and greatest obstacle, the book sketches an image of the early twentieth-century audience, the audience of the Machine Age, an impoverished middle-class demoralized by long periods of unemployment and war; vulgar, half-asleep, empty-minded. In the theatre, Ervine argued, the aesthetic of beauty was being replaced by a horrible contagion of commonness, a contagion which 'spreads itself over a modern community until at last people are so accustomed to ugly things that they are incapable of realising that they are ugly at all – are even capable of believing them to be beautiful'.[19] Ervine saw the modern English drama as typified by commonness, vulgarity and the comic light fare of the music hall, and subject to the prescriptive tastes of an undiscerning urban middle-class audience. This environment was not at all conducive to the creation of a dramatic exemplar like *Hamlet*. In contrast to popular comedies which were demonstrative of a culturally impoverished audience, great tragedy, the kind produced by a figure like Shakespeare, was seen to be the expression of individual genius: 'A man of genius is at once a sign of his own greatness, and a sign of his nation's greatness: he is the expression both of a unique personality and of a noble race.'[20] Such kind of genius represented the history of progress, 'the history of the heart-rending attempts made by determined individuals to overcome the sloth and opposition of multitudes obstinately resolved not to have any progress at all'.[21] Thus, the question Ervine posed was how to reorganize the theatre so that, should a young dramatist with the genius equivalent to Shakespeare come to London to begin a career in the theatre, he would find the equivalent conditions which would allow the kind of success Shakespeare had with such tragedies as *Hamlet* on the Elizabethan stage.

The idealization of Shakespeare as the exemplary symbol of genius and creativity in the English theatre was hardly unique to the twentieth century. But Ervine's elevation of Shakespeare to cultural and, more specifically, national and racial emblem, the cult of masculinity he seemed to advocate and, most significantly, his characteristically politicized rhetoric about the need for a radical response to middle-class culture – all of these traits exemplify early twentieth-century theatrical discourse. The nature, quality and legitimacy of dramatic art, and more importantly, theatrical art (the drama as produced in the theatre) had been a central preoccupation of theatre practitioners from the late nineteenth century. The need to define such a category, either within the terms of theatre art for theatre art's sake or within the terms of the theatre's potential for social enlightenment and education, became more necessary in what was unanimously agreed to be a period of epochal change, a period of unprecedented societal transformation. For Ervine, Shakespeare was a cultural exemplar who could unite a disenfranchised public under the aegis of nationhood, Shakespeare's individual genius and eternal value set against the image of a nation battling an effeminating loss of identity. This is a theme which recurs insistently throughout an expansive and largely undocumented body of writing about theatrical practice which, chronologically, charts the aesthetic and institutional transformation of the theatre in this period from the actor-manager system predominant in the nineteenth century to the state-subsidized national and repertory theatres established later in the twentieth century. Beginning around the time of Arnold's call in 1880 to organize the theatre, the numerous texts written by actors, producers and critics which addressed aesthetic and institutional reform constituted one long, sustained and unrequited plea unanswered until the legislation of the National Theatre Act in 1948. Occurring at a midpoint in 1924, Ervine's *The Organised Theatre* straddled the two categories of noticeably different kinds of writing on the subject; on the aesthetic debate, the kind of exposition which declared the art of the theatre or which supported various aesthetic movements; and on the more pragmatic question of the theatre's organization, that which proposed institutional reform, usually through advocacy of a national or repertory scheme. These two types of argument, however, were never really divided: the art of the theatre required a certain kind of institution, usually a state-funded repertory theatre, while those who advocated such an institution also advocated certain kinds of drama and certain dramatists to be produced, the new art of the theatre.

Though continuous with late Victorian cultural and social reforms, theatrical discourse by the early twentieth century increasingly sought to reconcile theatrical aesthetics with the socio-economic transformations of late industrial capitalism. Entirely distinct from, and arguably more imaginative and flourishing than, actual theatrical practice in England, the numerous works of theatrical theory articulated a collective and diverse politics of engagement which mirrored contemporary aesthetic and socio-philosophical discourse. What these diverse theatrical tracts shared was an ideological opposition to bourgeois capitalism and to the money-making actor-manager system which united their pleas under the banner of comprehensive theatrical reform, upon the general principles of which most were agreed. Most prominent in the theatrical reform movement were William Archer and Harley Granville-Barker, who endorsed the petition for a privately endowed repertory system in London as well as for state endowment of a national theatre. While more local campaigns for repertory theatre in the provinces looked to the experiments of Granville-Barker's Court Theatre seasons in London, also of considerable prominence was the Shakespeare Memorial National Theatre committee, combining the efforts of the London-based committee to establish a memorial monument to Shakespeare with the governing directors of the Shakespeare Memorial Theatre in Stratford who sought to establish a permanent, resident Shakespeare company for Stratford.[22]

Despite their diversity, where these various aesthetic and institutional campaigns coincided was in their attempt to regulate the production and reception of drama in the theatre by coding and institutionalizing an autonomous theatrical art to counter the threat posed by what were perceived to be the prescriptive tastes of an emerging mass culture audience. Commercial entertainment, either as represented by the large-scale theatres established in the eighteenth and nineteenth centuries for bourgeois audiences, the working-class music-hall venues, or the now well-established cinema houses, necessitated the legitimation of dramatic art as aesthetically exclusive and institutionally legitimate. As the calls for the reformation of theatrical practice in the early twentieth century became more persistent, the style of expensive and grand productions of Shakespeare, such as those of Sir Herbert Beerbohm Tree at Her (later His) Majesty's Theatre around the turn of the century, were regarded as being primarily commercially motivated. For the various proponents of theatrical reform, the actor-manager system represented theatrical production on a grand scale which not only was no longer viable, but more importantly, was not considered art. Even before Tree's film of *Henry VIII* in 1911, Edward Gordon Craig was criticizing the pageantry and spectacle of the degraded money-making theatre, 'the coloured Christmas card culture which in the teeth of common sense and conventional good taste displays its impertinence night after night, year after year upon our English stage and claims the right to be held as artistic'.[23] If the burning of Tree's film in 1911 reflected on one level an emerging conflict between the commercial enterprise of marketing Shakespeare and a notion of Shakespeare as theatrical art, by 1924, this conflict had expanded into a rhetorically complex debate.

Tree had by then been dead for seven years, but his lavish productions of Shakespeare, along with those of Henry Irving, still persisted in the public imagination as the most ornate and grandly histrionic productions of the contemporary stage. Tree was famous for the sheer scale of his theatrical productions, from the meticulously decorated and historically researched settings to the immense supporting casts of supernumeraries. Tree's attempt to recreate the renaissance in his stage production of *Henry VIII*, for example, required 380 expensive and ornate costumes for the cast of 172 actors. The pageantry and spectacle included, in one reviewer's opinion, 'kaleidoscopic tableaux such as have never been seen on any stage' (*Manchester Courier*, 2 September 1910).[24] Tree's contemporary actor-managers like Johnston Forbes-Robertson and Frank Benson could not parallel the scale on which Tree produced Shakespeare; indeed, his version of Shakespeare was so unapologetically grand and commercial that few producers could continue to follow that avenue successfully. For those who campaigned variously for the reform of the theatre, Tree's Shakespeare productions not only epitomized an outmoded histrionic style of acting largely descended from Victorian melodrama, but the unmitigated commercialism of his ventures was seen to accommodate the predominantly bourgeois tastes of his audience.[25] Actor-managers such as Tree were seen to have reduced Shakespeare to the level of expensive spectacle and pageantry, sacrificing their integrity to the 'profit-seeking stage'.[26] In his argument for the repertory system, P. P. Howe summarized the problem of treating the theatre as a trade to be exploited to the greatest possible profit: 'Everything tends to filter down to the level of the readiest possible popular acceptability. In other words, in the economics of the theatre it is the man in the street who is the residual claimant.'[27] For Howe, the phraseology of 'the man in the street' served to characterize a largely unintelligent and undiscerning, growing mass public audience; and for the majority of theatrical reformers, this mass public audience was symptomatic of what was, as early as Barker's 1911 film of *Henry VIII*, the firmly established cinema culture. Thus, where the reformers continued to promote, for example, the traditional antithesis between the theatre with working-class entertainments such as the music hall, the cinema threatened to absorb those social distinctions into a single mass commercial audience, represented allegorically by 'the man in the street'. T. S. Eliot, in one of his brief forays into social criticism for the American *Dial* magazine neatly, summarized the problem in England:

if it rejects with contumely the independent man, the free man, all the individuals who do not conform to a world of mass-production, the middle-class finds itself on one side more and more approaching identity with what used to be called the Lower Class . . . In other words, there will soon be only one class, and the second Flood is here.[28]

The emergence of film technology followed by the rapid commercialization of this technology in the cinema system in the early twentieth century initiated for the theatrical environment the same type of anxiety and ideological contestation which the introduction and commercialization of photography had earlier imposed upon the visual arts. As early as 1916, Antonio Gramsci was able to recognize and manipulate this growing anxiety about the threat of the cinema in his criticism of theatrical practice in Italy. Admonishing the theatre for trying to produce the same effects as the cinema, Gramsci, well ahead of his time, denounced the purely visual function of the film: 'It is silent; in other words it reduces the role of the artists to movement alone, to being machines without souls.'[29] For Gramsci, the film, lacking human content, was incapable of conveying the psychological truth, creative imagination and passion of genuine art. By 1936, Walter Benjamin was able to articulate more clearly this apparently antagonistic relationship between the work of genuine art to the work mechanically reproduced. Benjamin ascribed to the genuine art artefact an aura of authenticity; an aura of human creativity, genius, eternal value and mystery, a unique existence which withered when substituted with a plurality of identical copies.[30] Although written twelve years after Ervine's book and outside of England, Benjamin's theory arguably reflects what was a corresponding fear among theatrical producers in the period of film technology's impending effect upon theatrical art. Concentrating his argument on photography, Benjamin opposed the mechanically reproduced artefact to a notion of the authentic or the genuine artefact, defined by an actual presence in time and space, a 'unique existence at the place where it happens to be'.[31] In contrast, the mechanically reproduced artwork represented for Benjamin the potential for the limitless multiplication of the genuine artefact, a multiplication which was seen to jeopardize the authority, or more correctly, the 'aura' that inhered within the genuine art object. The work of art in the age of mechanical reproduction became the work of art designed for reproducibility, designed for multiplication into the greatest possible number of copies. In the age of mechanical reproduction, art was therefore seen to be preconditioned by the mass audience response it would produce, and was, consequently, subject to the tastes and desires of an uncritical public.[32]

Of course, in the English theatrical environment of 1924, the language of Marxist aesthetic theory had not yet been fully or completely articulated.[33] While many of those who campaigned for reform were members of socialist groups like the Fabians or retained associations with private literary and dramatic societies, in their critique of the commercial system of theatrical production they lacked a developed theorized vocabulary to articulate effectively what they perceived as the threat posed by a massified, industrialized society; still, the threat of the mass predominated the images and language used to describe the audiences of the commercial theatre. Whether described in visions of industrialized society or whether hypostasized as a mindless public audience, the threat of the mass was equated with the levelling of social distinction, with the sublimation of the individual and the genuine into an indistinct 'man in the street'. In his collection of essays *The Foundations of a National Drama*, for example, the dramatist Henry Arthur Jones qualified the great 'humanizing' force of dramatic art against the threat of an endlessly multiplied image of the urban middle-class: 'millions of our citizens living sedentary, monotonous lives in their little, square, drab, brick boxes'.[34] In architecture as in the theatre, Jones held that the aesthetic of beauty had been degraded by persistent repetition and replaced by a hollow, lifeless form. In his characteristic image of monotonous suburban life, the individual was endlessly multiplied into the mass characterized as mechanical, imitative, and lacking in thought, texture and life. Like the photograph, the man in the street was held up as a representative of the endlessly multiplying, and therefore threatening, mindless urban middle-class. In his analysis of the English stage at the turn of the century, Mario Borsa also provided a characteristically modern vision of London, 'where the life of the streets, with all its phases and episodes, melts, as it were, and merges into one single, immense, confused, tiresome roar . . . the crowd is so characterless and inscrutable'.[35] The tiresome roar is the anathema which echoes in the various hypostasized images of threat posed by the unintelligent and undiscerning mass culture audience. Those authors like Jones and Borsa who criticized the theatre using such terminology variously submerged the threat posed by a mass culture within different class associations, either criticizing the effete and imitative bourgeois society, the impoverished middle-class, or the 'lower instincts' of a working-class audience seeking pleasure.[36] Regardless, the 'mass' associations remained the same: undiscerning, unintelligent and in need of guidance.

A National Theatre: Scheme and Estimates – the 1907 treatise jointly authored by William Archer and Harley Granville-Barker – similarly expressed a fear of the growing predominance of the mass culture audience in the theatre. The scheme for a national repertory system employed a characteristically Fabian rhetoric to describe the effect upon theatrical art of the commercial system. The Fabian Society, among whose members the names Shaw and Granville-Barker were prominent, supported a mass democratic base of art institutions, though their aim, ostensibly to facilitate social levelling, was in reality to infuse mass culture with the precepts of traditional high art.[37] Disparaging the entrepreneurial commercialism of the theatre, Archer and Granville-Barker's scheme characterized the theatre as degraded by the social and economic relations of capitalism. In a preface to the scheme, Granville-Barker insisted that it 'is essential to break away, completely and unequivocally from the profit-seeking stage'.[38] In a similar vein, the poet and dramatist John Drinkwater warned that: 'All arts are in constant danger of becoming commercialized, and none more so than that of the theatre.'[39] In both cases, the exigencies of commercialism were seen to represent the greatest threat to the production of theatrical art: like the photograph, drama produced for the commercial theatre was the drama produced for reproducibility, for the long-run system. While these various theatrical discourses sought to define the crisis in theatrical production against the vicissitudes of the commercial mass market, the notion of a dramatic art transcending the conditions of its production and reception – the 'exigencies of the theatrical system'[40] and 'the limitations of its audience'[41] – was particularly problematic for the theatre. While popular art forms or entertainments such as the cinema (popular in the sense of having a wide appeal) were seen to be dictated by the tastes and frivolities of an undiscerning public and were therefore ordered below genuine art precisely because of their popular associations, the drama, insofar as it was produced for public performance and therefore depended upon a certain degree of popularity for success, could not easily escape the exigencies of the commercial theatre. As Howe reminded his readers, the theatre was ultimately a trade, and therefore, 'it must shape its policy in accordance with the general dictates of supply and demand'.[42]

For Archer and Granville-Barker and those who argued in favour of a nationally institutionalized repertory theatre, the solution to the problem of commercial theatre could be found on the continent in the examples of successful and, most importantly, 'popular' repertory theatres. Granville-Barker had visited both the Deutsches Theater in Berlin and the Düsseldorfer Schauspielhaus, and he greatly admired the work of producers such as Max Reinhardt. In the case of a National Theatre for England, Granville-Barker believed that it should be unmistakably a 'popular institution, making a large appeal to the whole community'.[43] In the context of this argument, the notion of a 'popular' theatrical art implied neither commercial motivation nor catering to the populist tastes of an undiscerning mass audience, but rather, the more continental sense of 'popular' as a representative and organic, community-centred culture. The establishment of a truly national theatre would transcend the commercial system of theatrical production, offering instead a popular theatre institution in the sense of being representative of the nation's people. For Granville-Barker, the mere promise of such an institution was already 'completing the belated conversion of the average public man from his steadfast belief that the Drama is nothing more than a twentieth-century substitute for cock-fighting'.[44] If there is a suggestion of elitism in his idea of the theatre as public property, in his later revision of the scheme after Archer's death, Granville-Barker provided a much clearer definition of what such non-commercial 'popularity' really implied: a national theatre 'must appeal to all sorts of people and to every sort of taste – except bad taste'.[45] Not unlike his Fabian contemporaries, Granville-Barker's socialism was decidedly idiosyncratic in its interpretation of the popular. In the scheme for a theatre which would be national, representative and popular, a privileged place was reserved for the dramatist and for the class of intellectuals who would ensure the intelligence of the fare provided. Exactly what was defined as popular, representative drama would in fact be limited and controlled by the proposed national theatre, an institution free from the strictures of commercial success, and governed by an 'imaginative minority' who would take upon themselves the representation of the silent majority.[46] The inherent elitism of the scheme was also reflected in Granville-Barker's plea for private patronage and the degree to which the plan vested the governing authority over the theatre in the nation's academic institutions. Most importantly, however, the undemocratic organization of the theatre was best exemplified in the scheme by the figure of the director who should have all executive power, 'who should have absolute control of everything in and about the theatre'.[47] Archer and Granville-Barker's scheme, rather than emancipate a 'popular' or representative aesthetic of drama from the limitations of an otherwise popular commercial theatre, or striving to represent a national ethos, instead invested authority in the leisured middle-class elite typical of the Fabian Society.

For the dramatists, producers and critics who advocated schemes for a national or repertory theatre, the threat posed by a homogeneous mass culture and the emergent forms of mass media would be answered by the state institutionalization of dramatic art. The primary objective of a national theatre would be to elevate the drama above popular amusements according to certain artistic principles. As William Archer argued: 'the acted drama of the English language ought to rank high among the intellectual glories, and among the instruments of culture, of the nation, or rather of the race'.[48] Archer here provided the appropriate language to characterize the movement: institutionalizing dramatic art, transforming the theatre into an instrument of culture, would provide a means of superintending the production and reception of drama, prescribing the ideal dramatic standard. State recognition would authorize dramatic art as national and representative, as a public social service. Similarly, Jones argued that 'if we wish to inflame these millions and millions of city dwellers with enthusiasm for great national ideas . . . what instrument could be so swiftly and surely operative to these ends as a wisely-conceived, wisely-regulated and wisely-encouraged national drama?'[49] The motive of the envisioned national repertory theatre as expressed by Archer and Granville-Barker in their scheme, as well as by Jones and Howe, 'the motive of securing a consecutive interest for intelligent people',[50] required that the intelligent drama be invested with an aura of artistic authenticity: 'The first demand of this theatre is that its plays be judged as art as distinguished from entertainment. All the plays of the free theatre have been marked by genuineness of substance and an artistic intent in composition.'[51] Thus, for the advocates of a National Theatre, the disorder and chaos of cultural and class dissolution would be answered by the integration of the mass culture into a national culture ordered and legitimated within state-sponsored national institutions such as the proposed theatre. This, in turn, necessitated the emphasis upon the cultural and racial superiority, the creativity and genius, of national dramatists like Shakespeare.

As probably the most successful actor-manager of the late nineteenth and early twentieth century, Tree himself was not ignorant of the debate around him, and he was also able to identify what he determined to be the sea-change which the world was undergoing in the same terms of class and industrialization used by his younger contemporaries:

the old landmarks are being swept away, the barbed wire fences which separated the classes are being relegated to the limbo of the human scrap-heap . . . Wherever we put our ears to the ground we hear a tiny tapping at the earth's crust; it is the upspringing of a new social creed; it is the call of a new religion; it is the intellectual enfranchisement of mankind.[52]

Defending himself from the charge made against the chief, commercially successful metropolitan managers of pandering to public taste, Tree was quick to note the intellectual snobberies of his adversaries, proclaiming himself reluctant to stamp the great mass of English theatre-goers as ignorant fools.[53] For Tree, the popular representation of Shakespeare was justified by the wide appeal it made: 'Thousands witness him instead of hundreds . . . Indeed, there should be more joy over ninety-nine Philistines that are gained than over one elect that is preserved.'[54] In his own way, Tree saw his commercial success not only as justifiable, but as a modernizing agent in the intellectual enfranchisement of the lower classes. So even Tree was aware, as early as his book's publication in 1915, of an ideological confrontation between the mainstream commercial theatre and the reform movement. He refused, however, to idealize his own sense of dramatic art as authentic and genuine by setting it against the unfolding menace of a spiritless modern industrialized society. Indeed, one might reasonably argue that Tree, through his forays into film, was more progressive and pioneering than his younger contemporaries. Although they reacted to the growing commercialization of the arts under the influence of a predominating mass culture in the modernized society of the early twentieth century, what their various calls for state-endowment or privately sponsored repertory systems, as well as the various demands for aesthetic ideologies, ultimately reinscribed were primarily romantic and, as Benjamin argued, outmoded concepts such as creativity, genius, eternal value and mystery, 'concepts whose uncontrolled (and at present almost uncontrollable) application would lead to a processing of data in the Fascist sense'.[55]

Although I would be cautious about suggesting this kind of causal association with fascism, nevertheless, many of these characteristics written through this body of texts about theatrical practice in early twentieth-century England – the rhetoric of nationalism, the demand for an elite leadership, the predilection for tragedy and violence, and the emphasis upon genius – would seem to infer some deeper, darker anxiety underneath the idealism of these writers. Perhaps this is the anxiety reflected in the burning of Barker's 1911 film of *Henry VIII*. The suggestion of a ritualistic and violent public display notwithstanding, this burning of the film might be seen, in retrospect, to symbolize the convergence of several 'hotly' contested issues in the English theatre of the period: the actor-manager system, the relatively new and increasingly popular technology of film production, the popularity and accessibility of Shakespeare in performance, the changing class associations of Shakespeare's audience – indeed, the entire apparatus of producing and marketing Shakespeare. For those who were witness to the destruction of Tree's film, Barker's stunt was a harmless publicity tactic and has since been remembered as one of the film industry's early curiosities. However, read within the context of the emerging debate about the commercial enterprise of marketing Shakespeare and early twentieth-century theatrical discourse, the burning of Tree's film becomes far more significant, an almost prophetic symbol of the paradigmatic sea-change which was engulfing the theatrical world of the early twentieth century.

EDWARD GORDON CRAIG'S SCENE

Several years prior to William Barker's film version of *Henry VIII*, in the earliest days of experimentation with film production between the years 1895 and 1896, the two French brothers Louis and Auguste Lumière produced a series of short demonstration films. Their intention was to demonstrate the capabilities of what was then their pioneering Cinemato-graph camera. This early lightweight form of motion picture camera, similar to the Kinetoscope developed a few years earlier by Thomas Edison, was a technology which had long been anticipated after the introduction of the still-frame camera earlier in the nineteenth century, and was therefore regarded largely as a natural development or next step in the mechanical representation of reality. The early films of the Lumière brothers, all ranging between five and ten minutes, were produced to display the technological novelty of capturing motion on film. One of their more well-known films, *La Sortie des Usines* (*Workers Leaving the Lumière Factory*, 1896), exemplifies the sense of attraction which filmed movement offered to the uninitiated pre-cinema audience. In this film, the camera remains positioned in a stationary place to view the doors of their factory, with various figures filmed entering and leaving the viewed space. Unlike the conventional film to which we are accustomed, the workers are not linked by a narrative other than their movement, nor do they possess identity other than that which may be inferred by viewing them in the context of that space. Rather, typical of this early genre of non-narrative filmic demonstrations, the movement of the workers is

Figure 3.1. Still image from Louis and Auguste Lumière's 1895 film *La Sortie des Usines*
(*Workers Leaving the Lumière Factory*, 1895).

itself the subject, the multiple directions suggesting a fixed spatial location; a space containing transition, defined by depth, and not framed, but
ordered by the unseen surrounding environment.[56]

While movement supplies the revolutionary context of the new technology, movement also radically alters the nature of photographic perspective, displacing the conventional subject on display in pictorial
representation with a perspectival space in which transitory objects are
seen. The stationary perspective in the film was unavoidable given that the
Lumière cameras were heavy and cumbersome, and therefore immobile
during filming. This sense of perspective allowed by these early cameras
was perhaps a part of the attraction of early demonstration films, the
audience wanting to see how a machine 'sees'. Still, the perspective of
spatial order imposed by the stationary camera, which heightened the
subjectivity of the viewer's perspective and suggested the depersonaliza-
tion of, for example, factory workers, anticipated the 'machine aesthetic'
of later modernist and avant-garde art movements such as expressionism
and futurism. The figures which appear in the viewed space, while

animated by their movement, are ultimately depersonalized bodies moving in and out of, participating in, the view of the viewer.

Move forward a few years to 1905 when Edward Gordon Craig produced a series of four drawings titled *The Steps*. Craig was a talented artist praised for his bookplates and woodblock figures. Periodic gallery exhibitions of his work helped to supplement his modest income. His artworks, however, never ventured far from his real occupation in the theatre and from the volumes of prescriptive theatrical discourse which he wrote. As with most of his art which served primarily to augment his theories and designs for the theatre, most often as a preliminary model for a scenic design or performance, Craig offered *The Steps* as a conceptual drama. Insofar as the drawings represent a contribution to the theatre, I would suggest that this series occupies a similar revolutionary context in relation to the theatrical arts as the early demonstrations of film to the photographic arts. The drawings are presented as four individual images representing different moments in a fixed location, the architectural structure of steps. As with *Workers Leaving the Lumière Factory*, the four images offer neither a central subject on display nor a panoramic view. Each image is divided into three distinct spatial areas. The steps themselves occupy the centre and offer the only sense of a frame, two walls whose ability to demarcate a central subject is limited by the imposing open sky above. The closest area, the broad open space in front of the steps further serves to disengage the figures who appear on the steps by the illusion of distance from the viewer. The figures are largely interchangeable, faceless bodies engaged in uncertain activities, bodies which seem to move, as in the Lumière film, in and out of the single fixed perspective. The third spatial division, located beyond the steps, is the backdrop which reflects light to suggest time of day. Though filmic, the scenic space also anticipates the modernist theatrical space: the steps, a multi-level playing area dominating centre-stage, are offset by the large empty forestage and a simplistic backdrop used for lighting and shading effects.

Rather than frame a realistic pictorial scene in the style of a nineteenth-century proscenium arch stage, the four drawings capture the fluidity of film by the manner in which they seem to express both depth and movement: the varying positions and postures of the figures create the impression of a fixed spatial perspective which witnesses multi-directional movement. The four individual images neither narrate a story nor do they imply any relation between the figures who occupy the steps at different moments; instead, they represent 'different moods' linked sequentially by what we might infer from the use of shadowing is a single day.[57] As with

Figure 3.2. (a) Edward Gordon Craig, *The Steps 1* (1905). (b) Craig, *The Steps 4* (1905). (Reproduced by kind permission of the Edward Gordon Craig Estate.)

the early demonstrations of film, the movement of the figures rather than the figures themselves serves as the subject. The non-impressionistic stylization, the long shadows of the stark impersonal bodies which are dwarfed by a geometric structure of steps and blocks, the use of sharp angles and a deep perspective all suggest an expressionist influence, expressionist in the sense that the four images create a highly subjective perspective, the drama as a dream of images. This drama is not self-explanatory; rather, as we perceive the images, we share our perspective with an inferred viewer who is the absent-presence for whom the significance of the view is intended. The idea of a subjectively constructed aesthetic was not an invention of the late nineteenth century. Nevertheless, what the Lumière film demonstrates is that even from the earliest pre-narrative demonstrations of film, the sense of an auteur giving shape and providing meaning was embedded within the film medium, the invisible film author or auteur imposing a largely inescapable and more invasive perspectival subjectivity unparalleled in the more static visual arts. So too did Craig's *Steps* series, read as a drama, impose a subjective perspective upon the viewer, one ordered by a similar unseen auteur. This coincided with his ideas of theatrical production in his writing: for Craig, the auteur or theatrical producer, the *metteur-en-scène*, served to define his revolutionary art of the theatre.

The revolutionary context which the Lumière film and the drawings share, then, would appear to be a perspective of spatial order, the presence 'behind the camera' an integral component of the view. Exactly how four static coloured pencil sketches, in a traditional medium of the visual arts, comprise a drama is left ambiguous in Craig's accompanying commentary, and here the comparison between the Lumière film and Craig's drawings seems untenable: whereas film technology constituted a temporal reorganization of two-dimensional images to create the impression of fluid movement, a drama composed of four drawings would seem to have served exactly the opposite effect. I would argue, however, that the comparison between the Lumière film and Craig's early drawings usefully demonstrates that theatrical design in this period, at least in theory, shared some of the fundamental aesthetic attributes of an emerging film art; in the example above, the redefinition of perspectival space and movement according to the vision of the auteur or director. This correlation is perhaps nowhere more evident than in the influence expressionist stylization, with its invasive subjectivity, had on contemporaneous film and theatre in the 1920s and 1930s. The filmic nature of the modern theatrical space would reflect in Craig's own Shakespeare designs, designs which would influence and inspire twentieth-century Shakespeare production from that of Konstantin Stanislavsky to Peter Brook. More importantly, however, while the Lumière demonstrations advertised a technological development in the mechanical representation of reality and ushered in the age of cinema, in the same manner, Craig's visionary designs and polemical pronouncements on the art of the theatre, perhaps more than those of any of his English contemporaries, radically transformed English theatre design and announced the arrival of English theatrical modernism.

Craig's career also demonstrates the dramatic gulf between the works of theatrical theory and design which proliferated in this period and actual theatrical practice, a division which problematizes the question of his influence.[58] Indeed, influence is itself a problematic concept, but especially in the case of Craig insofar as the concept imposes the sense of a unified discourse (his 'thought' or his 'work') and diminishes the specificity of an incredibly varied body of writing and theatre work in a narrative of successive related phenomena.[59] Craig was a prolific writer on the subject of the theatre, having produced an almost immeasurable volume of essays and short articles (always polemical, often difficult or contradictory) under numerous pseudonyms. He collected the most significant of these essays in two full volumes, *On the Art of the Theatre* in 1911 and *The Theatre Advancing* in 1919.[60] Throughout his writing, he repeatedly proclaimed himself an authority on the theatre, though the difficulties which beset each of Craig's few theatre projects derived from an inability to realize pragmatically his impossibly grand theoretical models and designs. Especially in his later designs for the theatre such as those for Herbert Beerbohm Tree, Max Reinhardt and Stanislavsky, the technology to implement the designs did not exist, they remained too abstract and impractical for the producers who commissioned them, or Craig withdrew from the project for fear of his ideas being compromised. Craig's theory made his practice impracticable. While his theatrical designs and theories were among the most discussed and controversial in early twentieth-century English theatrical culture, during the most productive period of his life in which he produced the body of his writing and the majority of his sketches and woodblocks, between the years 1906 and about 1940, Craig lived in self-imposed exile in Europe, mostly in Florence, far removed from the English theatre scene.

Son of the famous Ellen Terry and well-known architect and scenic designer Edward William Godwin, Craig trained from an early age under Henry Irving at the Lyceum, about whom he wrote a biography in 1930.[61]

Even as a young actor, Craig was receiving favourable reviews for his stage performances. After a brief acting career though, he turned his attention to producing, soon establishing his reputation as an imaginative and energetic young producer. Together with the musician Martin Shaw and a committed company of amateurs, Craig produced a few short operas and masques to critical acclaim, the most notable including Purcell's *Dido and Aeneas* (1900) as well as a financially disastrous production of Handel's *Acis and Galatea* (1902), whose debts Ellen Terry helped to bail out post-production. Despite the financial difficulty, many of the reviews for these early experiments were very favourable. The *Review of the Week*, for example, emphasized the triumph of Craig's approach to design in *Dido and Aeneas*: 'The real triumph of the setting was. . . in the use of light and shade; it was as carefully considered as in a wood engraving, and added immeasurably to the tragic simplicity of the whole performance.'[62] As much as Craig's sketches and woodblock designs were self-stylized dramas, this reviewer was wise to note the pictorial quality of what Craig termed his 'theatrical vision'.[63] Experimenting with the recently developed technologies of stage lighting, Craig's design corresponded with the work of the Swiss Adolphe Appia who similarly used 'sculptured' beams of light to achieve simple illusionistic effects. In 1903, Craig then produced Ibsen's *The Vikings at Helgeland* (1903) at the Imperial Theatre, in which his mother acted the lead female role of Hjordis. The reviews once again emphasized the 'unexpected and bizarre' effects Craig achieved through the use of light and shading.[64] But though these early experiments were critical successes, they failed to attract sufficient audiences: *Acis and Galatea* closed after one week and *The Vikings* failed to make a profit after three. Though remarkably innovative in their stylistic design and use of relatively recent theatre technologies, Craig's early productions were quite marginal, little more than fringe productions to the mainstream English theatre. Their subsequent afterlife in the English theatre was therefore greatly limited by their scale.

In 1903, in order to recoup their financial loss from *The Vikings*, Ellen Terry convinced Craig to mount a production of *Much Ado About Nothing* using stock costumes and a simple setting, and featuring Terry as Beatrice, a role she had played to much acclaim at the Lyceum. While the production was a greater, though still modest, financial success and was later toured in the provinces, Craig believed his aesthetic ideals had been compromised by the necessity to produce a commercial success, and he later disowned his role in the production. Still, his involvement epitomized his approach to theatrical production and the ideas which would resurface persistently in his later writing and designs. Despite the minimal amount of stage setting he could afford to employ, Craig achieved an innovative and effective use of the mostly open space with what would become some of his trademark techniques, giving shape to the stage simply and abstractly through the use of plain classical pillars and colonnades, lit cycloramas and large swathes of hanging cloths. Craig found the inspiration for the design of *Much Ado About Nothing* in the Italian renaissance, having acquired Sebastiano Serlio's *Five Books of Architecture* (1545). Copying Serlio's simple design, he constructed five Tuscan pilasters, each measuring eighteen feet in height, which were then manipulated in different positions on the stage for different scenes, the spaces in between them filled with curtains and balustrading.[65] The illusionistic effect achieved by the design was augmented once again by Craig's use of focused coloured lighting. This application of evocative patterns of light was most effective in the suggestion of a church interior in which an imaginary stained glass window above was suggested by the projection of a pattern of coloured light on the stage floor. Even Bernard Shaw was to admit that 'as usual, Ted has the best of it. I have never seen the Church scene go before – didn't think it *could* go, in fact.'[66] Though he had little control over other elements of the production such as costumes and style of acting, both the setting and lighting exemplified Craig's trademark theatrical vision.

His desire to implement a personal vision to give shape to the play was finally mitigated, however, by the lack of control over the production which his mother, who controlled the play's finances, allowed. In a letter to Martin Shaw, he wrote of the numerous changes made to the production by the actors while on tour: 'Each time I see it a viler gaiety is added – speech is noisier & action floppier – thought infrequent, and taste unknown . . . They come off the stage and seriously take as final verdict, the applause of a kind audience. This is Hell – I know of nothing more tormenting.'[67] Craig's relationship to his mother made the issue of his control particularly acute. While he worshipped 'little Nelly', the private Ellen Terry who he remembered as the loving and caring mother of his childhood, Craig was resentful of the famous actor, the public Ellen Terry, the woman to whom he had played the subordinate throughout his early acting and producing career.[68] Disheartened by these difficulties, *Much Ado About Nothing* was to be Craig's last production for several years and the beginning of his self-imposed exile from the English theatre. His desire for absolute control as scenic producer, a control unimpeded by the commercial system of production, by the egos of actors or by the tastes of audiences, dictated his decision to abandon theatrical production in favour of writing about the theatre. Applause and financial success came to signify aesthetic failure, failure to emancipate his ideals of theatrical production from convention. After his earlier productions, Craig increasingly turned away from working on any project which he felt would compromise his absolute control. Consequently, he spent much of his time in relative isolation, writing his theory and publishing his periodicals, supplementing his income by making bookplates, and experimenting with working models of his scenic designs.

In the autobiography which he published late in his life, *Index to the Story of My Days*, Craig failed to remember the tormenting hell of working with other people which drove him out of practice and into theory. Instead, he remembered:

This year 1900, when I began as *metteur-en-scène*, what was it that *urged* me? Theatre – scene – writing? I will sum it up in the word *affection*. I did all this because I loved it . . . I was practising *metteur-en-scène* long before I wrote about *l'Art du Thèâtre* – and I *did* then what I wrote of later – the theory came after the practice.[69]

That Craig's experience was in fact limited and that he turned from the English theatre frustrated by his thwarted attempts to assume absolute artistic control to become instead a self-proclaimed authority on the theatre was a contradiction not lost on most of his contemporaries. Nevertheless, Craig's theoretical essays were widely read, eliciting responses from nearly every important theatrical producer and writer in the period. For these critics, though his ideas of scenic representation were inventive and inspiring, what remained irreconcilable about Craig's writing was his increasing dehumanization of the theatre: the more he wrote, the more Craig turned his attention away from the idea of the producer as a manager of a theatre ensemble and towards his miniature scenic models – the woodblock figures he used for his print designs were themselves 'puppets' which he manipulated on a meticulously scaled model wooden stage – and marionette theatres in which he could play with and act out his ideal performances alone. In 1923, for example, Granville-Barker ridiculed Craig's series of designs for *Hamlet*: '"Hamlet" with the Prince of Denmark left out is too good a joke not to be taken in earnest sometime. Are we to have a company of mere human beings revolving around some mighty symbol of morbid indecision; a pillar of light, it might be, registering moods by ranging through the spectrum, with a little music to help?'[70] Disagreement such as this subsequently heightened Craig's indignation and furthered his interest in inanimate apparatuses of theatrical production such as lighting and mechanically operated mobile settings.

Perhaps the best known and most controversial of Craig's essays, 'The Actor and the Über-marionette', which most famously prescribed the replacement of the actor with the impersonal string puppet, would seem at first to have endorsed an aesthetic of mechanical representation. Craig's attempt to marginalize the human actor was, however, as he argued, part of his protest against the literal or photographic reproduction of reality. For Craig, the living figure of the actor confused the audience into connecting actuality and art; therefore, he emphasized the necessity to do away with realistic conventions such as the human body: 'do away with the real tree, do away with the reality of delivery, do away with the reality of action, and you tend towards the doing away with the actor'.[71] Reduced to theatrical instrument, hidden in a chorus of masked figures or, at the most extreme, substituted entirely with a wooden marionette, the physical body of the actor represented for Craig an intrusion of personality which threatened the scenic illusion of the stage: actors were prone to accidents and subject to vanity, and their penchant for displaying personality rendered them ultimately imperfect. The inherent weakness of the flesh was unable to convey the essence of the work or the soul of the artist. Instead of the actor, Craig offered an ideology of stage space and physical movement in which the body of the actor became a more symbolic representation of character, anonymous and stylized body-forms translating through suggestive action rather than acted roles the thoughts and passions of the play.[72] Between the years 1904 and 1906, the period of his affair with the celebrated dancer Isadora Duncan, Craig expressed an interest in the suggestive movements of dance. This interest was short-lived, however, and by 1911, the year in which Diaghilev's Russian Ballet made its first London appearance, Craig would criticize dance as an art of the body 'appealing to our senses, not through them'.[73] For Craig, the most ideal symbolic form replaced the actor altogether with the nobly artificial marionette: 'The applause may thunder or dribble, their hearts beat no faster, no slower, their signals do not grow hurried or confused . . . There is something more than a flash of genius in the marionette, and there is something in him more than the flashiness of displayed personality.'[74] The marionette became Craig's superior symbol, a perfect representation of and substitution for the human body.

The first English translation of Heinrich von Kleist's essay 'On the Marionette Theatre' appeared in a 1918 periodical which Craig titled *The Marionette*, a version of his longer running periodical *The Mask* dedicated solely to the marionette. Kleist's essay, written in 1810, compared the affectation of the actor to the weightless pendulum movements made by the artificial limbs of the marionette.[75] For both Kleist and Craig, the wooden figure offered a form without animate substance; lifeless, suspended by strings, governed by the laws of gravity, impervious to the reactions of the audience. The strings of the marionette represented the perfect instrument of artistic expression, a direct medium between the mind of the creator and the body on stage. In contrast to the imperfections of human flesh, the marionette stood as a symbol for the Creator above. Characteristically, Craig argued: 'Grace appears most purely in that human form which either has no consciousness or an infinite consciousness.'[76] Underlying the marionette theories was an implicit metaphor which suffused all of Craig's writing, a metaphor equating artistic creation with divine creation: hiding the person and personality of the actor behind masks and robes, or replacing the actor entirely with a new form, the artist would be 'following in the footsteps of nature where the Creator is always hidden'.[77]

While the articles written for and reproduced in *The Mask*, which Craig published irregularly between 1908 and 1929, bolstered a renewed vogue for the figure of the marionette in the early twentieth century, Craig's ideas of presentational acting also precipitated a considerable backlash. Once again, Granville-Barker, defending the heritage of the actor, criticized Craig's theory: 'Actors, remembering their great predecessors, must feel a little bored when they are recommended to be "presentational" or to wear masks, or, on occasion, to abdicate altogether in favour of marionettes.'[78] This rhetorical rivalry between Granville-Barker and Craig reflected an important facet of Craig's influence. As a dramatist, Granville-Barker was himself greatly influenced by his good friend George Bernard Shaw who, as noted earlier, was an enthusiastic advocate of naturalism.[79] The drama which both Shaw and Granville-Barker wrote and which Granville-Barker produced for The Court Theatre between 1904 and 1907 offered a considerable impetus to the naturalist movement in England. Throughout Craig's writing, in articles which he published in his periodicals and later collected into larger volumes, Craig maintained his criticism of naturalism, and he helped to circulate the ideas of symbolists such as Walter Pater and Arthur Symons. Like Pater and Symons, Craig was an enthusiastic advocate of this French pictorial and theatre art movement: 'Symbolism is really quite proper', he wrote in 1911 in *The Mask*, 'it is sane, orderly, and it is universally employed . . . It is the very essence of the Theatre if we are to include its art among the fine arts.'[80] Representation on the stage, he argued, rather than portray the mundane, conscious reality of life, should signify instead a fundamental content beyond the flesh and blood of actors, what he regarded as a transcendental spirit of death revealed through the symbol. In contrast to dramatists like Granville-Barker and Shaw, or John Galsworthy and Elizabeth Robins, who recognized explicitly the social power of the theatre, having produced decisively topical plays with names such as *Strife* (1909), *Justice* (1910), and *Votes for Women* (1909), the idea of symbolism as espoused by Craig provided a subtler means of coding and controlling meaning through representation.

Among the names of Pater and Symons, selections from the writings of Friedrich Nietzsche appeared often in *The Mask*.[81] The debt to Nietzsche in the idea of the 'Über-marionette' is obvious, and there is an unmistakably Nietzschean emphasis on genius in Craig's idealization of the theatre artist. Nietzsche's elevation of the artist figure to a quasi-religious status, particularly in his early writing, a 'cult of genius' status he would later criticize, echoed in Craig's elevation of the theatrical producer to artist of the theatre.[82] More importantly, however, Craig's sense of symbolic form seems to have derived from Nietzsche's cryptic distinction in *The Birth of Tragedy* between Apollonian and Dionysian consciousness. Pater, like Nietzsche, whose works were not translated into English until the early years of the twentieth century, had designated these two opposing deities as representing opposed artistic spirits in his essay 'A Study of Dionysus', published in 1876.[83] Nietzsche's *The Birth of Tragedy* was first published in Germany in 1871, and the English translation followed in 1909 when Nietzsche's works were beginning to receive a more common currency in England. Earlier in 1902, however, Arthur Symons wrote a review of *The Birth of Tragedy*, having read a French translation, in which he noted the similarity to Pater's discussion.[84] Symons was an enthusiastic advocate of Nietzsche's aesthetic philosophy, and perhaps Symons, who was an associate of Craig, was the source of Craig's interest in Nietzsche's writing. Typical of the Nietzsche enthusiasts reading Nietzsche in English translation in the first few years of the twentieth century, however, Craig's interest was primarily in Nietzsche's poetic ideas, though his understanding was characterised by subjective reactions and creative misunderstandings, reflecting the poor and incomplete translations in limited circulation until about 1909.[85]

Craig's creative interpretation of Nietzsche's Apollonian/Dionysian dichotomy was reflected in his arguments for symbolic form. The absence of what he described in abstractly metaphysical terms as a sense of form was, he argued, the problem with the commercial English theatre, a theatre which fraudulently paraded its drama as art: 'What the Art of the Theatre (or rather we must call it the *Work* of the Theatre at present) lacks is *form*. It spreads, it wanders, it has no form.'[86] Whereas Nietzsche regarded the Apollonian in art as the phenomenal representation of reality, Dionysian consciousness was seen conversely to express the fundamental meaning or spirit of the work. Nietzsche divided art into the dichotomous realms of lucid dream images which express, at the other end, intoxication and rapture. For Nietzsche, music served to exemplify this Dionysian element in art, communicating immediately and without the need for interpretive symbols the expression of the aesthetic will.[87] Wagner's music and his notion of the *Gesamtkunstwerk* are an important point of reference in *The Birth of Tragedy*, the book having been originally dedicated to him. Following Wagner's synaesthetic ideal, great art was held to be ultimately a synthesis of the two, the musical and the non-musical, the drunken Dionysian frenzy ordered and expressed through beautiful, sober images.[88] Short of being musical, great art would express a musical element or spirit which would serve to intoxicate the visually ordered work. Borrowing from Nietzsche, Craig's sense of form was similarly comprehensive or 'synaesthetic', incorporating every element of theatrical performance. This synaesthetic form would express the metaphysical or spiritual quality of the work. Following Nietzsche, but borrowing Pater's terminology, Craig identified this quality as the condition of music.[89]

Defining the new *Über*-artist of the theatre, the first and perhaps most important distinction Craig needed to make was that of scenic producer or *metteur-en-scène* versus playwright. By 1908, Craig had 'parted company with the popular belief that the *written* play is of any deep and lasting value' to the art of the theatre.[90] Privileging 'sound' or the voiced beauty of the soul above the 'word with its dogma', two euphemisms which would appear to stand for an esoteric performance aesthetic and the dogmatic authorial text, Craig was perhaps the only English theatre producer in the period to exclude written dramatic texts from the theatre altogether on the basis that they were literary as opposed to theatrical art (though one is reminded, from the opposite point of view, of Eliot and his closet drama). Such radical idealism was not characteristically English, but was rather more typical of European avant-garde movements such as dadaism and futurism. This is unsurprising given that Craig was living and writing in Florence at the time. Excerpts from the English translation of Filippo Tommaso Marinetti's futurist manifesto *Futurism and the Theatre* were published in *The Mask* in 1913. Though Craig was guarded in his appreciation of futurism, like the Italian Marinetti, he expressed his admiration for Mussolini's leadership and idealism.[91] Invoking a typically Nietzschean emphasis on leadership and personality, Craig praised such concepts as genius, creativity and order, concepts whose uncritical application, as Benjamin warned, would lead directly to fascist ideology. It was therefore with some surprise that Craig was forced from the fascist state in 1940, his library and designs at the Goldoni Arena in Florence where he made his home having been confiscated. Much of the material, including many of his early Shakespeare designs, was subsequently lost.

As with so many of his contemporaries, Craig's engagement with Shakespeare was traversed by different motivations throughout his career. On the one hand, Craig was an enthusiastic admirer of Shakespeare. *Hamlet*, in particular, remained a central interest for him, some of his most inspired woodcuts and sketches deriving from designs and costume sketches for this play. The advantage of Shakespeare's texts was that, although the more popular plays had become sedimented with convention in the commercial theatre through the nineteenth century, they were otherwise relatively open to the interpretive conception of the producer, unlike the more conventional realist and naturalist drama whose authors most often produced their own work. Craig advocated his own methodology for textual interpretation as a mediating process which would reconcile the written text with the art of the theatre, the playwright relinquishing control to the stage director. As described by Craig, the task of the scenic designer would be to inhabit the text, locate and envision the appropriate impression, draw forth the essential idea underneath the written words, and 'never lose hold of your determination to win through to the secret – the secret which lies in the creation of another beauty, and then all will be well'.[92] The precarious transition from essential Dionysian consciousness to beautiful Apollonian structure would be mediated by the scenic designer, whose keen and mystic perception would mitigate the dogmatic reality of the words in favour of the voiced beauty of the soul. Naturally, Craig's lack of regard for the authorial text incited a certain degree of outrage among the new class of respected playwrights in England, including Shaw, who commented: 'If he did that to a play of mine, I would sacrifice him on the prompter's table before his mother's eyes.'[93]

On the other hand, though, while Craig believed that Shakespeare produced great works, he argued that those works were ultimately poetic. *Hamlet*, for example, as well as

the other plays of Shakespeare have so vast and so complete a form when read, that they can but lose heavily when presented to us after having undergone stage treatment. That they were acted in Shakespeares day proves nothing . . . *Hamlet* was finished – was complete – when Shakespeare wrote the last word of his blank verse, and for us to add to it by gesture, scene, costume, or dance, is to hint that it is incomplete and needs these additions.[94]

This conviction persisted in his later writing, at which time Craig departed entirely from his earlier methodology of interpreting the authorial text, positing his new theory of the 'durable theatre' or 'monodrama'. Instead of written text, this ideal drama would be composed of a deliberate silence, a mode of presentation in which words would be substituted with physical gesture, light and the dynamics of space, an evocative rather than expressive text operating on a plane of sub-literal communication. Since the durable drama remained unwritten, Craig argued that it would never need to be rewritten into subsequent texts but would become one mode of presentation, 'one Drama, unchangeable. Such a drama would have to be beyond criticism, and would have to be what they assert the Shakespearean drama is – for all time.'[95] Seeking to establish the authority of his aesthetic will as he receded further and further from practical implementation of his theoretical models in the theatre, Craig's writing style became more eccentric and idiosyncratic, even anxiously neurotic at times. The more he wrote, the more he receded into the realm of his highly theorized conceptual drama, into his own impossibly grandiose fantasy theatre.

If in his later writing Craig became, like Nietzsche, neurotically obsessed with his aesthetic will, his hyperbolic rhetoric also became more vituperative and exclusive, damning not only of authors, but more interestingly, of women. Again corresponding with Nietzsche, Craig's aesthetic will was always 'his', necessarily male because the artist of the theatre was always male. On Cambridge University and its ban on actresses, for example, Craig commented:

it is an incalculable gain to the art in that it replaces a personality by a symbol. For men, when they act female roles, do not parody womankind as do women themselves when they let loose their silliness and vanity on the stage as representative of the beauty of the female sex. Nor do men representing women *pretend* to be women or to create an illusion. Rather do they present an idea, interpret the spirit of womanhood; and the power of that spirit is the more deeply felt by the audience in that it is unallied to any counter attraction of the flesh.[96]

Demonstrating moderation, control and precision in art instead of a reckless and excessive passion, Craig argued that the genuine artist would exhibit a masculine manner. In 'The Actor and the Über-marionette', Craig appropriated (or perhaps fabricated) an Eastern myth of dramatic origins to defend the marionette. In this myth, women were primarily faulted for having destroyed the noble tradition of puppet theatre by wishing to exhibit themselves on stage in place of the puppet: 'The actor springs from the foolish vanity of two women who were not strong enough to look upon the symbol of godhead without desiring to tamper with it.'[97] According to Craig, the drama of human actors was said to have originated as a result of two women in the East who desired to stand as a direct symbol for the divinity in man. Craig's durable theatre was a theatre of gender conflict and patriarchal subordination, of male versus female, the artist of the theatre versus the actor, true form versus imperfect representation. The truth or essence which the marionette and mask would represent, and which the actor, and worse the female actor parodied, was a masculine divinity for whom the artist of the theatre became a symbolic substitute. The blatant patriarchal bias of his theories, particularly the suggestion that women parody themselves when they act women's roles and that men somehow do not, seems particularly striking in view of the fact that his mother was a famous actor and his sister was a similarly visionary costume designer and stage director.

Craig's desire for an unquestioned, absolute, even monotheistic control as stage director in his theoretical writing was best exemplified in his designs for *Scene*, a scenic model for his monodrama. *Scene* began as a series of sketches and woodcuts which he produced between 1906 and 1908 which first depicted his conceptual model for a system of scenic design, though the idea was preceded by Craig's earlier production designs and by his interest in classical and renaissance architecture. As with *The Steps*, the conceptual designs for *Scene* are characterized by long shadows, beams of light, a deep perspective, impersonal figures, and sharp angles. The cubic structures which hover around the desolate figures were meant to represent plain and angular flats or screens. Proposing a single set design which could be universally employed in all dramas, Craig devised a system of moveable, free-standing, monochrome screens which found their inspiration in the essential features of all human dwellings;

Figure 3.3. Edward Gordon Craig, from his *Scene* (1907). Each plate, though titled *Scene*, was given a subtitle by Craig to help the publisher distinguish them, this one, 'Descent into the Tomb'. (Reproduced by kind permission of the Edward Gordon Craig Estate.)

flat walls, floor and ceiling.[98] Though plain and indistinct, Craig argued that the screens could be manipulated through movement and light to reproduce suggestively any scenic environment. As a result, *Scene* would

Figure 3.4. Craig, 'The Übermarionette', *Scene* (1907).
(Reproduced by kind permission of the Edward Gordon Craig Estate.)

be able to contain any moment or environment from any play, the design being both any scene, but foremost Scene, a physical unity endowed with animate presence: 'In the hands of an artist it is capable of all varieties of expression', he wrote, 'even as a living voice and a living face are capable of every expression. The scene remains always the same, while incessantly changing.'[99] *Scene* could contain a scene which expressed its own poetic particularity, but *Scene* would be foremost a unitary projection of all drama, the art of the theatre.

In his imagination, Craig envisioned giant suspended blocks seamlessly and effortlessly rising and falling, shifting and sliding across the stage, and he imagined himself coordinating the entire scenic operation upon a large organ-like machine. Unfortunately, however, Craig's own practical experiments with the design on a large scale were mostly unsuccessful. In 1909, Herbert Beerbohm Tree, although impressed, rejected an experimental design for *Macbeth* fearing the moveable screen system would be costly and difficult to manoeuvre. The cumbersome nature of the screens was the same reason Craig's mother rejected designs for *The Merchant of Venice* in the same year.[100] In 1911, Craig and Stanislavsky conjoined their efforts for a Moscow Arts Theatre production of *Hamlet* for the purpose of which Craig produced his most famous series of woodblocks and sketches. Later, Craig would develop his Moscow designs to produce a series of bookplates for the Cranach Press edition of *Hamlet*, published in German in 1928 and in English in 1930, one of the most beautiful and impressive editions of Shakespeare published in this period.[101] In print, Craig's designs remain visually impressive, capturing the modernist sense of the individual overshadowed by the external forces of society and tortured by psychological distress. In the Moscow production, however, Craig's designs were seriously limiting: the technology to give the screens the impression of effortless movement did not exist, and after several near disasters, the precarious screens were modified considerably by Stanislavsky, much to Craig's exasperation.[102] Following his attempt in Moscow, once again frustrated by his attempt to implement his theory into practice, Craig returned to the isolation of his theoretical models and designs.

Although *Scene* proved largely immobile and impractical in 1911, incapable of expressing Craig's grand symbolic movement, the design no longer seems as ill-conceived or impossibly grand. His innovative use of light and sense of stage architecture exemplified the kind of changing aesthetic practices which would later define the twentieth-century theatre. Moreover, as with *The Steps*, *Scene* seems to capture the fluidity of film, expressing a sense of depth and movement: the designs evoke a dream quality, the significance of the dream sequence retained by the imagined dreamer whose eye provides the subjective interiorized perspective. And yet, while his designs and theories might be seen to have engendered and energized the progressive scenic innovation of the early twentieth-century theatre, or made the theatre more contemporary in its association with the aesthetic practices of film, ultimately, Craig's theories reinscribed largely nineteenth-century patriarchal romanticist ideologies of art. Gauging his influence therefore requires the negotiation of a fine line between the visionary perspective of a theatre artist's 'eye' and the patriarchal and class bias of a dogmatically prescriptive 'I'.

THE THEATRE AND A CHANGING CIVILIZATION

The political doctrines of Mussolini, Lenin, Stalin and Hitler are the only ones in our time that have genuine idealistic foundations, a definiteness of aim and a constancy of purpose, all of which were so utterly lacking under the so-called democratic regimes . . . The idealistic foundations of the future of humanity lie in the programmes of the present European dictators.[103]

Writing in 1935, Theodore Komisarjevsky would have been unaware of the atrocities which would be wreaked by the totalitarian regimes of Mussolini, Stalin and Hitler during and after the Second World War. Unlike his contemporaries, we have a retrospective awareness of history which makes such thoughts – Hitler's definiteness of aim or Stalin's constancy of purpose – quite unsettling. The perspective of a Russian expatriate living in England in 1935, having emigrated one year after the Bolshevik revolution in 1917, would have differed considerably from that of his English contemporaries as well, but in 1935, his radical political thought would have found some sympathy there. For Komisarjevsky, the European dictators provided a model of rigorous idealism in contrast to what he regarded to be an age of degeneration and bourgeois decadence. However, what makes this reverence for totalitarianism more surprising is that it occurs in the preface to a book about the theatre, *The Theatre and a Changing Civilisation*, a treatise which outlines Komisarjevsky's own principles of theatrical production and which attempts to define the emerging role of the *régisseur* or director in the early twentieth century. Komisarjevsky, however, is not remembered for his forays into aesthetic theory, and the few extreme views expressed in his writing, but primarily for the six productions of Shakespeare which he directed at the Shakespeare Memorial Theatre (SMT) between 1932 and

1939. One of the twentieth century's earliest and more visionary directors of Shakespeare in the English theatre, Komisarjevsky is remembered for having brought to Stratford his innovative approach to stage design, shocking the sedate audiences – grown accustomed to the stultified traditions of Shakespeare in Stratford – with his avant-garde stylization. Thus, even while the remarkable comments in his writing are rarely noted, Komisarjevsky's aesthetic radicalism continues to be discussed by contemporary historians and performance critics in the context of a 'Shakespeare revolution' in twentieth-century performance.[104]

Komisarjevsky, like Craig, is a fascinating figure in the history of English theatre, not least because he pioneered uses of stage space and lighting which would become standard technique of more contemporary Shakespeare production. More significantly, though, Komisarjevsky's writing on the theatre underscores a central problematic of modernism: the point where the utopian dimension of an aesthetic idealism becomes political idealism, and how this subsequently crosses over into and is potentially perpetuated by the actual aesthetic artefact. Part of that problematic is the complicating moral dimension offered by historical retrospect, the legacies of fascism and communism which, in the case of Komisarjevsky's writing, amplify the striking incongruity of Mussolini, Lenin, Stalin and Hitler's presences there. One is reminded of Ezra Pound's connections to Italian fascism and the tarnished reputation of the *Cantos*, or the Nazi associations of Wagner's music. Until only recently, although surrounded by much controversy, the Israelis observed an informal ban on the public performance of Wagner because of the Nazi and neo-Nazi associations (Wagner was passionately anti-Semitic and Hitler was an ardent Wagnerian). In this case, the stigma of association, respect for the memory of holocaust victims, would seem enough to complicate the performance of Wagner's music. But the question of whether the music itself continues to perpetuate an anti-Semitic ideology points to a more complicated part of that problematic: the degree to which aesthetic ideologies openly committed to flawed political ideologies produce actual aesthetic commitments, resulting in, for example, a fascist or anti-Semitic art. The ideological legacy of anti-Semitism is no less resonant in the case of Shakespeare's *The Merchant of Venice*, which Komisarjevsky also happened to direct in 1932 at the SMT. The production was praised in the reviews for having reversed the theatrical tradition established by Henry Irving and continued by subsequent actor-managers such as Tree of portraying Shylock sympathetically. In contrast, Komisarjevsky directed Randle Ayrton to play Shylock as he supposedly would have been played on the renaissance stage, a heavily accented comic villain stereotype, an unsympathetic Jewish usurer. In *The Theatre and a Changing Civilisation*, although he expressed his regret for the confinement of Jews, not to mention the 'disposal' of Russians, Komisarjevsky also argued that mass progressive movements in the history of humanity required bloodshed and injustice to be inflicted on certain groups of people: 'however sentimental we may be', he argued, 'our feelings must not be allowed to blind us to the positive and progressive sides of the Fascist, Communist and Nazi movements'.[105]

Theatrical records rarely speak immediately or transparently of a given artist's or production's ideological commitments. While most reviews of *The Merchant of Venice*, for example, noted the shift in Shylock's portrayal, in the conservative environment of the SMT in 1932, English sensitivity to European anti-Semitism was overshadowed by the sheer radicalism of the production. One reviewer succinctly related Komisarjevsky's impact: 'It is brave business to have a bit of fun with Shakespeare in Stratford, where William suffers the sacrosanctity of monarchy and where the ritual of ceremonial veneration has reached its most dismal superfluities' (*Weekend Review*, 30 July 1932). The style which Komisarjevsky introduced to Stratford was decidedly new and different and this came at a very auspicious moment in the history of the SMT. After the long reign of Frank Benson's touring company at the SMT between 1886 and 1918, a permanent resident company was established in 1923 under the direction of W. Bridges-Adams. During this period, the SMT relied on private subscriptions and ticket sales for survival, which greatly amplified the pressure to accommodate an audience grown accustomed to Benson's traditional style. In March 1926, however, a fire destroyed the old SMT building. For the intervening years while the theatre was being rebuilt, Bridges-Adams and his company worked and performed in a temporary theatre which was otherwise the Stratford Picture House. The new theatre, meanwhile, was being built at great expense according to the architectural designs, chosen by open competition, of the young architect Elisabeth Scott and was aggressively modern, the art deco stainless steel and red brick contrasting sharply with the quaint Warwickshire buildings of historic Stratford. Dubbed the 'jam factory' in the local papers, it also boasted a revolving stage, impressive fly-space and a state-of-the-art lighting system. To accompany the inaugural season of the new SMT, the board of governors decided that something radically different was required to stir interest and to demonstrate the capabilities and justify

the expense of their controversial new theatre.[106] One of the plays subsequently included in the 1932 season was Komisarjevksy's *The Merchant
of Venice*. This production answered the need for international cosmo-
politanism and stylistic currency in Stratford after the impressive ex-
penditure on the new theatre. As the first star producer to be invited
to Stratford and, more significantly, a Russian, he represented the shift
occurring in the administrative policy of the theatre. The media recognized that: 'As a child of the Continent, he is free from the Shakespeare-
worship which has stultified dramatic development in this country for so
long' (*Birmingham Gazette*, 26 July 1932). The presence of a Russian
director would invigorate the new stage with the possibility of what was
deemed the dramatic development occurring in Europe, the stylistic
novelty and daring experimentation of the European theatrical avant-
garde. However, for the governors of the SMT, more important than
artistic integrity, the idea of the avant-garde in Stratford inspired hopes
of impressive box office returns. Whether the novelty of the new theatre
or the presence of Komisarjevsky, *The Merchant of Venice* fulfilled such
expectations, breaking all of Stratford's box office records.[107]

　　Komisarjevsky was born into a prominent aristocratic theatre family in
Russia. His father, Fyodor Petrovich Komissarzhevsky, was a famous
operatic tenor for the imperial Mariinsky Theatre in Saint Petersburg,
while his half-sister, the equally popular Vera Komissarzhevsky, was a
repertory actress at another imperial theatre, the Alexandrinsky.[108]
Though he enjoyed some success on the Russian stage in the relatively
new field of directing (he had worked with both Stanislavsky and
Vsevolod Meyerhold in Moscow), he emigrated from Russia in 1918
because he felt that communism was artistically restrictive, particularly
for the formerly imperial theatres in which he enjoyed working, with
their rapidly diminishing bourgeois audience base. Following his flight,
Komisarjevsky toured Europe where he visited various experimental
and repertory theatres, witnessing the work of directors such as Leopold
Jessner and Max Reinhardt firsthand.[109] Once he arrived in England,
bringing with him the notes he had accumulated while in Europe, he
began to establish a reputation for himself in London. Between the years
1925 and 1936 in particular, his reputation as a stage director in England
grew when he produced all of Chekhov's plays on the London stage to
critical acclaim. By the time he was preparing to work in Stratford, the
Birmingham Weekly Post was heralding the arrival of the greatest 'producer' in the world, suggesting that: 'It is by such methods that the intrinsic
value of the Festival and the Memorial Theatre can legitimately be

reinforced with an eye to attracting support other than that of the fervent Shakespearean enthusiast' (2 July 1932).

But while the London audiences would tolerate the suggestion of continental influence in the naturalist style of Chekhov, initial reaction to Komisarjevsky's 'pranks' with Shakespeare in Stratford was more apprehensive and guarded. The *Daily Express*, under the headline ' "Crazy Night" at Stratford', wrote: 'The pillar of St Mark's leaned drunkenly against a nightmare Venetian tower surrounded by a confusion of flying bridges. The set was riotously out of perspective and bathed in a pink glow' (26 July 1932). Set against the opening backdrop of a comically misshapen Venetian street scene, the production began with a harlequin-ade masque played to Bach's Toccata and Fugue in D Minor, during which Lancelot Gobbo, dressed as Pierrot, slid down from the gallery at the side of the stage on a rope.[110] The carnivalesque quality was further emphasized by the colourful eclectic mix of costumes. The whole tone was comic romance: 'When somebody gave him the script of the play', wrote the *Birmingham Gazette* (26 April 1932), 'he read it, and remarking, "This fellow is a fine poet, but this is a rotten play," he proceeded to turn it into musical comedy'. Other pranks included the Prince of Morocco in black-face with thick red lips supposedly looking like Al Jolson but wearing a sombrero, and over-sized owlish spectacles for Portia in the trial scene. Setting these stereotypes in a comic reinterpretation of the play, Komisarjevsky was clearly exploiting the latent racial and patriarchal contexts of Shakespeare's writing. Unused to such interpretive heavy-handedness, *The Times* called it 'Komisarjevsky on Shakespeare' (26 July 1932). Komisarjevsky's anti-traditional vision thus proved disruptive and hostile for many of the major press critics. The production 'failed in miserable confusion' (*Daily Express*, 26 July 1932) and was 'reckless and affected' (*The Times*, 26 July 1932). Theatre critic W. A. Darlington wrote: 'It has been his weird fancy to be completely inconsequent' (*Daily Telegraph*, 26 July 1932).

Still, though *The Merchant of Venice* was widely considered one of the least impressive plays in the canon, the production drew record numbers to Stratford. The central attraction was the theatre itself, and the new technology which he exploited to great effect. None of the characters, for example, entered from the wings, but were instead revealed in waxwork-like tableaux as the large settings were shifted back and forth from Venice to Belmont. In the first scene change, the Venice setting was divided in the centre, half sliding off on each side, with the Belmont scene rising slowly from a well in the stage to reveal Portia, Nerissa and attendants

Figure 3.5. The opening set for Theodore Komisarjevsky's 1932 production of *The Merchant of Venice* at the Shakespeare Memorial Theatre, Stratford-upon-Avon.

frozen in position. 'Full of glee at finding himself in charge of the finest set of stage machinery in England', wrote Darlington, 'he does everything he can with it' (*Daily Telegraph*, 26 April 1932). The effect supposedly wore as the play continued, the set changes becoming often clumsy and time-consuming. But while the effects may seem unimpressive now, for audiences accustomed to painted cloths and footlights, the exploitation of the new theatre technology, like the initial demonstrations of film, was an attraction in itself, and coupled with Komisarjevsky's directorial vision, helped to create a setting for Shakespeare in Stratford strongly reminiscent of Granville-Barker's illusionistic productions between 1912 and 1914 at the Savoy Theatre in London. *The Merchant of Venice*, embracing the spirit of innovation and technological modernity, was

Figure 3.6(a). The set for Komisarjevsky's 1933 production of *Macbeth* at the SMT.
Shakespeare Centre Library, Stratford-upon-Avon. Notice the similarity to Edward
Gordon Craig's earlier design, figure 3.6(b).

seen to liberate Shakespeare from the stagnating traditions of theatrical
production in Stratford.

While his first production at the SMT met with a reception mixed with
surprise and wonder, the imposition of what was deemed an extra-textual
vision upon Komisarjevsky's second production, *Macbeth* in 1933, proved
more obtrusive for many of the critics, *The Times* having dubbed it
'Producer's Shakespeare'.[111] The strength of that vision lay primarily in
the austere and aggressive set, a construction of steps and pillars in
burnished aluminium dissected by sharp angles and shadows. The design
relied heavily upon steps and levels set against a cyclorama used for
various lighting effects. The influences here were perhaps expressionist
and constructivist, particularly in the suggestion of *Jessnertreppen*, Jessner's
trademark step design used to create multiple acting areas and spatial
perspectives. More immediately, though, Komisarjevsky's design for
Macbeth appears to have drawn inspiration from Edward Gordon Craig's
designs for the play – again, arguably expressionist, perhaps having influenced Jessner – reproducing the block-set offset by sharp angles and
illuminated by beams of light. Not unlike Craig's screens, the set could
be divided and repositioned around the stage to create different acting
spaces. The press also described this *Macbeth* as futurist, perhaps due to

Figure 3.6(b). Edward Gordon Craig, *Macbeth* (1906).
(Reproduced by kind permission of the Edward Gordon Craig Estate.)

the suggestion of a machine aesthetic in the metallic set – the *Birmingham Mail* compared it to Fritz Lang's 1926 film *Metropolis* (19 April 1933) – or to the intimation of the previous war. Komisarjevsky's *Macbeth* presented a 'dark, ferocious world in which human beings fluttered as the impotent victims of storms too vast for their comprehension or resistance' (*Manchester Guardian*, 20 April 1933). The witches, speaking in strong Scottish accents, resembled 'old crones, plundering not only corpses but skeletons on the battlefield, under the shadow of modern guns, while steel-helmeted soldiers carrying rifles pass on into battle'.[112]

Earlier in 1928, the Birmingham Repertory Theatre had similarly overhauled the interpretation of the play, dressing Macbeth in a modern khaki military uniform. Komisarjevsky also sought to remove the play from the traditional Caledonian setting, but not with the aim of simply modernizing the play. Referring to Barry Jackson's 'modern-dress' productions, he derided: 'Hamlet in plus fours or Macbeth in khaki uniform cannot sound or look otherwise than a skit or parody.'[113] In contrast to Jackson, Komisarjevsky's resetting had an ideological rather than merely aesthetic function. 'He produced a *Macbeth*', wrote *The Times*, 'with the supernatural elements "reduced", as theologians would say, to suit an age dominated by psychological conceptions' (21 April 1936). In the banquet scene, Macbeth's shadow, reflected disproportionately large against the back wall, served as the ghost of Banquo. The same effect was used later in the play when Macbeth, rather than visit the witches, was visited by them in a dream, their shadows projected on the wall behind his bed. Komisarjevsky also dressed Macbeth and his soldiers in evidently German-style military uniforms and apparently directed the cast to speak in a 'metallic and explosive staccato' (*Birmingham Gazette*, 19 April 1933). Emphasizing the psychology of war – the insatiable and immoral desire for power which drives tyrants to slaughter and self-destruction – in a proto-fascist German setting, Komisarjevsky's *Macbeth* was an extraordinary commentary on the contemporary European political theatre. The point was perhaps too subtle for English audiences in 1933: 'Macbeth becomes no closer to us if he is transformed into a species of Hitler, surrounded by a bodyguard of steel-helmeted warriors' (*Manchester Guardian*, 20 April 1933).

Komisarjevsky's talent for shocking the audiences of the SMT continued with his 1935 production of *The Merry Wives of Windsor*, a production which was universally panned as an artistic failure. The style of suggestive eclecticism which had worked for *The Merchant of Venice* in 1932 proved unsuccessful here: there was little rationale for the garish costumes and setting which mirrored the Venetian fashions of Komisarjevsky's first attempt at Shakespeare in Stratford. The fact that a single set served both for a street and for the living room in Mrs Ford's house, in particular, was seen to place too many demands on the capacity of the audience to understand scenic place and time. At the end of the play, Herne's Oak was an oversized trunk, behind which was a Venetian-style pergola surrounded by slender marble columns. Again, the general opinion was that there was little justification for wrenching this most English of plays out of its traditional setting: 'A bold experiment, but artistically a failure. Good fun for the unsusceptible, but likely to offend the sober Shakespeare lover' (*Yorkshire Post*, 20 April 1935).

The failure of *The Merry Wives of Windsor* perhaps explains the comparative simplicity and austerity of Komisarjevsky's next production, *King Lear* in 1936. This was the first production to establish Komisarjevsky's reputation as a Shakespearean and to demonstrate the viability of his directorial approach. One important reason for that success was the casting of Randle Ayrton as Lear. Ayrton had played Lear to critical acclaim under Komisarjevsky's direction earlier in 1927 for the Oxford Union Dramatic Society, and having repeated the role for Bridges-Adams in 1931 and 1932, he therefore brought to Komisarjevsky's Stratford production the confidence and polished delivery of an established repertory actor. The main reason for the success of the production, however, lay in the simplicity of the stage design and the subtlety of the effects. Komisarjevsky had stated his intention to emphasize the quality of acting rather than the scenography, and thus, in his design, though still removed from the traditional Celtic setting, he refrained from imposing the kind of stylistic eccentricities or 'tricks' which the press might then scandalize.[114]

As with *Macbeth*, the set was composed of a flight of steps designed to provide multiple acting levels and differing angles all ascending to a central point which was dominated by an oversized throne in the opening scene. The main effects, though, were achieved through the use of focused and coloured lighting, particularly against the cyclorama. The storm scenes offered the most visually impressive use of such lighting with 'scudding green and black clouds' swirling in the background. 'The beauty of the thing is that the atmosphere is achieved almost without noise, so that this Lear in his great speeches does not suffer the fate of so many of his predecessors of being forced to outbellow the hurricane', wrote Darlington in a rare moment of praise: 'he has shown us what can be done with modern stage machinery by making use of colour and lighting in a way I have never in my life seen equalled' (*Daily Telegraph*, 21 April 1936). Sharply focused beams of light were also used to suggest the physical structure of the hovel, an effect which drew some criticism in 1936, but which set a precedent for later productions in Stratford. The Royal Shakespeare Company's 1985 *Othello*, directed by Terry Hands and designed by Robert Koltai, for example, used similarly 'sculpted' beams of light on an open stage to great effect.[115] The more obvious legacy of the

production, however, was the effective use of 'empty space' as advocated
by Peter Brook in the 1960s.[116] While Komisarjevsky's earlier productions
had been constrained by short rehearsal periods and the often clumsy use
of the new theatre machinery, *King Lear* demonstrated the fluid incorpor-
ation of his prominently visual stage effects with the more traditional style
of acting Shakespeare in Stratford. If the production achieved less critical
attention than his first three, what this fact demonstrated was the degree
to which modern theatre technology and European-influenced stagecraft
were being integrated into more mainstream Shakespeare theatre in
England.

After *King Lear*, Komisarjevsky would go on to direct *A Comedy of
Errors* in 1938 and *The Taming of the Shrew* in 1939. By this time, he had
become a genuinely popular Shakespearean, one of England's first and
highest profile celebrity stage directors. Though the press generally
employed the label of expressionism to describe his artistic ideology, the
use of the term did not invoke the stringent principles pioneered in
Germany.[117] Indeed, for the press, the particularities of expressionism
were hardly differentiated from those of other movements like symbolism
and futurism. What was regarded as Komisarjevsky's 'flair for expressionism and burlesque' (*Daily Express*, 26 July 1932) suggested a general
modernizing principle as opposed to a commitment to a specific aesthetic
doctrine or anti-establishment ideology. Komisarjevsky himself was reluctant to endorse any specific movement and preferred to think of his own
approach as a kind of aesthetic synthesis, borrowing from different avant-
garde movements discriminately to create his own eclectic stage compositions. The 1938 production of *A Comedy of Errors*, widely praised as
Komisarjevsky's finest achievement in Stratford, perhaps best demonstrated this synthetic principle at work. The characters in the production
sported an eclectic mix of costumes ranging from mock Elizabethan to
contemporary fashion, a mix which offered no immediate rational order,
but instead, helped to create a fantasticated, comical world in which the
details of place and time were subordinated to the playing and rhythm of
the action. Reflecting the motley eclecticism of the costumes, the set was
'a market place crowded with a kaleidoscopic jostle' of houses and shops
(*News Chronicle*, 13 April 1938). *The Times* wrote: 'Mr Komisarjevsky sees
the play as a fantastic pattern of farcical incidents . . . and he offers it to us
as a piece of theatrical *bric-à-brac*, all the characters having a brilliant
artificiality appropriate to a Goldoni interlude' (13 April 1938). While this
pasting together of period and locale evoked the roughly contemporary
works of collage by pictorial artists such as Picasso, Komisarjevsky's

Figure 3.7. The eclectic ensemble for Komisarjevsky's 1938
The Comedy of Errors at the SMT.

emphasis on aesthetic synthesis – the disparate elements held together by the composition's constructive principle as orchestrated by the director – suggests more the idea of montage.[118] In the cinema, montage was quickly established as the predominant filmic device, the auteur composing and editing the view. Montage was a similarly important feature of both the symbolist and expressionist movements. But for Komisarjevsky, the use of montage, uniting disparate fragments or components into a stage com-position, suited his own directorial synthesis, and underscored that sense of auteur mediating between authorial text and audience.

Komisarjevsky's writing on the theatre is primarily centred on the concept and promotion of this synthetic principle. In addition to *The Theatre and a Changing Civilisation* and a handful of variously published essays, Komisarjevsky authored two earlier books about the theatre in English. His first, *Myself and the Theatre*, published in 1929, is an auto-biographical account of his exodus from Russia to London. This volume is the first to outline the idea of a synthetic theatre uniting all theatrical forms at once, with the theatrical producer or director coordinating the composition. The second volume, *The Costume of the Theatre*, published in 1932, chronicles, as its title would suggest, the history of theatre costume, as well as contemporaneous stage design movements.[119] Here as well, Komisarjevsky was unwilling to commit himself to a given aesthetic ideology, and he was wary of the avant-garde's emphasis on form as content, an extremity which entailed the distortion, rather than the interpretation, of the play's inner meaning or philosophical content. Thus, he argued that, whereas Russian symbolism failed to touch upon the essence of theatrical art, the expressionist and constructivist movements, as a rule, turned 'stylised principles into sore deformity'.[120] Even worse, the futurists and cubists had paved the way in art for the Bolshevik revolution in life: their hatred of nature, contempt for style and history, love of destruction and ugliness, and mechanical and geometrical outlook upon life, he argued, 'could not but plunge the stage into a morass of soullessness and often of gross stupidity'.[121]

In his earlier writing, Komisarjevsky sought to dissociate his own work from the extremity of the European avant-garde, and in particular, its emphatic anti-institutionalism. Instead, he advocated a broadly symbolic approach, selecting and synthesizing the aesthetic particularities of each movement into this sense of creative composition. In a posthumous collection of his work, Komisarjevsky's wife defined this synthetic principle: 'The word "synthetic" is used in the Hegelian sense whereby all the elements of a production – visual, aural, and dynamic – become *synthesized*, or, in Komisarjevsky's own words, "united harmonically into a single artistic demonstration".'[122] The idea of stage art as 'composition' meant both amalgamation and creation: multiple forms of art would be synthesized on the stage into an original, organic composition. That composition, coordinated by the director, would express the inner rhythm or music of the play: 'a work of art', Komisarjevsky himself wrote in 1938, 'is a creative composition, subordinated to and expressive of the ideology and emotions of the creator, and is therefore always *romantic* in its essence'.[123] This emphasis on synaesthesia, the stage as a symbolic metaphor demonstrative of the play's inner meaning, an essentially romantic expression of a musical element which animated the artwork, and the emphasis on the director as master artist of the theatre, all suggest a direct lineage from Wagner's notion of the *Gesamtkunstwerk* to Nietzsche's aesthetic philosophy in *The Birth of Tragedy*, and through the writing of Walter Pater and Arthur Symons in England, to Edward Gordon Craig.

As noted earlier, Komisarjevsky's designs for *Macbeth* starkly resemble Craig's earlier designs for Shakespeare.[124] Komisarjevsky, not unlike Craig, despised what he called the gambling spirit of the commercial theatres in England and expressed his hope for an 'idealistically large and heroically powerful theatre created by the people', a theatre with a modern spirit.[125] And like Craig, he regarded the plastic features of the stage as a creative composition in their own right, an abstracted expression of the play's inner meaning and music rather than a realistic reproduction of objective fact. Accordingly, Komisarjevsky summarized his aspiration for the theatre: 'The real function of the theatre is not to copy life, but to interpret plays, in which life and characters are recreated by the imagination of the dramatist, and to find for each of them a suitable form of artistic expression on the stage.'[126] But while he acknowledged his debt to Craig in particular, Komisarjevsky also emphasized that: 'As to Craig's theories, these had not actually very much influence on the practical side of the theatre of the twentieth century.'[127] Both Craig and Komisarjevsky advocated equally the importance of the stage director as the master artist of the theatre who, using the stage as a visual symbolic metaphor, revealed the inner spirit or music of the drama. Thus, particularly in Komisarjevsky's early works, the influence of Wagner and Nietzsche resonates in this emphasis on synaesthesia and the importance of the director's artistic expression, his aesthetic will to power. Komisarjevsky, however, refused to abandon the theatre, and unlike Craig, whose few practical attempts at theatrical production never quite paralleled his heroic ideals, Komisarjevsky's practical work in the English theatre remains more immediately impressive than his theoretical writing.

The symbolist movement in England thus provides the context for Komisarjevsky's first two books. When he first arrived in England, Komisarejvsky found an environment more suited to his own conservative tastes, and though the press exploited his apparent affinity with the European avant-garde, in his writing, Komisarjevsky maintained his distance by criticizing the extremism of European art movements, cultivating his own interests in the more poetic ideas of nineteenth-century German aestheticism after the fashion of Edwardian England's theatrical elite. Defining his idea of synaesthetic composition, the stage as a metaphor expressing the inner spirit of the work, Komisarjevsky denied any explicit political affiliation, maintaining instead the essentially romantic essence of art: 'Life is life and art is art, and, as Tieck said, each of them holds its own truth.'[128] By the mid-1930s, however, the direction of the theatre was shifting. Komisarjevsky's own experience of the Bolshevik revolution in 1917 had demonstrated the pervasive influence of communism on every level of cultural production. By the 1930s, other European countries were experiencing a reinvigorated political and nationalist solidarity under the emerging totalitarian regimes. In the art world, this sense of an emerging new world order precipitated a renewed interest in the pre-war quasi-political avant-garde movements, though they now assumed a more politically radical temper. The aesthetic idealism of the European avant-garde, though less pronounced, was also impacting upon the English theatre. Along with the renewed campaign for a national repertory theatre, local repertories and workers' theatre groups were expressing more emphatically the same socialist and anti-capitalist ethos as the initial efforts for theatrical reform, inspired now however by genuine socialist aesthetics and ideologies of the avant-garde rather than by the problematic socialism of elitist groups like the Fabians.[129] English theatre practitioners were not only looking to the successful German and Russian repertory theatres as models for England, they were also finding inspiration in the success of European art movements. As in the case of Komisarjevsky, these art movements were gradually appropriated and cross-fertilized in the work of more mainstream producers in the English theatre.

By *The Theatre and a Changing Civilisation*, then, Komisarjevsky would argue that: 'It is absurd to assert, as some do, that the art of the theatre is a purely aesthetic function and has nothing to do with "propaganda," either moral, religious, or political. The theatre has everything to do with all that concerns the life of mankind, whether rational or irrational.'[130] Although he continued to emphasize the romantic essence of art, the practice of art, and particularly the art of the theatre, was to be understood in specifically politicized rather than romanticized terms. And thus, the preface to the book invokes the political doctrines of totalitarian regimes for the purpose of analogy, an analogy which suggests the revolutionary context for his own writing about the theatre. This seemingly contradictory dissociation of real political organization from an art defined simultaneously by an apolitical aestheticism and by an ideological rigour is characteristic of numerous avant-garde movements in the period.[131] As the avant-garde increasingly advocated the aesthetic as an alternative to the political realm, this alternative would become increasingly political, and, by analogy or direct association, would draw strength from contemporary political movements such as communism and fascism. This is clearly the direction in which *The Theatre and a Changing Civilisation* turns.[132]

Still, while the period in which he wrote provides a basic context for
understanding the analogy initiated in *The Theatre and a Changing Civilisation*, Komisarjevsky's praise for Mussolini, Lenin, Stalin and Hitler
remains perplexing. The most obvious incongruity is the pairing of communism and fascism, which would seem to suggest, despite his personal
experience of the former, a political naivety or ambivalence. All of these
leaders were also highly suspicious of contemporary art movements.
Many of Komisarjevsky's theatre contemporaries, both continental Euro-
peans and English ex-patriots, were persecuted or jailed, or were forced to
flee the fascist and communist regimes particularly during the war: Jessner
left Germany in exile in 1933, soon to be followed to America by Max
Reinhardt; Meyerhold was imprisoned under ambiguous anti-communist
charges and then shot in Soviet Russia in 1940; Craig was forced out of
Florence in 1940. And yet, even though Komisarjevsky felt himself a
victim and political exile of Bolshevism, what he admired about the 'more
positive and progressive sides of the Fascist, Communist and Nazi movements' was their unrelenting commitment to ideologies which had the
potential to reorder the future relations of society.[133] Although he had fled
Bolshevik Russia, he still regarded such mass progressive movements as
'powerful forces which will help to open up the road towards a new life of
cultured, disciplined *individuals*, united in corporations under the leadership of enlightened men for social, scientific and artistic work'.[134] If this
was not confusing enough, he also claimed: 'To last, human civilisation
should strive to become the civilisation of the masses composed of
cultured individuals and not of a single class whether of workers or
profiteers and parasites.'[135]

The title of the book clearly initiates a context for discussing theatrical
practice in politicized rather than merely aesthetic terms, a context which
is developed in the book itself through a series of aphoristic declarations
characteristic of the avant-garde manifesto. The argument, however,
ultimately resists any extended examination of the theatre in the context
of contemporary political movements. As a manifesto on the theatre, *The
Theatre and a Changing Civilisation* lacks the cogency and explanatory
power of contemporary aesthetic theory such as that of Walter Benjamin.
Writing in 1936, the year of Komisarjevsky's *King Lear*, Benjamin was less
reluctant to explain what he determined to be the changing status of the
work of art under conditions of capitalism. Referring specifically to European art movements, Benjamin expressed his concern about 'aesthetic
theses' which outlined 'the developmental tendencies of art under present
conditions of production' (what would seem to be an oblique reference to

the manifestos of futurism, and possibly, expressionism) with their insistence upon the outmoded concepts of genius, eternal value and mystery, concepts whose 'uncontrolled (and at present almost uncontrollable) application would lead to a processing of data in the Fascist sense'.[136] Benjamin was thus warning that the politicization of the aesthetic – the idealization of individual genius and art as utopian alternatives to the degrading forces of capitalism – would lead to a necessary association with fascist politics.

Earlier in 1934 (one year after Komisarjevsky's production of *Macbeth*), another Marxist theorist, Georg Lukács, writing about the significance and decline of expressionism, similarly criticized the problematic idealism of contemporary art movements and their ideological proximity to fascism.[137] For Lukács, expressionism shared with fascism an abstract opposition to 'middle-classness', a superficially Marxist critique of the bourgeoisie and the 'bourgeoisification' of the masses, what he termed a 'romantic anti-capitalism'. Instead of detailing the class antagonism between the bourgeoisie and the proletariat, he argued that the doctrines of expressionism idealized an 'eternal' or 'philosophy-of-history'-based antithesis between the middle-class and an elite, intellectual league of the 'non-middle-class'. Lukács concluded: 'The next and positive step is of course the demand for this "non-middle-class" elite to take the leadership of society into their own hands.'[138] Although expressionism advocated the political left, Lukács argued that the progression of expressionist ideology would necessarily lead to the reactionary extremity of fascism.[139]

Komisarjevsky's writing in *The Theatre and a Changing Civilisation* and elsewhere echoed the anti-bourgeois sentiment and the less theorized, more figurative vocabulary of his English contemporaries writing about theatre reform. In *The Costume of the Theatre*, for example, he argued: 'In the majority of "civilised" countries men go to the theatre nowadays mostly to be amused and to divert their minds from their everyday occupation of "making money".'[140] Women, by comparison, went to the theatre to ape the fashionable costumes and manners of the actresses: the 'costumes of modern revues and musical comedies, like the plays themselves, satisfy the hypocrisy, the lightness of mind, the sexual instincts, and the taste for luxury of the present bourgeois generations'.[141] In contrast to the bourgeois theatre, his ideal theatre would be run by an intellectual or artistic elite, by those who 'enjoy the *art* of the theatre and its endless inventive possibilities, who are stirred by *ideas*'.[142] Later in *The Theatre and a Changing Civilisation*, Komisarjevsky would denounce, in the language of European socialism, the stifling traditions of the capitalist stage in contrast to the real modern spirit, 'seeking its expression in an idealistically large and heroically powerful theatre created by the people'.[143] Even if such a theatre were merely for amusement, however, Komisarjevsky argued, quoting the eighteenth-century German theorist Lessing: 'it would still be important not to allow it to be run by idiots and vulgarians who have no regard for spiritual values . . . its potentiality for good is rendered vain by the shallow and ignoble and by those not trained to its true principles'.[144]

From his earlier period in London and throughout his reign in Stratford in the 1930s, Komisarjevksy was a decidedly popular producer whose various appropriations of avant-garde stylization were quickly absorbed into the mainstream theatre. His anti-bourgeois rhetoric is therefore ironic given the commercial success of his productions. The apparent elitism of his 'heroically powerful' theatre also echoed the elitism of his contemporaries in England, especially Shaw and Granville-Barker, advocating a non-commercial repertory theatre whose 'popular' content would be determined by an elite class of artist-intellectuals. As with his contemporaries, Komisarjevsky adopted a politicized rhetoric about the need for a radical response to a growing and uncritical middle-class culture. But most importantly, Komisarjevsky's writing, more than that of any of his contemporaries in England, demonstrated how a broadly Nietzschean cult of artistic genius as appropriated into English theatrical culture through figures such as Symons and Craig would mirror the cult of leadership and authoritarian control of the contemporary European political theatre. This is the context of the analogy between theatre director and dictator initiated by the preface to the book: the emphasis on leadership and control, the art of the theatre a synthetic composition coordinated by the director which would then reveal some apparently essential truth or inner meaning of the work otherwise hidden from the ordinary person. For Komisarjevsky, the analogy served to justify the artistic will of the director to create and impose meaning.

Warning of the avant-garde's ideological affinity with fascism, Lukács argued that the expressionists cultivated an exaggerated subjectivism in their art, abstracting objective reality into an image of chaos, the task of the artist thus being to inject meaning into this 'meaninglessness' and reorder reality according to the artist's subjective perspective.[145] Similarly, for Komisarjevsky, the unification of seemingly disparate elements on the stage into a transparently synthesized composition, the ordered chaos of a drunkenly skewed Venice or an eclectically motley Ephesus, and according to a subjective rationale, was justified by the principle of theatre art: 'The production of a play is, like every work of art, a *composition* devised by the producer and subordinated in all its elements to his understanding and feeling of the play.'[146] Komisarjevsky regarded the interpretation of the text as a process of composition carried out by the producer or director whose invisible presence would be manifest in the perspective constructed. The analogy between director and dictator thus exemplified this aesthetic principle: 'An enterprise, particularly an idealistic one, requires a leader who either enjoys the confidence of the people or knows the secret of how to enforce his ideology upon them. A crowd left to itself is guided chiefly by emotions and passions and very often by confused personal instincts.'[147]

Imagine Komisarjevsky secretly forcing his ideology upon a confused and misguided audience by subordinating the elements of the stage to his own understanding of the play: this is a powerful image which suggests a fairly obvious correspondence between his own aesthetic doctrine and the political doctrines of totalitarian dictators. Of course, how we choose to read the significance of these comments depends entirely upon a series of related questions about the relationship between art and the social and political contexts of its making and remaking, questions which continue to complicate the discussion of and distinction between modernism and the avant-garde. On the one hand, Komisarjevsky's analogy is eccentric, a rhetorical flourish in the writing of a relatively minor and certainly unusual figure in the early twentieth-century English theatre. On the other hand, his writing also belongs to a body of theatrical discourse which initially provided the rationale for the contemporary national theatre culture in England as well as the working model for its organization – non-commercial exclusive institutions funded by public money and led by visionary artistic directors. The possibility that this is one of modernism's legacies in the contemporary theatre – a romantic anti-capitalist or anti-bourgeois ideology coupled with a cult of artistic genius leading to a culture of leadership and control – and is only one step removed from the legacies of European totalitarian politics is darkly disturbing and unsettling, not unlike the presences of Mussolini, Lenin, Stalin and Hitler in a book about the theatre.

CHAPTER 4

Shakespeare's text in performance, circa 1923

The Shakespeare renaissance in America, which I mentioned the other day, coincides very admirably with the three hundredth anniversary this year of the publication of the First Folio, as Mr William Poel reminds us. We owe to Heminge and Condell, those two obscure actors of Shakespeare's company, the volume which, next to the Bible, is the most cherished in existence. I think we in England might aptly celebrate the occasion by a short revival of certain notorious Shakespeare productions.

For example, there is Granville Barker's 'Midsummer Night's Dream' with its astonishing gilt fairies. There is Tree's (or was it Oscar Asche's?) 'As You Like It' with the real rabbits frolicking in and out of the Arden groves. There is Miss Viola Tree's 'Tempest' which was rather like a selection of refined music-hall turns. And there is an extraordinary production of 'Hamlet' in New York at the moment with Reinhardt-Craigish effects and queer, solemn eccentricities which would make Shakespeare gasp.

Finally, we might have one – just one – of the plays as Shakespeare wrote it.

(*Daily Express*, 9 January 1923)

Despite his understated sarcasm, the dramatic columnist for the *Daily Express*, writing early in the January of that year, astutely characterized the popular cultural complexion of Shakespeare in England in 1923. This was indeed the tercentenary year of Shakespeare's First Folio, and while Shakespeare's canon as represented by that volume still maintained an unparalleled appreciation in England, this critic was clearly envious of the Shakespeare renaissance occurring in the American theatre. The growing domination of American cultural exports certainly contributed to a characteristically English fear: that of losing their most valued cultural possession, particularly as original editions of Shakespeare continued to migrate in the opposite direction across the Atlantic to the libraries of wealthy Americans. And in 1925, John Barrymore would bring his New York

production of *Hamlet* 'with Reinhardt-Craigish effects' to England with
the intention of effectively conquering the renownedly fickle London
stage. The problem, however, was largely home-grown. The 'notorious'
Shakespeare productions of Tree and Granville-Barker, as well as the more
radical experimentation and theory of Poel and Craig, though they still
dominated the public memory, were old. Since the war, the few significant productions of Shakespeare had failed to reinvent Shakespearean
theatrical practice. Thus, citing the example of the Americans was only
one way of inciting a broader public anxiety about 'losing' Shakespeare.

1923 was in fact a significant if not pivotal year in the cultural history
of Shakespeare's texts. That 1923 was also the tercentenary of the Folio,
the anniversary of the publication of a book, was not merely coinci-
dental. The events and publications whose purpose was to commemorate the Folio not surprisingly functioned to focus attention upon the
cultural practices of reproducing Shakespeare's texts, either as edited
into book form or as represented in the theatre, and therefore reflected
the increasingly problematic issue of textual authenticity, the growing
fissure between the material artefacts descended from Shakespeare's
writing and the representation of an authoritative ideal text.[1] The public
focus upon the Folio effectively publicized and brought to the fore-
ground the work of the increasingly influential New Bibliography. The
research and the methodology of textual evaluation pioneered by, in
particular, A. W. Pollard, W. W. Greg, R. B. McKerrow, and, to a lesser
extent, J. Dover Wilson, spanned the first half of the twentieth century.
Their contributions to the examination of Shakespeare's texts were
unprecedentedly methodological and thus radically transformed not
only editorial practice, but the broader issue of textual authenticity
and its application to various forms of textual representation. Pollard
and his associates established the foundation for a bibliographic study of
early printed texts: 'the method followed in bibliography being first to
get all the information possible from the book itself and then to
interpret this information in the light of all we know as to the methods
of book production at the time that it was printed and published'.[2]
Their contributions to bibliographic scholarship, among numerous
volumes of textual study, were often published in the periodical the
Library, the journal of the Bibliographic Society which was under the
editorship of Pollard between 1903 and 1934, and they also established
the Malone Society in 1906 which was dedicated to the editing of early
printed texts and manuscripts.

Sir Israel Gollancz, the presiding chair of the Shakespeare Association and the chair of the Shakespeare Day Committee in 1923, established the tone for the year in the annual lecture of the Literary Society, 'Shakespeare: the Book and the Man'. His petition to have an appropriate commemorative event for the First Folio instigated the tercentenary celebrations held in April, in conjunction with the customary birthday celebrations, and also led to the publication of a commemorative volume by the Shakespeare Association with essays from some of the most recent and influential textual scholars including R. Crompton Rhodes, Dover Wilson and Greg.[3] Also in 1923, Rhodes published his study, *Shakespeare's First Folio*.[4] 1923, the year of a heightened public recognition of Shakespeare's Folio, was also the year in which Pollard delivered the Annual Shakespeare Lecture of the British Academy which he titled *The Foundations of Shakespeare's Texts*, a revision of his earlier position from the larger 1909 publication, *Shakespeare's Folios and Quartos*.[5]

The year prior, 1922, saw the publication of two highly influential literary texts, James Joyce's encyclopaedic work of fiction *Ulysses*, published by the Shakespeare and Company bookshop in Paris, and T. S. Eliot's poem 'The Waste Land', first published in the literary magazine *Dial*; and for this reason, 1922 has come to be known as the pinnacle of high modernism. A similarly auspicious year for the New Bibliography was 1923, especially insofar as that field of study reacted to the coinciding progression of literary criticism as championed by Eliot. Eliot was an enthusiastic fan of the Phoenix Society whose namesake bird symbolized their project of dramatic revival, mounting productions of non-Shakespearean Elizabethan and Jacobean drama. Eliot had also helped to revive the popularity of Shakespeare's lesser known contemporaries, his critical evaluation of renaissance drama influencing the generation of Shakespeare critics which emerged in the early twentieth century, the New Criticism of, among others, G. Wilson Knight and L. C. Knights.[6] In his contentious essay on *Hamlet*, Eliot had also praised the work of Shakespeare critic J. M. Robertson. In 1922, Robertson began publishing his series, *The Shakespeare Canon*, comprising perhaps the most controversial and influential of what would come to be labelled by E. K. Chambers in 1924 as 'disintegrating' criticism.[7] In an attempt to construct a measure of textual authority through a comparative literary and stylistic analysis of Shakespeare's plays, disintegrationists such as Robertson and E. E. Stoll were criticized for excluding suspect texts from the canon by relying upon their own subjective literary taste. The New Bibliography thus responded to such impressionistic attribution studies with their own empirical investigations into the processes of textual production and transmission which emphasized the texts as products of institutional practices and mechanical procedures.[8]

Then as now, conflicting claims as to what constituted authentic Shakespeare, the plays as he wrote them, dominated the critical environment, though in this period, those claims seem to have been polarized in schools of wholly differing methodologies. Certainly, the disintegrationists were in methodological alignment with the New Criticism insofar as both made their plea for the liberty of interpreting the text; that is, liberty from the kind of scholarship which would otherwise historicize or problematize the cultural status of Shakespeare, a status which overshadowed the status of his texts. Suspect texts could be included or excluded from the canon according to a predetermined and personally subjective sense of Shakespeare's writerly ability. For the New Criticism, archaeological consideration of the texts was superfluous: what could the study of typeface, textual transmission or holograph reveal about the essence of Shakespeare to bring us closer to what he actually wrote? This question was largely answered by the appearance of a study which suggested the possibility of Shakespeare's holograph in the manuscript for *Sir Thomas More*, a study published by, among others, Pollard, Greg, and Dover Wilson, once again, in 1923.[9] The claim of Shakespeare's holograph had been suggested earlier, most notably by Richard Simpson in 1871 and E. M. Thompson in 1916.[10] This new attempt to identify the author's hand (although primarily palaeographic rather than bibliographic and admittedly impressionistic in places) must have been a vindication for the New Bibliography, a demonstration of their competency, the impact of which would be weighted by the array of influential contributors. Whatever the possibility of Shakespeare's hand in the manuscript of *Sir Thomas More* represented to the literary interpretation of his printed texts, the short passage, inasmuch as the claim was verifiably true, was the most demonstrably authentic Shakespeare.

While the New Bibliography developed various procedures for investigating the complexities of and determining textual transmission, the question of authenticity to the representation of Shakespeare was no less relevant in the theatre. The year 1923 was also the year in which H. K. Ayliff produced his modern-dress *Cymbeline* for the Birmingham Repertory Theatre, perhaps the first self-stylized 'modern-dress' production in twentieth-century England and the production which led to the popular catchphrase, 'Shakespeare in "Plus Fours"' (*Daily Express*, 10 April 1923).

Under the direction of Barry Jackson, the company's later productions of *Hamlet* in 1925, *All's Well That Ends Well* in 1927 and *The Taming of the Shrew* and *Macbeth* in 1928 were equally unapologetic in their sartorial contemporaneity. But in 1923, there was little else to rival the aggressive modernity of the stylization. For Jackson, Shakespeare's popular status as the greatest dramatist legitimated the free interpretation of the text: 'My theory is that Shakespeare is so great that you can do anything you like with him . . . Human nature has not changed, and the great types that Shakespeare created are about us in the world today' (*Daily Express*, 10 April 1923). For the more conservative dramatic critics, however, what was seen as the 'inevitable incongruity' (*Daily Express*, 23 April 1923) between Shakespeare and the contemporary setting revived the debate which had surrounded William Poel's Elizabethan production of *Hamlet* in 1881 about what constituted an authentic representation of Shakespeare. Jackson's desire to eschew the kind of archaeological accuracy recommended by Poel in favour of his own more liberal interpretation played out the same dialectic at work in textual studies of Shakespeare.

The desire to represent Shakespeare's texts accurately, and more specifically, that imperative across textual studies to establish the parameters of Shakespeare's canon, was also reflected in theatrical practice. Again in 1923, Lilian Bayliss and her repertory company at the Old Vic completed the first-ever cycle to perform all of Shakespeare's canon under one management. On 7 November, one day prior to the official tercentenary day of the publication of the First Folio, the day in which Heminge and Condell applied to the Stationer's Hall for a licence, the company celebrated the Folio with a performance of *Troilus and Cressida*, the last play in their cycle and, incidentally, the last play to be included in the Folio. As in the case of the modern-dress *Cymbeline*, the performance of the entire canon by the Old Vic company demonstrated some concurrent sense of what constituted performative authenticity. But in the case of the Old Vic, that sense of authenticity was aligned quite identifiably with the printed text: the Folio maintained an iconographic significance which was seen to bear upon the representation of Shakespeare's texts in the theatre.

Now, the point of connection between all of these occurrences, and this should be obvious by now, is 1923. Unlike Edmond Malone's edition of 1790, no single event or text wholly transformed the representational practice of Shakespeare's texts, either as edited in book form or performed on the stage. On the contrary, if anything, the numerous events and publications which commemorated and thus idealized the Folio further

complicated discussions of textual authenticity. Nor would 1923 appear to
have been an exceptionally outstanding year either with regard to the
intellectual development of the New Bibliography or to theatrical practice. But at a time when these spheres of Shakespeare production were
being dramatically transformed by various new practices – New Bibliography, New Criticism, New Stagecraft, New Drama – what we find in
1923 are different approaches to representing the text engaging with and
intersecting at the idea of performance. In fact, what makes 1923, the year
of Folio commemorations, a particular critical juncture in the history of
Shakespeare's texts is the degree to which performance, in its various
material and metaphorical applications, problematized the idea of text –
as authorial script, as dramatic script, as edited, and as performed – thus
opening its representation out to dramatically different possibilities.[11] In
bibliographic scholarship, for a brief moment in 1923, a window would
appear to have been open to the possibility of recognizing Shakespeare's
plays as performative texts, performative in the sense of having been
derived from playhouse material which had been used for performance
and which was, therefore, more variable and fluid than a single authorial original. This more fluid (undefined) sense of textual authenticity
was reflected in contemporary editions of Shakespeare which, though
they reinscribed the values of authorship traditionally imposed upon
printed texts, were simultaneously committed to exploring the material
production of the text; that is, the text as conditioned by its reception in
the theatre and production/reproduction in print. In the theatre, the
coinciding desire to authenticate performance by returning to the text
elicited the same kind of dual and problematically intertwined commitments to Shakespeare the book and Shakespeare the man; on the one
hand, advocating a historical or methodological consideration of the
material text and its representation, while, on the other, simultaneously
re-inscribing assumptions inherited from the nineteenth century about
the nature of Shakespeare's writerly ability.[12] The parallel here is not quite
balanced, except insofar as this ambiguous and loosely metaphorical
relationship between text and performance – text as performance, text
in performance – characterizes the point where different practices of
textual representation meet in 1923.

THE 1623 FOLIO AND THE 1923 NEW BIBLIOGRAPHY

Among the more memorable and publicized Shakespeare-related events of
1923 were the numerous birthday celebrations held variously in Stratford

and London on 23 April. Throughout the early twentieth century, the birthday celebrations held a much greater stature as a national event, the annual pinnacle of Shakespearean events widely reported in the national newspapers, and the beginning of the Shakespeare Memorial Theatre season, the only Shakespeare programme sanctioned by the committees advocating a national or Shakespeare theatre.[13] In 1923, however, the tercentenary year of the Folio, the birthday celebrations were more historically significant. Seven years later than the tercentenary of his death in 1916, celebrations which had been regretfully muted by the war, the celebrations of 1923 were subsequently heralded as a more fitting tribute to the lasting memory of Shakespeare. Sir Israel Gollancz, writing in an article for *The Times* two days prior, termed the occasion 'the tercentenary of his living fame' (21 April 1923). This praise for the Folio as Shakespeare's living fame signified the regard in which this particular volume was held. The Folio was seen to have descended from Shakespeare, the product of his achievements and, moreover, a collection of 'the greatest achievements of the human mind' (*The Times*, 21 April 1923). The magnitude of this esteem made Shakespeare's First Folio, a book which was neither terribly old nor impressively and meticulously put together, one of the most important volumes of early printed material, the *Daily Express* rating the book as 'the volume which, next to the Bible, is the most cherished in existence' (9 January 1923). This strangely misguided emphasis on the book gave rise to a singularly unique tone for the birthday celebrations that year, the desire to commemorate something of Shakespeare's which was relatively concrete, 'the presentments which his pen left us' (*The Times*, 23 April 1923), resulting in a rather fetishistic celebration of the Folio which obscured, if only for the duration of the celebrations, the more complicated question of that text's authority.

Besides the new season of the SMT festival, the most publicized event of the 1923 celebrations was the luncheon hosted by the Shakespeare Association, this year in historic conjunction with the Stationer's Company of London. Here was a significantly symbolic meeting-ground for text and theatre where some of the most influential scholars and actors of the day gathered to commemorate the tercentenary. Descriptions in the press which covered the event characterized the meeting in the tone of political entente. The reputable actor and occasional writer, John Drinkwater, proposing a toast during the luncheon to Shakespearean scholarship suggested that there were two distinct branches of study, that of the theatre and that of the printed book: 'And the hope of all those who

cared very much for the theatre was that in the immediate following years
an endeavour would be made towards the unification of those two
branches of Shakespearean scholarship' (*Daily Telegraph*, 23 April 1923).
In response, Sir Sidney Lee replied that: 'Scholarship would in due time
make Shakespeare on the stage all that it ought to be.' The reason for this
strange moment of entente between scholars and actors during the Folio
tercentenary was perhaps that, insofar as the commemoration of the
Folio celebrated an icon of Shakespeare, the commemoration also paid
tribute to the two common actors of Shakespeare's company, Heminge
and Condell, who made the Folio possible by collecting the plays for
publication. In his address at the Wren church of Aldermanbury in
London where the memory of the two actors was preserved in a stone
memorial, the Archbishop of Canterbury summarized the debt of gratitude which the theatre owed to the preservation of Shakespeare in Folio
book form: Heminge and Condell, Shakespeare's admiring colleagues,
felt that what Shakespeare 'had written for the boards must not perish in
the using. They saw it to be a possession for all time, and they resolved
that it should be set forth for good in no ephemeral play copies, but in
solid form' (*The Times*, 23 April 1923). While the representatives of the
theatre were willing to recognize their debt to the study of the text, to the
preservation of their art in solid form, what made this moment of entente
dramatic was the degree to which scholarship was willing to recognize the
Folio as a particularly performative or dramatic text in the sense of having
been derived from playhouse prompt-copy.

Certainly by the time of the tercentenary a shift in attitude towards the
Folio had become evident as the circulation and price inflation of particular copies of Folio originals generated a public interest which, in turn,
further inflated the status and value of those originals. The national
newspapers regularly noted the prices which various Folios would fetch
at auctions and private purchases. Certain copies like the Burdett-Coutts
and the Bodleian even maintained a small degree of fame not only among
academics and enthusiasts, but in the press as well. The late nineteenth
and early twentieth centuries saw a dramatic inflation in the value of Folio
originals as academic libraries and private collectors sought to complete
what was considered to be the cornerstone of a good library, a complete
set of the four Folio editions from 1623, 1632, 1663 and 1685 respectively.[14]
Possession of a Folio original, or better yet, many Folio originals, signified
not only individual wealth, status and cultural sophistication, but also
national wealth and status. In 1902, as a supplement to his facsimile
edition of the Folio, Lee published a catalogue of the Folios known to

exist.[15] His concern for the condition and location of Folio originals undoubtedly contributed to that anxiety which was prevalent in 1923 about the tendency of privately owned copies to migrate to the United States. The most well known of Folio enthusiasts, the American Henry Clay Folger, with his passion for collecting numerous copies, had obtained more than thirty by 1923 and a total of seventy-nine by 1930.[16] As the status of the Folio became more embedded within public regard in England in the early twentieth century, and most notably acute in 1923, the mass migration of the Folios proved a distressing point. Manifest in the First Folio, Shakespeare's genius was regarded as 'in a true sense the property of his fellow-countrymen' ('Shakespeare First Folio, Address by Sir Sidney Lee', *The Times*, 22 January 1923).

While possession of a Folio original outwardly indicated a keen scholarly interest in Shakespeare, such demonstrations remained out of reach of all but wealthy individuals and institutions. Nevertheless, ever-improving methods of book printing and photographic reproduction secured the larger public's imperative to own or witness even reproduced images of the original printed text. In 1806, the first hand-set type facsimile of the First Folio was produced and in 1866, around the same time that Cambridge University began publishing their first scholarly edition series, the first widely available photolithographic facsimile entered the book market under the direction of Howard Staunton.[17] The subsequent proliferation of photographic reproductions, of which Lee's own collotype facsimile of the Chatsworth edition of the Folio was but one, possibly accounted for the public's increased interest in and familiarity with Shakespeare's original printed texts. More importantly, however, the photographically precise reproduction of the Folio's text demonstrated the integrity and authority of the original, unhampered by the literary tastes of eighteenth- and nineteenth-century editors and also unhampered by cuts, additions, and adaptations made in the theatre.

By 1923, the age of mechanical reproduction was helping to transform public awareness of Shakespeare's extant texts and the status of the edited text. With improvements made in printing and book production technology, Shakespeare editions had been multiplying at an ever-increasing rate since the late eighteenth century. These editions were mostly inexpensive pocket and abridged or expurgated family editions, but also included the elaborately illustrated decorative and performance editions of the nineteenth century. The growth of a mass market for editions of Shakespeare reflected not only the introduction of Shakespeare into the national school curriculum in the nineteenth century, but more broadly, and especially by the early twentieth century, the assimilation of working-class and bourgeois culture in a growing urban middle-class culture in which Shakespeare proved a respectable and entertaining pastime.[18] While print mechanization coupled with the growth of a domestic reading culture were diversifying the edition and expanding the mass market audience for Shakespeare, the increasing dissemination of photographic reproductions of sixteenth and seventeenth-century printed texts – ostensibly 'genuine' with their visibly old type-face and spelling – exposed contemporary stylistic superfluities such as bowdlerization, extra-textual illustration and editorial emendation as inauthentic, making contemporary popular editions less than satisfactory as academic or authoritative editions. The unmediated photographic reproduction of what were still largely regarded with an eighteenth-century pessimism to be corrupted texts, also magnified the necessity to establish criteria for modern editing and textual production.[19]

Academic scholarship would increasingly seek to contain the ever-expanding diversity and heterogeneity of the Shakespeare edition. This would give rise to the specialized scholarly editions of the late nineteenth and twentieth centuries, editions which would seek to secure the tastes and values of a traditional literary high culture against a threatening mass culture. The New Bibliography emerged out of the confrontation between technological development in photographic and print media, the commercial diversification of the edition and the romanticist belief in Shakespeare as the unitary imaginative and intellectual centre of the canon, a canon conveniently, but not unprobematically, symbolized by the Folio. Though committed to illuminating 'original' texts, the New Bibliographers recognized the disparity between extant early printed texts, whose errors and typographical irregularities represented what they repeatedly referred to as 'the veil of print', and the authorial copytext thought to be hidden underneath that veil.[20] What they were seeking to establish exactly around this time of 1923 was a bibliographic methodology for verifying the authenticity of original printed texts against an as yet undefined notion of what constituted textual authenticity. This task, moreover, had not yet translated into a protocol for editing those texts. So while the appearance of photographic reproductions exposed the bias of popular abridged, embellished and expurgated editions seeking to represent stylistic superfluities as authentic Shakespeare, simultaneously, the dissemination of photofacsimiles, which reproduced the veil of print without intervention, magnified the necessity to establish criteria for editing Shakespeare's texts.

Published in 1935, McKerrow's *Prolegomena for the Oxford Shakespeare* was the first systematic consideration of editing practice to define explicitly an editing procedure against a bibliographic criterion of authenticity. The ideal text, McKerrow argued, 'should approach as closely as the extant material allows to a fair copy, made by the author himself, of his plays in the form which he intended finally to give them, and . . . should not in any way be coloured by the preconceived ideas or interpretations of later times'.[21] However much McKerrow's definition of an ideal text was still open to ambiguity, that ideal would approximate a final written fair copy or manuscript which then proceeded to the playhouse. While the idea of editing the text according to a conjectured authorial fair copy was an evident, though ambiguous and unwritten, objective in the earlier work of the New Bibliography, where the research of Pollard in particular differed was in the absence of an imperative to define explicitly an 'ideal text' or to establish an editing protocol. Pollard's study was primarily an investigation of the authority of Quarto and Folio editions, descended almost directly from and responding to Malone's edition. Editors like Malone from the seventeenth through to the nineteenth centuries were mostly pessimistic about the authority of the Folio, their valuation hinging upon the prefatory material ascribed to Heminge and Condell and, in particular, the one line which referred to previously published Quarto texts as 'diverse stolne and surreptitious copies'.[22] For Malone, this condemnation of the Quarto texts was a transparent commercial strategy: 'The players, when they mention these copies, represent them all as mutilated and imperfect; but this was merely thrown out to give an additional value to their own edition, and is not strictly true.'[23] More importantly, according to Malone the editors of the Folio compromised their integrity and the integrity of the Folio text by privately using the very Quartos they wholly condemned as copytext. Where Malone inherited a certain degree of the contemporary prejudice regarding the character of actors, Pollard effectively redeemed the reputations of Heminge and Condell by reinterpreting 'diverse' to mean 'some' as opposed to 'all' of the Quarto copies, distinguishing between good Quartos which the Folio editors did use for copy and the bad or surreptitiously published Quartos which they did not. Pollard and his associates were therefore able to read the First Folio 'with all the more confidence because we need no longer believe that its editors in their preface were publicly casting stones at earlier editions which they were privately using, often with no very substantial modification, in constructing their own text'.[24] Rethinking what Pollard termed the foundation of the text as understood by the prefatory material built a stronger case for the authority of the Folio.

While Malone was cautious in his collation of the Folio variations, the primary effect of Pollard's redefinition of 'diverse' was to question the nature of the changes and corrections of the Quartos made in the Folio. According to Pollard's reasoning, if, in their collection of copy for the Folio, Heminge and Condell had selected with discrimination, then perhaps they had also provided the printers with either manuscript or playhouse prompt-books against which the Quartos could be checked. Not only would corrections in the Folio possibly be authorial, they would also possibly reveal valuable information about the way the plays were performed, recording alterations which may have been made after performance. According to Pollard, the 'foundations of Shakespeare's texts must have been laid in his study and in the playhouse'.[25] Rather than evaluate the authenticity of the Folio text against a problematic and ideal authorial fair copy, Pollard's study offered the possibility of recognizing the now positively valued Folio texts as both authorial and theatrical documents, texts written by Shakespeare and subsequently conditioned by their performance in Shakespeare's theatre. This possibility of theatrical intervention would later evolve in the late 1910s and early 1920s into what would come to be known as the doctrine of 'continuous copy', the suggestion being that copytext used in the printing-house would have undergone various degrees of potentially non-authorial alteration, insertion and revision after leaving Shakespeare's study for a length of use in the theatre.

Pollard's theories had been tested in a series of articles jointly written with Dover Wilson for the *Times Literary Supplement* in 1919.[26] This series of five articles was concerned primarily with the transmission of the 'bad' or surreptitious Quartos as categorized by Pollard in 1909; though, significantly, insofar as the three Quarto texts discussed were derived from 'shortened versions of the plays used by Shakespeare's company on tour' (*TLS*, 19 January 1919), they therefore also reflected performance versions of the plays. Moreover, argued Pollard and Dover Wilson in the following week, the bibliographical links between the bad and the good Shakespearean texts proved 'not only that the former were to some extent derived from playhouse manuscript, but that these manuscripts possessed some kind of organic connexion with those which formed the copy for the latter' (16 January 1919). The articles generated a significant interest insofar as they explained the 'corruption' of the surreptitious texts in the context of piracy, which Pollard had initially proposed in his 1917 *Shakespeare's Fight with the Pirates*, but also in the possibility of theatrical revision.[27] In further suggesting that the bad texts possessed an organic connection with the good, these initial articles established a strong correlation in all the extant texts between textual mutability and performance.

In 1924, one year following Pollard in 1923, E. K. Chambers delivered his British Academy Lecture whose title, 'The Disintegration of Shakespeare', neatly categorized a range of textual activities associated with the reattribution of Shakespeare's plays to non-Shakespearean sources. Included among these was the doctrine of 'continuous copy'. As Chambers noted, this doctrine was based primarily on the principle of theatrical precaution and economy: the copytext used by the printers for the 'good' Quartos reflected the fewest possible number of expensive transcriptions, and were, therefore, primarily authorial fair copies. Given the fear of printing piracy, these manuscripts were closely guarded by the theatrical companies over long periods of time, and, subsequently, reflected the numerous, possibly non-authorial, revisions occasioned by revivals and provincial tours. Returning in 1923 to the question of the Folio's authority, Pollard thus surmised that, when the copytexts used by the printers were not the revised authorial fair copies themselves, then the earlier 'good' Quartos used as copytext may have either served as playhouse prompt-books, which would then bear the marks of dramatic revision, or may have been checked against authorial or revised manuscript or playhouse prompt-books. In any case, the Folio text might reveal important information about the way the plays were performed, recording alterations which had been made in performance. Thus, the 'foundations of Shakespeare's texts' demonstrated a continuity between authorial and performative versions. In 1923, Pollard's *Shakespeare's Hand in the Play of Sir Thomas More* offered the extant manuscript of *Sir Thomas More* as the most concrete evidence of such theatrical revision. Insofar as the claim of Shakespeare's hand was true, then it represented the possibility that the copytexts used by the printers for Shakespeare's First Folio were, like the manuscript of *Sir Thomas More*, socially conditioned, possibly multi-authored, and dramatic in nature.

'Continuous copy' was a fairly divisive theory in the ranks of the New Bibliography. Chambers, himself an editor, derided: 'and so we arrive at the notion of the long-lived manuscript in the tiring-house wardrobe, periodically taken out for a revival and as often worked upon by fresh hands, abridged and expanded, recast to fit the capabilities of new performers, brightened with current topical allusions, written up to date to suit new tastes in poetic diction'.[28] Greg would later deride 'continuous copy' as a figment of the editorial brain, 'according to which an old play-book might undergo almost any amount of alteration, cancellation, and addition, and still remain in use as a prompt copy'.[29] Greg also noted later in 1955 that both Pollard and Dover Wilson would also seem to have withdrawn from the idea after 1924, the latter writing in his introduction to the New Shakespeare *3 Henry VI* that 'continuous copy' was 'a doctrine which the said Wilson long since abandoned, without, to the best of his recollection, ever consciously holding it'.[30] The possibility of socially conditioned and multi-authored texts like *Sir Thomas More* no doubt augmented the anxiety about losing Shakespeare; and perhaps the idea of continuous copy is one reason McKerrow set about defining an ideal text to mean explicitly an authorial fair copy which then entered the theatre, though even he admitted that it was 'very doubtful whether, especially in the case of the earlier plays, there ever existed any written "final form"'.[31] Nevertheless, Pollard and Dover Wilson's earlier suggestion opened out a possibility to which later editors after McKerrow would return; that is, that the authenticity of a text was not necessarily corrupted by alterations and adaptations made in the theatre, or that a more fluid notion of performative copy could be the basis for an edited text.

Thus, having established the necessity to consider the performative qualities of the text, the high-profile work of Pollard and his contemporaries had readied the stage for entente with the actors by 1923. The New Bibliography had almost singlehandedly redeemed the integrity of Shakespeare's fellow actors as editors. In the Shakespeare Association's commemorative tercentenary collection of essays, Dover Wilson observed this newly recognized correlation between the authenticity of the Folio's texts and the integrity of Heminge and Condell, suggesting that their prefaces were 'the title-deeds of our greatest national possession; and our views upon the integrity of the Folio texts depend in a large measure upon the views which we believe Heminge and Condell themselves took of their responsibilities'.[32] At the luncheon in the Stationer's Hall, John Drinkwater similarly affirmed this strengthened affiliation between text and theatre, suggesting that actors, after the example of Heminge and Condell, were to be regarded as symbolic stewards of the text, while scholars of a liberal and humane mind were to check the actors in this matter (*Daily Express*, 23 April 1923). So by the time of the tercentenary celebrations, Pollard and his associates had not only redeemed the authority of the Folio, but they had also announced the beginning of academic interest in the performance of Shakespeare's texts within both the

Elizabethan/Jacobean and contemporary theatres, while also establishing the desire or need to explore the possibility and nature of a performative text, a text conceived as the product of, and intended for, theatrical use.

One important point to remember about the New Bibliographers is that, despite their methodical discipline, they were still largely regarded by their contemporaries to be the least conservative of textual practitioners and, though references were often made to their comparatively unconventional conclusions in textual notes, they were not directly associated with the established editions of Shakespeare in 1923. The two major edition series of the period, the Arden Shakespeare begun in 1891 under the general editorship of W. J. Craig and the American Yale Shakespeare begun in 1917, remained cautious in their application of the New Bibliography's speculations. Both nearing completion in 1923, these two series represented the second generation of academic edition series after the landmark nineteenth-century Cambridge Shakespeare. A third ongoing major series in 1923 was The New Shakespeare, also published by Cambridge University Press and begun in 1921. Under the editorship of Arthur Quiller-Couch and Dover Wilson, this was the only edition series to acknowledge an intellectual debt to the New Bibliography: 'No moment', Quiller-Couch wrote in his general introduction, 'has been more favourable for auspicating a text of the plays and poems than that which begets the occasion of this new one.'[33] Clearly, the editors conceived of their series as an answer to the contemporary popular editions, the next generation of *new* Shakespeare texts informed by the twentieth-century scientific approach of the New Bibliography.

In his review of the first edition for the series, *The Tempest* (1921), Sidney Lee praised the scientific principles which the editors endeavoured to employ, but Lee remained far more cautious about Dover Wilson's controversial textual theories.[34] Dover Wilson held, for example, that the punctuation of the extant Folio texts for the most part reproduced the punctuation of the prompt-copy and, furthermore, reflected the dramatic quality of that copy. The punctuation, he argued, represented Shakespeare's instructions to the actors: 'The stops, brackets, capital letters in the Folio are in fact stage-directions in shorthand. They tell the actor when to pause and for how long, they guide his intonation, they indicate the emphatic word, often enough they denote "stage-business".'[35] Chambers was also cautious about Dover Wilson's theory of theatrical revision in the transmission of the play, this idea of 'continuous copy'. For both Chambers and Lee, Dover Wilson's conclusions about the dramatic quality of the text rested not on empirical deduction, but on 'unstable foundations of conjecture and hypothesis'.[36] Moreover, far from being a performance-oriented text, reviewers also noted the editors' proclivity for narrative elaboration, demonstrated especially by the frequent 'supererogatory' stage directions inserted into the text for the benefit of the modern reader.[37] Thus, despite the pseudo-scientific methodology advocated by the editors, the Arden remained the more conservative and reliable series of Shakespeare editions.

In contrast to the major Shakespeare editions of the period, only one series seems to have applied an academic interest in performance to the actual practices of book production. One project undertaken by the publishing house of Victor Gollancz in 1923, once again to commemorate the tercentenary, was a series of typographic reproductions of the Folio notably titled *The Players' Shakespeare*. As an eminent actor and director of Shakespeare, Harley Granville-Barker was commissioned to write a number of prefaces for this single-play edition series which set about to reprint the text 'literatim' from the Folio.[38] Like the original Folio at the time of its production, this series was intended as an expensive and exclusive commemorative edition, with a limited publication of 100 signed and 450 unsigned copies. Each volume furnished with illustrations by a contemporary artist, *The Players' Shakespeare* differed significantly from photographic reproductions of the Folio, the ornamented and embellished volumes attempting to represent the original printed text within a decidedly dramatic or performative context. Having solicited Granville-Barker, who made his reputation directing innovative productions of Shakespeare at London's Savoy Theatre in 1912 and 1914, the publishers were seeking to compose an edition 'from the point of view of their performance on the stage'.[39] While the venture, largely a commercial failure, sustained the publication of just seven volumes between 1923 and 1927, Granville-Barker's prefaces were later reorganized, rewritten, and expanded to be published with Sidgwick and Jackson in a new series appropriately titled *Prefaces to Shakespeare*.[40]

A comparison of a page from this series with a contemporary photo-facsimile text, for example, the 1928 Faber and Gwyer photofacsimile of *Macbeth*, demonstrates immediately the greater degree of intervention and revision between the typographic reproduction of *The Players' Shakespeare* and a photographically reproduced original printed text. The print of the typographic editions is proportioned evenly, buffeted

Figure 4.1. Design for *King Lear* by Paul Nash, from William Shakespeare, *King Lear, Newly Printed from the Folio of 1623*, The Players' Shakespeare Series.

by a generous use of blank space, and printed on expensive rag paper. The presentation of the volumes combined with the addition of large colour illustrations suggests a performative quality, meant not simply to be read, but to be appreciated for the many visual and tactile elements. The prefaces written by Granville-Barker indicate, however, that this series sought to achieve more than a dramatic visual presentation. Informed by Granville-Barker's experience in the theatre, the emphasis in the prefaces on the ideal dramatic presentation of the text provided an unprecedented orientation towards performance. The illustrations as well, contributed by the well-known artists Paul Nash and Charles Ricketts, the latter of whom was also a designer for the stage who had worked with Granville-Barker in both 1907 and 1914, demonstrate the performative quality of the edition, offering costume and scenic designs and explorations rather than narrative pictorialization.[41] Ricketts' illustrations for *Macbeth*, for example, are characterized by elements of

Figure 4.2. Design for Peter Quince's house by Paul Nash, from William Shakespeare, *A Midsommer Nights Dreame, Newly Printed from the Folio of 1623*, The Players' Shakespeare Series.

modernist theatre design such as tall pillars, steps and levels dominating the upstage area, and an abundant use of hanging cloths. As artists 'interested in the modern stage, whose object has been in creating for the reader the atmosphere of the ideal dramatic representation', these designs for the stage typify the innovative non-pictorial principles of stage production in the period: favouring a simple and uncluttered central acting space; emphasizing light sources emanating from different directions; and using geometric shapes and structures like pillars and blocks to provide an illusionistic suggestion of the setting.[42]

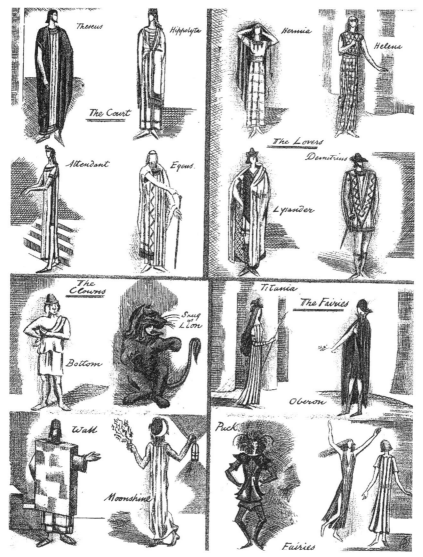

Figure 4.3. Costume designs by Paul Nash for *A Midsommer Nights Dreame.*

In compiling the prefatory material for *Macbeth*, Granville-Barker chose to reproduce Henry Cuningham's reading of variants and misprints in the 1912 Arden edition.[43] This would seem to suggest that Granville-Barker fulfilled some capacity as an editor of the text, if only to note the

Figure 4.4. Design for *Macbeth* by Charles Ricketts, from William Shakespeare, *Macbeth, Newly Printed from the Folio of 1623*, The Players' Shakespeare Series.

variants and misprints in the preface, though the volumes otherwise fail to identify the editor or editors of the text. Insofar as the idea of editing still primarily implied the selection of texts, the publishers may have genuinely believed that a series of Folio reproductions, photographic or typographic, was not edited, though some copytext must have been selected by someone appointed with that task. Even Lee's facsimile edition cited the Chatsworth copy of the Folio, so in the case of this typographic reproduction, the failure to identify the copytext seems conspicuous. The omission of editorship also evidences their stated objective, to represent an unmediated or original printed text, the Folio 'literatim'. To admit to the task of editing the text was to defeat the purpose, to mitigate the authority of its 'original' status; and compared to the characteristic contemporary editions, this series was relatively unmediated. *The Players' Shakespeare* fell somewhere between a photographically precise reproduction of an original printed text and the presentation of a beautifully uniform and decorative text.

Since McKerrow, the task of editing has come to be recognized explicitly as a process of reading the errors and irregularities of extant texts with the aim of reconstructing a non-existent manuscript or revised playhouse script.[44] Editors represent their uniform texts as verifiably corrected editions of an early printed text which approximate to a non-existent original, authenticated by a catalogue list of collation and emendation. The interpretation of textual irregularity and error is thus indicative of the differentiation between authorial fair copy or playhouse manuscript and extant printed text. The editors of *The Players' Shakespeare* had some sense of this correlation between textual irregularity and authenticity, since, though they chose to normalize the text, they maintained certain textual irregularities and errors, though they seem to have corrected or excluded other typographical irregularities, particularly those which might be argued to have resulted from the inconsistent practices of printing. What the editors of the series were attempting to achieve was an idealized version of the Folio in which the textual markers of authenticity were represented as unaltered or unmediated; in other words, the authenticity of their edition was physically demonstrated by the reproduction of certain authenticating textual irregularities. Characteristics of the original not normally reproduced by contemporaneous editions, such as inconsistent speech headings and spellings, were fastidiously and precisely reproduced throughout the series perhaps because they were seen to reflect the words as Shakespeare wrote them. The editors also reproduced precisely the Folio's scanty stage directions, Granville-Barker suggesting in the preface that the absence of consistent or narrative and scenic elaboration, as compared with that in contemporary editions, startled and made keen again the too accustomed eye: 'This printing of the plays, with its modest nomenclature, scanty directions and ignoring of all scenic impedimenta – compare it with our modern elaborations! – does so much to give us Shakespeare as Shakespeare was.'[45] What makes these editions of the plays unique is Granville-Barker's willing recognition that Shakespeare wrote playhouse scripts which achieved their final form in the playhouse, and the result of this attitude is a fluid and natural fluctuation between the 'words as Shakespeare wrote them' and the copytext derived from the prompt-copy of theatrical use. For Granville-Barker, the Folio's printed text, devoid of narrative elaboration and supererogatory insertions, was demonstrative of the acting material which Shakespeare provided for his company.

In contrast to the editions' representation of authenticating irregularity, other textual characteristics and inconsistencies which were deemed the products of irregular Jacobean printing procedure, typographical irregularities such as typeface, lineation, pagination, and the distribution of type and space, were uniformly normalized. The editors also chose to retain the Folio's act and scene divisions as a matter of convenience even though Granville-Barker admitted that 'taken together the attempt at uniformity and the failure to achieve it do not smack of Shakespearean authority'.[46] Evidently, the editors had some procedural criteria for editing the text. They clearly regarded the interventions of editing as compromising to their text, and they were more inclined to retreat from textual complexities and print errors which required decisive and conspicuous editorial intervention. One such complexity involved the lineation of prose passages. In the first of *The Players' Shakespeare* series, the edition of *Macbeth*, the lineation of prose passages does not match the Folio, but rather flows freely according to the type space available, suggesting that the editors followed a standard editorial practice like that of Cuningham in the Arden edition. However, by the last in the series, *The Tragedie of King Lear*, the lineation of both verse and prose matches the Folio exactly. Of course, most editions in the period collated the 1608 Pied Bull Quarto, so there were few or no precedents to follow in the reproduction of the Folio text. What this change in practice between the first and last editions would, therefore, seem to have demonstrated was their increasing unwillingness to deviate from and, therefore, actively edit the Folio text.

The unusual criteria according to which the seven editions in this series were produced clearly make *The Players' Shakespeare* one of the more unique contributions to the Shakespeare book market. Of course, what must be remembered is that, while *The Players' Shakespeare* purported to be an edition for practical theatrical use, the venture was a commercial failure, sustaining the publication of only seven volumes, and had little recognizable impact on Shakespearean theatrical practice. Though initial reviews of the series praised the high standard of book production and the commendable illustrations, the emphasis upon the aesthetic beauty of the editions defeated their intended purpose. Arthur Reed noted the discrepancy: 'Beautifully printed at the Shakespeare Head Press, Stratford-on-Avon . . . these handsome quartos are, we understand, intended for the hard usage of the theatre.'[47] Large and heavy, expensive, and impractical for theatrical use, that the volumes were impressive as books was self-defeating. The stated intention of the series to present the plays 'from the point of view of their performance on the stage' was undermined by their book-ness.[48] Was this not the problem across all editions of Shakespeare, the problem which *The Players' Shakespeare* was attempting to counteract, the inclination towards story-telling and picture-drawing imperative in the book?

Still, *The Players' Shakespeare* series was oddly representative of the complex issue of textual authority in 1923. The publicity focused on the Folio during the tercentenary year had functioned to re-affirm the iconographic importance and centrality of the Folio as a symbol of national wealth and status. The appearance of numerous photographic and typographic reproductions had further served to augment the 'original' status of early printed texts. As a decorative and illustrated commemorative edition series which claimed to reproduce the Folio's text typographically, *The Players' Shakespeare* idealized and, therefore, promoted the status of the Folio as an original text. Simultaneously, the unnamed editors had some procedural criteria for editing their text; but rather than normalizing the text, they chose to demonstrate the authenticity of the 'original' by reproducing textual irregularity. By this token, *The Players' Shakespeare* text also represented the idealized text from which the extant Folio texts were derived. This series therefore demonstrated the degree to which the notion of textual authenticity straddled differing concepts of the text: as a material object in history, as an idealized work of the author, and as the indeterminate potentiality of performance.

GRANVILLE-BARKER'S EXEMPLARY THEATRE

Despite the failure of *The Players' Shakespeare* project, 1923 was nevertheless a significant juncture for Granville-Barker insofar as his first preface to *Macbeth* marked the beginning of his career as a writer of Shakespeare criticism. While many of his theatrical contemporaries such as George Bernard Shaw and Edward Gordon Craig were also prolific writers, Granville-Barker's more balanced success demonstrated his equal ability in the theatre – as an actor, dramatist, director and theatre critic – and as a writer of Shakespeare criticism, whose *Prefaces to Shakespeare* remain in print. Moreover, with his emphasis on the plays as, above all, material for acting, placing primacy upon the performative quality of the texts, Granville-Barker's scholarly writing is often credited with having ignited a strain of performance-oriented criticism.[49] Also in 1923, alongside the publication of *The Players' Shakespeare* series, Granville-Barker published an article, 'Some Tasks for Dramatic Scholarship', which rehearsed the commonly held perception of a divide between scholar and actor and which detailed a new project of scholarly cooperation.[50] On the possibility of a new kind of Shakespearean study, Granville-Barker proposed an alliance of mutual help: 'we might project a Variorum edition of a new sort, one that would epitomise Shakespeare, the playwright'.[51] Even while Granville-Barker was writing and publishing his prefaces in *The Players' Shakespeare* series, he was simultaneously considering the possibility of a different edition which not only fulfilled, perhaps more fully, his criteria for an ideal performative text, but also detailed a new kind of study. Scholarship's new task, continuing as well the effort of bibliographic examination to provide a stable and accurate text, would be to uncover the conditions of the Elizabethan stage and record the details of consequential productions throughout history. While the theatre had need of scholarship's services, Granville-Barker here argued that the full life of the play was only realized in the theatre. Accordingly, he held: 'The putting of a play to the proof of its acting *ought* surely only to be a help and not a hindrance even to the acutest critic. Any other contention must finally involve us in the wildest sort of paradox.'[52]

Ideally, the practices of the theatre and the practices of textual criticism and examination would serve mutually validating functions, both 'un-editing' the adaptations and transfigurations of the eighteenth and nineteenth centuries by returning to the extant texts and by reconsidering Shakespeare's plays archaeologically, as they would have been performed in their day. Although a prominent voice, Granville-Barker was not alone in advocating a return to the text in 1923. For Lilian Bayliss at the Old Vic, representing Shakespeare according to an authoritative text in the theatre, unedited in the sense of relatively uncut and unadapted, meant producing the entire canon, representing not just the full text but the full text to mean all of the texts, thus demonstrating some projected idealization of Shakespeare as canonical author.[53] Performances of the inferior plays of the author's work in particular, plays which were only viable in repertory and could not sustain a long commercial run, were demonstrations of Shakespeare's deliberate experimentation or were examples of early points in his artistic development or maturation. The completion of the canon cycle could claim performative authenticity by historical precedent, achieving what no management had achieved since Shakespeare's age, returning the canonical text to the stage. Not long after the Old Vic began this endeavour, Granville-Barker produced his three epochal productions of Shakespeare at the Savoy theatre in London: *The Winter's Tale* and *Twelfth Night* in 1912, and *A Midsummer Night's Dream* in 1914.[54]

In contrast to both the Old Vic's as well as the SMT's more traditional staid and subdued interpretations, Granville-Barker's use of unconventional sets and costumes, patterned materials, and the overall eclectic stylization of his productions, were highly praised by his contemporaries. Reviewers were quite right to note the stylistic similarity of his productions, especially *A Midsummer Night's Dream*, to those of Max Reinhardt at the Deutsches Theater in Berlin which he had visited in 1910.[55] Granville-Barker, however, was the first English director after Craig (and certainly more successful) to apply modernist theatre design to the production of Shakespeare in London. His abundant use of geometric shapes, especially for the dizzying backcloths of *Twelfth Night*, and his principle of eclectic synthesis mirrored the cubist works of artists such as Pablo Picasso and Georges Braque working in this style from about 1908. His productions sought to achieve the same kind of perceptual discordance, only in relation to Edwardian pictorial theatre rather than impressionistic painting. More importantly, his stage implemented the three-tier design, including a forestage extending over the orchestra, a central and largely open playing space and a raised platform upstage. All three of the productions also employed tall pillars and hanging cloths to create illusionistic suggestions of time and place. The effect was a kind of modern Elizabethanism. While for Granville-Barker authenticity in performance meant discarding the vagaries and traditions of the Edwardian stage, of actor-managers like Tree and Irving, in favour of innovative contemporary design, representing the plays as Shakespeare meant them to be also demanded reincorporating some of the performative conditions of Shakespeare's stage.

Practical experimentation with speculative reconstructions of the Elizabethan stage had begun in the early nineteenth century: in Germany, Karl Immermann incorporated the Elizabethan staging theories of romantic critic and Shakespeare translator, Ludwigvon Tieck, in his few Shakespeare productions at the Düsseldorf Theatre between 1834 and 1837; and in 1889, the stage designers Jocza Savits and Kurt Lautenschläger designed a structure that came to be known as the 'Shakespeare-stage' for the Munich Theatre; in England, Benjamin Webster and J. R. Planché staged *The Taming of the Shrew* at the Haymarket in 1844 on an open stage using only a backcloth depicting Elizabethan London and the Globe Theatre.[56] Principles of Elizabethan staging, however, gained their greatest momentum in England under the direction of William Poel, who chose Granville-Barker to play Richard II in his 1899 production of the play. Granville-Barker clearly integrated some of his predecessors' principles into his own production style, principles which he would modify and adapt, and which he would continue to advocate throughout his writing career.[57] As with Poel, his priority was to insist upon the integrity of the text uncut and unadapted, and on the text as material for acting: 'It may be far more, but it must be that to begin with. The actor brings it to technical completion.'[58] In terms of the playing space, Granville-Barker advocated an open platform stage with a central unclut-tered acting area. Setting designs would make economic use of non-pictorial scenery which was not obstructive. The staging of the plays was to be clean and simple, without the conventional 'business' that had come to be associated with certain plays during the era of actor-managers. In his capacity as director, Granville-Barker coached the actors with emphasis upon their speech, encouraging a clear and precise delivery and a more naturalistic pace and intonation above the presentational embellishments of the actor-managers. Like the pace of delivery, the pace of the entire play was to be quick and uninterrupted, scenes following one another with little disruption of the play's continuity. For Granville-Barker, the drama's strengths were, 'First, the fellowship set up between actors and audience on the strength of the fellowship between the actors themselves. Next, the power of the spoken word. And in these two things the power and the quality of the art must lie.'[59]

Even by 1923, when Granville-Barker had just begun his prefaces to Shakespeare, his staging principles had become widely influential. For as much as Barry Jackson, for example, with his modern interpretations, claimed that 'Shakespeare is so great you can do anything you like with him', all of the Birmingham Repertory's modern-dress productions im-plemented what had become the established 'Elizabethan' criteria. Ac-cordingly, these productions were played on relatively open stages, where possible with platforms extending out from the proscenium arch, with little or no interruption, the scenes played continuously one after the other, and with a naturalistic style of verse-speaking.[60] In 1923, his modern-dress *Cymbeline* was heralded as the funniest melodrama of the contemporary stage (*Daily Express*, 23 April 1923). However, Jackson achieved wide acclaim with a modern-dress version of *Hamlet* which opened at the Kingsway Theatre in London in 1925. The *Daily Mail*, writing of the 'Success of Sir B. Jackson's Experiment' (26 August 1925), underscored the sense of radical innovation with which the production was greeted: 'The whole thing soon ceased to be a freak, a curiosity, it became a gripping story with nearly every character the sort of person you might know or read about one day.' Before the opening, Jackson had prepared the London audience by deliberately publicizing his intention to use contemporary fashions: 'Our effort at the Kingsway', he stated in an interview before the production, 'is aimed at making the people of England believe to-day that the plays of Shakespeare are good stuff – the right thing.'[61] Still, the headlines of the reviews were dominated by the sense of sartorial radicalism: 'Hamlet in "Plus Fours" with Ophelia in Short Skirts' (*Daily Mail*, 25 August 1925) and 'Hamlet with a Cigarette' (*Daily Express*, 26 August 1925).

Coming on the heels of Barrymore's touring production, one of the most significant deviations of Jackson's from previous productions, besides the modern dress, was the absence of star actors in the major leading roles. Rather than have the play serve as a vehicle, his intention was to remove the emphasis from the main character, returning the focus back to the dramatic apparatus of the play. Jackson argued that the conventional emphasis upon Hamlet and his epic dilemma interposed a veil between the author's intention and the average spectator who would come away 'with an increased feeling of almost superstitious awe but no understanding that he has been witnessing a real conflict of credible human beings'.[62] The modern costumes, the unadorned and unostentatious setting, the relatively natural delivery of the lines with unemphatic gestures all emphasized the contemporary currency of the play and the prosaic credibility of the characters. This contrast between credible ordinariness and the histrionic presentational styles of dramatic tradition was best demonstrated by the staging of 'The Murder of Gonzago', a caricatured portrayal of the kind of theatrical convention Jackson's *Hamlet* was intended to replace. In the scene, the modern King and Queen, seated downstage, were cast in silhouette against the brightly decorated internal play, characteristically nineteenth century with elaborate medieval robes, footlights, a pictorial drop curtain and exaggerated elocution and gesture.[63] In what one observer termed a Pirandellian confusion, the new observed the old in a self-referential representation of theatrical practice.

In a letter to Jackson praising the production, Poel heralded Jackson's achievement: 'I don't think that a nearer approach to an Elizabethan rendering of the play on the stage has before been reached by a producer.'[64] Poel saw the modern reinterpretation of *Hamlet* as a discarding of the detritus accumulated during the eighteenth and nineteenth centuries. Although Jackson held that Shakespeare was essentially modern, 'about us in the world today', his productions conformed to what Poel and Granville-Barker advocated as authentically Shakespearean principles of production. Granville-Barker's staging principles did not imply, however, that Shakespeare was to be regarded as some antiquated museum relic. On the contrary, like Jackson, he regarded Elizabethan and Jacobean drama as most apt for the expression of modern life: society, radically altered in the previous one hundred years, required reinterpretation by the vivid art of the theatre through the medium of Shakespeare.[65] Scholarship's share in the reformation, made possible by the significantly new studies of Pollard, Greg and Dover Wilson, would aid in rescuing Shakespeare from the nineteenth century, bringing the author into a new relationship of proximity with contemporaneity. The production of Shakespeare according to Granville-Barker thus required negotiation between the historically informed and performance-oriented text and a more visceral and experiential exploration of the essential ageless drama underneath.

What makes Granville-Barker's Shakespeare criticism relatively unique among that of his contemporaries is this commitment to the idea of the drama as a performance text, individual plays interpreted according to performance choices and motivation. Indeed, despite a tone of erudite academism, his prefaces reflect the actor and director Granville-Barker, as well as his lifelong commitment to theatrical reform in England. Prior to 1923, he had written about the theatre at great length. In 1907, he published his scheme for a national theatre, jointly authored with William Archer, a campaign which he continued to wage through the 1930s.[66] Granville-Barker had also visited and written about established repertory theatres on the continent such as the Deutsches Theater in Berlin and the Düsseldorfer Schauspielhaus. In 1922, one year prior to the first of *The Players' Shakespeare* series, he published *The Exemplary Theatre*, a treatise which outlined his own dream of a theatre experiment free from the exigencies of the commercial theatre production system and the demands placed on it by its bourgeois audience. What Granville-Barker found most offensive about the commercial theatre was the appeal it made to the mass audience: 'My first complaint', argues a fictional character who represents the theatre in dialogue with the Minister of Education, 'is of the mob appeal, the mob standard of success, and the ever-growing confusion of purpose that results'.[67] His own ideal theatre would be governed by a select minority of elite intellectuals and professionals who would prescribe theatrical culture for the larger public. Championing the theatre as the rightful place for the drama, *The Exemplary Theatre* goes on to criticize academic scholarship: 'once we give authority to professors to spread abroad some complicated lingo', argues the Minister of Education this time, 'for their own greater credit they'll go on complicating it indefinitely'.[68]

While Granville-Barker's various writings would seem to suggest a kind of schizophrenic division between Granville-Barker the theatre practitioner and Granville-Barker the scholar, they also reflect, once again, that dichotomous thinking about textual authenticity, circa 1923, opened out by the ambiguity of performance. On the one side of this dichotomy was Granville-Barker's commitment to a methodology of evaluating and performing the text. This involved variously a recuperated respect for the text uncut and unadapted, the historical consideration of the text in performance, an informed awareness of textual bibliography, an insistence upon the text's performativity, and a distrust of literary idealization. This return to the text required scholarship's participation, but unlike the 'mystery-mongering' of traditional academism, Granville-Barker's approach to the historical consideration of Shakespeare was centred on the pragmatic negotiation of the text. Between Shakespeare and the contemporary theatre, he argued, is an aesthetic chasm: 'Its bridging is a matter of convenience and compromise. What has to be decided is how far we can and must adapt our consciousness to the essential theatrical conditions of that time.'[69] At the same time, however, Granville-Barker remained wary of scholarly historicism and even while he advocated the necessity to explore the conditions of Shakespeare's stage, he argued that Shakespeare's dramatic art was ahistorical, transcending the material conditions of its production: 'But Shakespeare's art at its greatest – this is the plea – so utterly transcends the material circumstances of its creation that these can now be, and had better be, neglected altogether, and the essential drama somehow isolated in its purity.'[70] The other side of this dichotomy, then, involved a more traditional appreciation of Shakespeare's essential character and artistry and a sense that his art was perpetually living and contemporary. The task of associating with Shakespeare as if the author were still alive meant 'breaking through the thicket of circumstances which keeps the authentic Shakespeare from our sight, and to bring all of us – Tom, Dick and Harry – into full and free association with him'.[71]

The idea of a living Shakespeare associating fully and freely with what are ostensibly representatives of a twentieth-century mass public audience would seem to conflict with the idea of an ornately embellished and

unusually expensive commemorative limited edition of Shakespeare's
works. As noted earlier, though he endorsed his scheme for a National
Theatre which was decidedly anti-capitalist and popular, a theatre
in which Tom, Dick and Harry could associate fully and freely with
Shakespeare, Granville-Barker's scheme invested authority in his intellectual minority, the leisured middle-class elite who would extend their own
values and tastes to the growing mass audience or mob. A further point to
note is that Tom, Dick and Harry are all male, a point which would also
seem to imply that associating with Shakespeare was a kind of historicist
male-bonding exercise. Certainly for Granville-Barker, the acting of
Shakespeare was best left to men, or in the case of female roles, to boys.
In the General Introduction to *The Players' Shakespeare* in particular,
Granville-Barker maintained that Shakespeare's verse found a more 'full
and free' expression in the voice of a boy actor, a voice not charged and
coloured by the extremely personal attractions of women: 'Even now,
though these social conditions have changed, the plays remaining as they
were written for those original circumstances, it behoves the most devoted
actress to remember that in the acting of these parts her sex is more a
liability than an asset.'[72] He would not go as far as Craig to recommend
the exclusion of female actors altogether. Nevertheless, just as Tom,
Dick and Harry represented his idea of the Shakespeare audience,
Granville-Barker's idealization of Shakespeare in performance – drawing
equally on textual precedent and a more visceral experience of the drama
underneath – functioned to shape his ideas of how to represent
Shakespeare's texts authentically.

While this short review of his writing inadequately summarizes the
diversity of his work and complexity of his writing, the point to note
here, especially given this emphasis on 1923 as a meeting-ground for
text and performance, is that Granville-Barker was himself an exemplary figure: at the centre of various campaigns and schemes to reform
twentieth-century theatrical practice, particularly those which sought to
create a viable repertory theatre system, especially for Shakespeare, and
to institute a national theatre; as a visionary director of Shakespeare
who advocated a return to the text, as well as a return to the conditions
of the Elizabethan stage; and as an early advocate of a new kind of
performance-oriented textual criticism. The example of Granville-Barker,
particularly in 1923, would also appear to demonstrate the many ambi-
guities to which the idea of performance as a textual practice gives
rise, especially insofar as performance conflicts and divides the text

between various idealizations of author and representation. Indeed, Granville-Barker's participation in *The Players' Shakespeare*, and his subsequent move from the theatre to the study, perhaps demonstrates that inevitable association of performance with the production of text. And yet, while the semantic play of performance/representation points to the complex interrelationship between the various practices which make up and condition the text, what the year 1923 would also seem to demonstrate are the latent possibilities opened up by performance, in this case, resulting in several unique contributions to the history of playing with Shakespeare.

CHAPTER 5

How many children had Virginia Woolf?

In 1933, L. C. Knights asked in the title of an essay, *How Many Children Had Lady Macbeth?* The function of his title was to trivialize the style of what he termed 'pseudo-critical investigation', the character-oriented studies dominated by psychological readings and extrapolative profiles of Shakespeare's characters which still predominated Shakespeare criticism, from the popular volumes by early nineteenth-century essayists such as Coleridge and Hazlitt still in frequent reprint to, more recently, the influential studies of Swinburne and Dowden.[1] The 'most illustrious example' of character criticism, Knights argued, was A. C. Bradley's renowned study of tragic heroes in *Shakespearean Tragedy.*[2] First published in 1904, the popularity of Bradley's work was evidenced by the numerous reprints which appeared nearly every year throughout the early twentieth century, his study having achieved no less than nineteen reprints by the time of Knights' essay. Bradley's collection of detailed and methodical character studies was an acclaimed pinnacle of Shakespearean scholarship which, though clearly descended from the stylistic and topical orientation of nineteenth-century essayists, was also demonstrative of the rigorous and non-impressionistic methodology of an early twentieth-century style of academic writing. For Knights, however, Bradley's criticism was singularly old-fashioned and tiresome in its insistence upon interpretive literalism. Asking a question to which no reasonable answer could be given, the title of Knights' essay deliberately, and perhaps somewhat unfairly, ridiculed the character orientation of Bradley's criticism. Even Bradley, whose discussion of Lady Macbeth's possible children was little more than a footnote to his main argument, admitted that this particular question was immaterial and did not concern the play.[3] Nevertheless, such questions were, for Knights, completely banal (and consequently, beyond the title Lady Macbeth's children do not reappear). Before he turned to deride Bradley, however, Knights began by responding to Ellen Terry's recently published lectures on Shakespeare.[4] For

Knights, Terry's written lectures, adapted from a series of oral lectures she presented to audiences over a period of several years, also demonstrated a propensity for asking irrelevant and distracting questions: 'To her the characters are all flesh and blood and she exercises her ingenuity on such questions as whether Portia or Bellario thought of the famous quibble, and whether it was justified.'[5] The essay goes on to state: 'Ellen Terry of course does not represent critical Authority; the point is not that she could write as she did, but that the book was popular.'[6]

While he dismissed her writing as non-authoritative, Knights did not trouble to make any allowance for Terry when he might have distinguished her more personal reflections and recollections as a famous Shakespearean actor from the critical inquiry of an established professional academic like Bradley. As her lectures descended through years of presentation and transformation, so too were Terry's character sketches the culmination of practical experience. The lectures were, as a reviewer for the *Daily Telegraph* duly noted after seeing an early version delivered in 1911, a gallery of portraits reflecting the marvellous art of her acting.[7] Terry herself felt the need to distinguish her lectures as the reflections of an actor from more scholarly criticism: 'I leave theories to scholars. An actress does not study a character with a view to proving something about the dramatist who created it. Her task is to learn how to translate this character into herself, how to make its thoughts her thoughts, its words her words.'[8] For Terry, her intense character analyses were indispensable to her work at the Lyceum with Irving, a theatre where she had built her international reputation upon roles such as Lady Macbeth. In *How Many Children Had Lady Macbeth?*, however, Terry's acting career remains unmentioned. More surprising, though, are the words 'of course' when Knights argues that 'Ellen Terry of course does not represent critical Authority', the positive valuation of that authority emphasized by its capitalization. Exactly why Terry is not a 'critical Authority' remains unarticulated, substituted instead by the suggestion that Terry's popularity as a writer, rather than her character criticism, is the cause for greater concern. While the essay goes on to consider Bradley's writing in greater detail, by dismissing Terry as a matter 'of course', her critical commentary (like the question of Lady Macbeth's children) is omitted from his consideration, Knights himself being, one presumes, a 'critical Authority'.

Two years later in 1935, Virginia Woolf completed the second draft of her only extant play, *Freshwater*, for which the life and identity of Ellen Terry served as her subject. Although usually considered a minor work, the composition history of the play, spanning the early 1920s to the mid-1930s, offers a fascinating study in the intellectual development of Woolf's writing. Woolf began working on *Freshwater* some time before 1923, the date of her first draft, with the intention of writing a comedy about her great-aunt Julia Margaret Cameron and husband Charles. Through the mid to late nineteenth century, the Camerons were well-established society figures with a reputation for characteristically Victorian eccentricity. Julia Margaret was born in India to a family of seven sisters, the daughter of James Pattle, employed by the East India Company.[9] In 1848, she and her husband, Charles Hay Cameron, left India for England, finally taking up residence in Freshwater Bay on the Isle of Wight. After emigrating, Cameron began experimenting with a camera given to her by her daughter and she made a small reputation as a photographer in the late nineteenth century. In 1926, a small collection of her photographic portraits and allegoric compositions was published for which Woolf wrote a short, rather unreliable, biographical essay.[10] *Freshwater* incorporates details of this biography, dramatizing the period leading up to the Camerons' dramatic final departure to Ceylon (bringing with them two coffins for fear of finding none there) from Dimbola, their residence at Freshwater which serves as the setting. In her diary, Woolf imagined the superb possibilities of Freshwater for a comedy, with the eccentric Camerons deciding to proceed to Ceylon, 'taking their coffins with them, and the last sight of Aunt Julia is on board ship, presenting porters with large photographs of Sir Henry Taylor and the Madonna in default of small change'.[11] While she was certainly inspired by the reputed eccentricity of the Camerons, the idea of Freshwater also provided Woolf with a counterpart to her own Bloomsbury as a coterie of artists and intellectuals united into a geographical and social hub. Cameron and her sisters helped to coordinate an impressive social circle that included the most influential intellectuals and artists of Victorian society. Cameron's portfolio of close-up photographic portraits recorded in silver chloride imprints the scope of her social influence, including the heads of such famous men as Sir John Herschel, Charles Darwin, Robert Browning, Alfred Lord Tennyson, Henry Wadsworth Longfellow, G. F. Watts and William Holman Hunt.[12] In a second preface to the collection of Cameron's *Victorian Photographs of Famous Men and Fair Women*, Woolf's friend and collaborator Roger Fry mockingly criticized the photographic allegories Cameron composed by manipulating her often recalcitrant subjects into tableaux such as 'The Passing of Arthur' or 'The Death of Elaine'. For both Fry and Woolf, Cameron's photography inadvertently caricatured a typically nineteenth-century sentimentality about art: 'There is something touching and heroic about the naive confidence of these people. They are so unconscious of the abyss of ridicule which they skirt, so determined, so conscientious, so bravely provincial.'[13] This same condescending attitude characterizes Woolf's play, the snap-happy Cameron and her drowsy husband, together with the foppish Tennyson and the melancholy Watts providing what Woolf saw to be a characteristically Victorian backdrop.

Although Woolf was clearly interested in Cameron as a female artist and a little-appreciated pioneer of the photographic arts in the nineteenth century, it was the young Ellen Terry whom she chose as the female subject of her play. After a modestly successful career as a child actor, in 1864, at the age of sixteen, Terry married the artist Watts who was her senior by nearly thirty years. She then moved to Little Holland House, Cameron's sister's Freshwater residence, where Watts lived and where the impressionable Terry was first acquainted with the unconventional Camerons and their artistic and literary friends. The marriage of Watts and Terry, however, attracted a public attention which was greatly amplified when the two separated a mere ten months later. Woolf's play combines the departure of the Camerons, complete with their coffins, with a fictional account of the relationship between Terry and Watts. The character Terry's flight from Dimbola with the fictional character Craig alludes to the real Terry's second relationship with the artist and architect Edward William Godwin, whom she first encountered in the same year she first met Watts and by whom Terry later had two children, Edith and Edward Gordon, both of whom adopted the surname Craig. Incorporating a loosely biographical account of Terry and Watts in *Freshwater*, Woolf actively re-imagined the early life of her female subject in order to thematize the idea of female subjectivity in art, Terry abandoning her role as an idealized object of characteristically male art to adopt and identify her own female subjectivity.

In October 1923, Woolf wrote to her sister to express doubt about her manipulation of the material into comic form: 'I rather doubt its worth going on with. It seemed to me, when I read it last night, that its so much of a burlesque, and really rather too thin and flat to be worth getting people together at infinite trouble to act.'[14] In the ten-year interim leading up to the 1935 text of *Freshwater* during which she had abandoned writing the play, Woolf had become more confident both as a writer and as a feminist, and perhaps with this confidence, she ventured to complete and revise the earlier draft. Moreover, a number of books had been published which served to revitalize the reputation of Terry. In 1931, Edith Craig and

her female partner, Christopher St John, published the letters between
George Bernard Shaw and Terry, a move which angered her brother
Edward Gordon Craig and provoked him to write his own biographical
account of his mother.[15] In 1932, Terry's much-acclaimed lectures on
Shakespeare were published, and in 1933, riding on the wave of this
renewed interest in Terry's writing, St John and Edith Craig revised and
supplemented Terry's 1908 autobiography, *The Story of my Life*, under the
title *Ellen Terry's Memoirs*. Thus, by 1933, the year in which Knights made
his criticism of Terry, her reputation as a great Shakespearean had been
re-invigorated by her new reputation as a talented and engaging writer.
St John noted that: 'Her old fame as a great actress and a great personality
has been renewed after death by her fame as a writer, and possibly will be
kept alive by it.'[16] Certainly, this renewed public interest in Terry helped
to propel and shape Woolf's subsequent draft of the play and inspired her
interest in Terry as an artist.

1935 was also a very different time politically from 1923, especially with
regard to the status of women. While the 1918 Representation of the
People Act had extended the vote to some women of property who were
over the age of thirty, the amended 1928 Act had enfranchised all women
over the age of twenty-one giving them 52.7 per cent of the total voting
electorate.[17] By 1935, women were sitting in parliament and legislation was
increasingly reflecting the rights of married women and mothers and the
status of women in the workplace.[18] The increased advocacy of the
women's movement no doubt shaped the feminist dimension of Woolf's
later writing, and so the later text is more confidently experimental as well
as more didactic in its thematic structure. Both the 1923 and 1935 texts of
Freshwater are a comic sendup of the artistic pretensions of the male
characters, both texts written in the drawing-room comedy style of the
Edwardian stage. The Dimbola drawing room of *Freshwater* is peopled by
burlesque caricatures of the Camerons and their friends. The 1935 text is
also a drawing-room comedy in the sense of having been written for a
private performance which was given in Vanessa Bell's drawing room
during a private party for family and friends.[19] Thus, although the 1935
text reflects Woolf's later maturity and confidence as a writer in the post-
equal-franchise period, at the same time, replete with Bloomsbury in-
jokes and semi-private allusions, *Freshwater* seems less polished and
somewhat more dated and intractable than the writing Woolf actively
published. This is the context in which Woolf's Terry is re-imagined:
from the public sphere of Terry's theatrical performances and published
writing to the semi-private sphere of Woolf's dramatic imagination. So

while the real Terry's writing was excluded as a matter of course from the consideration of a critical authority, her perspective entirely dismissed by Knights, in *Freshwater*, Woolf's Terry rejects the frame of male perspective to discover and empower her own artistic identity. In this context of dramatic imagination, the play explores and dramatizes the possibility of a positively valued female artist like Terry, questioning the relationship between identity and art, or more particularly, between gendered identity and the institutional apparatus of art, in a way which is unique among Woolf's other non-dramatic texts.

LAIUS AND OEDIPUS AT THE CROSSROADS

Surprisingly, Shakespeare is entirely absent from the play, an absence which seems not a little conspicuous given the real Terry's later fame as a Shakespearean. Woolf might have incorporated, for example, the numerous sketches and paintings begun by Watts during their marriage and completed in the early 1880s after she had established her success in the role at the Lyceum. This absence differentiates *Freshwater* from, for example, the more polemical *A Room of One's Own* (1928), Woolf's most celebrated feminist text, and a text which idealizes Shakespeare as a 'naturally creative, incandescent and undivided' artist.[20] The question of whether *A Room of One's Own* represents a correctly feminist text has generated a vociferous debate, the extremes of position perhaps most famously exampled by the two diverse and equally feminist critics, Elaine Showalter and Jane Marcus. For Showalter, Woolf's flight into her supposedly radical gender concept of androgyny – a sexually neutral and gender-balanced ideal demonstrated in art by an author like Shakespeare – was an attempt to transcend or escape, even while Woolf addressed, feminist conflict.[21] Showalter argues that the impersonality of Woolf's unintrusive 'I's, the three identities of Mary Beton, Mary Seton and Mary Carmicheal from whose perspective the book is narrated, splinters and fractures the narrative voice leaving the reader without a single subject position with which to identify. Woolf's own experiences as a woman remain obscured. Whereas for Showalter, the slippage and evasion evident in *A Room of One's Own* make it a 'teasing, sly, elusive' book in which Woolf denies any 'earnest or subversive intention',[22] for Marcus, in contrast, the slippery quality of Woolf's narrative identity demonstrates her subversive feminist technique.[23] *A Room of One's Own* begins by appropriating male strategies of narration and discourse, deconstructing them and finally subverting the insistent 'I' of male authority. For

Marcus, the typically male identification between reader and author is
a phallocentric textual process. She continues by suggesting that, with
Woolf: 'What some readers have seen as her incapacity to create character
is not an incapacity at all but a feminist attack on the ego as male false
consciousness.'[24] In contrast to Showalter, Marcus argues that the plural-
ity of slippery narrative identities is an empowering subversion of male
authorial identity.

The description of these multiple narrative 'I's as either a subversion of
or a fractured substitute for male authorial identity re-enacts the interpretive ambiguity of Joyce's 'I' equation in *Ulysses*. Both Woolf and Joyce
were, not dissimilarly, exploring and subverting the conventions of narrative identity in their writing, a largely stylistic experimentation which is,
perhaps, too easily interpreted as a metaphor for their own psychical
projection into their texts. Read in this Freudian context, however, the
thematization of creative process in *Ulysses*, as noted earlier, functions to
project the Freudian family romance upon literary authorship, thus
negotiating Joyce's place into a generational literary canon. Harold Bloom
has also appropriated the Freudian model of authorial inheritance by
embracing the metaphor of Oedipal anxiety, describing the artist's relation
to his precursor as a 'battle between strong equals, father and son as mighty
opposites, Laius and Oedipus at the cross-roads'.[25] Bloom's metaphor of
literary paternity, generating an 'anxiety of influence' among the literary
inheritors, though it concisely typifies the modernist self-perception of art,
renders problematic the position of the female artist.

This idea of a gendered modernism is supported by Sandra M. Gilbert
and Susan Gubar with the claim that: 'as much as the industrial revolution and the fall of God, the rise of the female imagination was a central
problem for the twentieth-century male imagination'.[26] Early twentieth-
century feminism, the measured success of the Suffrage movement and
the attendant implication of a growing number of women entering
traditionally male institutions and employments including the literary
and academic establishment (which, incidentally, is the subject of *A Room
of One's Own*) undoubtedly provided one impetus for modernism. Gilbert
and Gubar explain further that the metaphor of author as father to a text,
as a progenitor and procreator, prefigures the artist as male, 'an aesthetic
patriarch whose pen is an instrument of generative power like his penis'
and who (re)produces by responding 'to his muse's quasi-sexual excitation' with an outpouring of aesthetic energy.[27] Though they recognize
that the aesthetic practices of modernism or the avant-garde functioned to
occult language for a privileged male literary elite, in so doing, Gilbert

and Gubar pave the way for discussing the more pioneering and feminist modernism of a woman like Woolf: 'For inevitably, the "ideal order" of patriarchal literary history was radically "modified by the introduction of the new (the really new) work of art" – and, as Woolf remarked, that "really new work" was women's work.'[28] Appropriating the Freudian language of Oedipal anxiety, they argue that the radical modernism of a female artist such as Woolf involved her overcoming her anxiety as a woman writing in a predominantly male environment, Woolf breaking with the pattern of patriarchal authorship as exemplified by someone like Shakespeare, to invent her own matrilineage.

In *A Room of One's Own*, Woolf's narrative identities, if not a projection of her own psychological anxieties, inarguably exemplify her transformation or rewriting of such literary teleology. In fact, what makes *A Room of One's Own* unique among contemporary modernist texts is Woolf's attempt to re-pattern a sense of literary influence for women writers and readers in a process of thinking 'back through our mothers'.[29] This need to establish a female literary tradition or ancestry, as much as it reproduces the strategies of Woolf's male contemporaries, seems a reasonably feminist project. Yet, the success of this project in *A Room of One's Own*, I would suggest, is complicated by the central importance of a male author to the work. Woolf's modernism problematizes her feminism, her matriarchal order of authorship. Shakespeare stands at the beginning, the first precursor of a literary tradition whose origin is located in the Elizabethan period. Consequently, while she contemplates the lack of books by women writers on her shelf, the narrator states: 'If ever a human being got his work expressed completely, it was Shakespeare. If ever a mind was incandescent, unimpeded, I thought, turning again to the bookcase, it was Shakespeare's mind.'[30] While the narrator mourns the impossibility of a Judith Shakespeare, a female equivalent of Shakespeare living and writing in the sixteenth century, similarly incandescent and unimpeded, the comparison the text inevitably sets up is with her more successful brother. Ultimately, Shakespeare exerts an anxiety of influence upon Woolf's writing, a disturbing shadow of metaphor lingering in the image of the pen the author is holding.

Following the path beaten by Showalter and Marcus, more recently, Beth Schwartz has tried to resolve this apparent contradiction by making of Shakespeare a literary mother. Schwartz begins by summarizing Woolf's feminist project: 'by thinking back through our mothers, Woolf aims to establish the mother as the repository of memory and as the source of poetic inspiration for women writers by locating her at the core

of the creative impulses'. She then addresses the conflicting centrality of
Shakespeare by stating that 'rather than figuring as a fatherly source of
inspiration or anxiety, Shakespeare seems to play the part of a maternal
muse in Woolf's creative process, as well as to help shape her feminist
vision and agenda'.[31] Schwartz makes this statement possible by drawing a
comparison across a number of Woolf's texts in which Shakespeare is seen
to have exerted a mothering influence, from *A Room of One's Own* and
Orlando to one of the essays Woolf was writing at the time of her death,
'Anon'. A nameless and genderless literary archetype imagined by Woolf
to embody an abstract pre-industrial spirit of art, Anon is the anonymous,
androgynous figure whose death, at some point in the late Elizabethan
period when the vicissitudes of print culture necessitated the author's
name to be attached to the book, signalled the beginning of a patriarchal
order of authorial identity: 'Anonymity', Woolf argued, 'was a great
possession. It gave the early writing an impersonality, a generality.'[32]
Here, Woolf took her cue from Eliot in privileging the drama of the
Elizabethan period as one of impersonality and sensibility, identifying a
primitive, universalized tradition exampled by Elizabethan drama and
recovered from the degradations of the eighteenth and nineteenth centuries by the early twentieth-century artist. Woolf departed from Eliot,
however, by attempting to re-gender that essential ideal, which she
personified as the creative spirit called Anon: 'Anon is sometimes man;
sometimes woman.'[33] After making the connection between Woolf's idea
of Anon and Shakespeare, Schwartz continues her argument by drawing a
further parallel between Woolf and Freud; more specifically, Woolf's
concept of an anonymous archetype embodying the qualities of both
the male and female imagination, and Freud's concept of a pre-Oedipal
order which he began to use to explain female sexuality at around the
same time as the first publication of *A Room of One's Own*. Schwartz
argues that both metaphors posit a matriarchal world which pre-exists and
influences the patriarchal history of Oedipal civilization. Shakespeare,
whose Hamlet figured so prominently in Freud's description of the
Oedipal order, is Woolf's pre-Oedipal Anon: 'Anon or his/her avatar
Shakespeare serves as a vehicle for recovering the suppressed world that
exists before sexual difference, discrete ego-boundaries, and entry into the
symbolic order of language and social convention.'[34]

   In describing Woolf's act of transgression – stealing, re-imagining and
re-gendering Shakespeare for the female tradition – Schwartz commits her
own series of ironies, not the least of which is that, in patriarchal fashion,
she commits the anonymous Anon to a male name and identity. Still, the

comparison between Woolf's Anon and Freud's pre-Oedipal order is compelling. Woolf's interest in Freud has been well documented, and the fact that the Hogarth Press was responsible for printing many of Freud's essays in English implies that Woolf would almost certainly have read the 1932 English translation of Freud's treatise on 'Female Sexuality'.[35] What Schwartz glosses in her description of Freud's pre-Oedipal phase is the teleology implied by the term 'pre-Oedipal'; for while the pre-Oedipal is characterized by the maternal bond, Freud argued that the pre-Oedipal soon progressed to the Oedipal phase at which time the female acknowledged 'the fact of her castration, and with it, too, the superiority of the male and her own inferiority'.[36] The Freudian implication here is that Woolf, in her characterization of Anon/Shakespeare, arrested the female in the pre-Oedipal phase. When we follow Freud through, we find that the female who suppresses her transition to the Oedipal is led to cling with defiant self-assertiveness to her threatened masculinity:

To an incredibly late age she clings to the hope of getting a penis some time. That hope becomes her life's aim; and the phantasy of being a man in spite of everything often persists as a formative factor over long periods. This 'masculinity complex' in women can also result in a manifest homosexual choice of object.[37]

While neither Woolf nor Schwartz intended to characterize Anon in the terms of a 'masculinity complex', I would also like to believe that Woolf would have avoided such an unapologetic phallocentrism as a model for her theoretical writing. Even Freud himself acknowledged that feminists would 'hardly fail to object that such notions spring from the "masculinity complex" of the male and are designed to justify on theoretical grounds his innate inclination to disparage and suppress women'.[38] One also fails to imagine Shakespeare clinging to the hope of getting a penis some time. However, the phallocentrism of Freud's narrative of psychological development remains implicit, particularly in *A Room of One's Own*, as the text attempts to invert and re-gender the concept of literary inheritance in the project of looking back through one's mother, while simultaneously clinging to a paragon of the patriarchal, symbolic order. Indeed, if we were to consider Freud's earlier sexual theory – in particular, his description of the female's 'castration complex' and attendant 'penis envy', two concepts which appear throughout his earlier work and which had considerable currency by the time of Woolf's writing *A Room of One's Own* – what we find is a potentially more disturbing

Freudian interpretation of Shakespeare's presence in *A Room of One's Own*.[39] According to Freud, the female's repressed wish to possess a penis like a man is transformed through the course of the female's normal mental development into two corresponding desires, the wish for a man and the wish for a baby. Both figuratively phallic, the man and the baby displace the penis as the object of desire and, therefore, the female's transference of desire onto them represents the course of normal sexual development. Conversely, the absence of a maternal instinct in a female's later life, which often corresponds with a masculine disposition, demonstrates some form of mental neurosis or sexual inversion (read homosexuality).[40] Short of suggesting that Woolf's idealization of Shakespeare reflects her desire for a penis or, conversely, her homosexuality, the phallocentrism innate in the choice of Shakespeare becomes acute, particularly against the concept of literary motherhood as a kind of psychical/historical transference of the female literary imagination. The suggestion is that, by re-gendering the model of literary teleology typical of her contemporaries, Woolf transformed the model of literary succession to suggest the equally patriarchal imperative for women, if only metaphorically, to bear children, a development which, in the Freudian narrative, is nevertheless indicative of her inferiority complex and penis envy.

There is an absurdity in the extremity of this argument, in the parallel with Freud which suggests that gender identity is at stake in *A Room of One's Own* because Shakespeare wields a phallic presence over the text. I would hesitate to argue uncompromisingly like Showalter that in 'Virginia Woolf's version of female aestheticism and androgyny, sexual identity is polarized and all the disturbing, dark, and powerful aspects of femaleness are projected onto maleness'.[41] Nevertheless, the narrative strategies of *A Room of One's Own* would appear to enact, if not a pre-Oedipal desire for maleness, then at least a confusion regarding the nature of gender identity as either essential or socially determined. This confusion results in a very literary, richly suggestive, but also highly ambiguous, conceptual model for gender identity. Rather than transform Shakespeare into a maternal muse, a female-coded archetype, the text transforms the failed Judith Shakespeare, whose explicitly invented life and death comprise a non-identity, into Shakespeare, his 'mind as the type of the androgynous of the man-womanly mind'.[42] The predominance of the masculine also characterizes Woolf's Anon, a figure identified consistently by the male-gendered pronouns 'he', 'him' and 'his'. As much as this was an established writing convention, the predominance of masculine language in a universalized ideal nevertheless demonstrates and reinscribes the innate privileged status of the male. In a work like *A Room of One's Own* in which gender privilege is forthrightly contested, the innate phallocentrism in the choice of an archetype like Shakespeare becomes even more conspicuous. Woolf's concept of anonymous androgyny, if we accept that parallel across her different texts, is overshadowed by the male-gendered symbols, language and narrative styles she chose to appropriate.

To be fair, the problem of gender and androgyny in *A Room of One's Own* reflects the largely gendered history of literary creativity, as well as the problematically essentialist nature of language – the system of gendered pronouns, for example, which Woolf's writing fails to acknowledge or subvert – rather than her personal phallocentrism. The result, however, is the same. Consider one of the narrators in *A Room of One's Own* reading a male author's novel in a later section:

Back one was always hailed to the letter 'I'. One began to be tired of 'I'. Not but what this 'I' was a most respectable 'I'; honest and logical; hard as a nut, and polished for centuries by good teaching and good feeding. I respect and admire that 'I' from the bottom of my heart. But – here I turn a page or two, looking for something or other – the worst of it is that in the shadow of the letter 'I' all is shapeless as a mist. Is that a tree? No, it is a woman.[43]

At first, the narrator begins by contrasting two different forms of textual experience, the male author's use of a persistent narrating 'I' through whose limiting perspective the experience of the text is channelled, versus her own use of the eponymous 'one'. This is the 'one' of the title whose universality is meant to embody and contain the experiences of both male and female, thus typifying Woolf's androgynous ideal. Rather than oppose categories of male and female, the comparison between 'I' and 'one' opposes an incomplete, one-sided, male-centred textual experience which conceals woman in a shapeless mist, to an impersonal, universalized whole experience. Shakespeare's writing is androgynous in *A Room of One's Own* because Shakespeare, so Woolf argued, is concealed completely in his own writing: 'his grudges and spites and antipathies are hidden from us. We are not held up by some "revelation" which reminds us of the writer.'[44] His writing is universal and undivided, open to male and female experience equally, because the author is absent. However, even while the narrator objects to the insistence of the male 'I', that insistence quickly invades the narrator's own position as the experience of 'one' unfolds as the experience of 'I'. The narrator states: 'I respect and admire that "I" from the bottom of my heart. But – here I turn a page or two, looking for something or other.' The private and personal experience of turning a page or two subsumes the experience of the reader within the experience of the narrator. As the objective, universal 'one' yields to a deluge of 'I's, the narrator's 'I' and the emphatic male 'I' resonate together until they become, except for the use of quotations, indistinguishable. Ultimately, Woolf adopts the style of phallocentric narrativity she simultaneously condemns. Admittedly, I have been discussing Woolf's activity and the narrator's activity interchangeably despite the fact that, at the beginning of the essay, the 'I' which writes denies any substantial identity altogether, stating: ' "I" is only a convenient term for somebody who has no real being. Lies flow from my lips, but there may perhaps be some truth mixed up with them; it is for you to seek out this truth and to decide whether any part of it is worth keeping.'[45] That 'I' is then fractured between the three fictional Marys. Yet, the insistence of the 'I's experience consistently throughout the essay, the lecturing and pronouncing which denies the reader any experiential autonomy in relation to the text, finally unifies and channels the whole text through a single perspective which would seem inseparable from that of the author. In this way, the narrative identities would seem no more than a ruse to disguise Woolf's own identity as the author of the text. Or we might say that, as a female author, Woolf's use of the masculine narrative 'I' effects a kind of literary cross-dressing.

Throughout her writing career, Woolf herself experimented with the ideas of transvestism and transsexualism as a means of addressing issues of gender; even in *Freshwater*, in the early version of 1923, Ellen Terry appears in the last few moments of the play before her departure dressed in men's clothing. For Woolf, the mutability of gender identity embodied in the metaphor of transvestism provided a symbolically powerful means of bringing into question sociocultural constructions of gender, sartorial transition a way of transgressing the gendered roles rigidly prescribed by social custom. Transvestism provided an alternative metaphor for identity as a multiple and mutable layering. But underneath the idea of transvestism, the metaphor of gender as socially constructed apparel, lay the far more problematic model of the essentially androgynous being. This Woolf used throughout her writing, in some places referring to androgyny, and in others bisexuality. Woolf's model of a bisexual universal spirit or state of mind vacillating between male and female, as demonstrated by a figure like Anon or Shakespeare in *A Room of One's Own*, although mutable and anonymous in the sense of being universal and multiple, is essentially gendered, made up of equal, intrinsically and inescapably male and female components. The androgynous model is not androgynous in the sense of lacking sexual signifiers, but in possessing two complete and competing gender identities, the dominance of one at any given time not necessarily coinciding with the outer gendered apparel.

Perhaps her most complete and most imaginative representation of the bisexual being is *Orlando*, published one year prior to *A Room of One's Own* and serving as its fictive, less didactic counterpart. Woolf bisected her fictive biography structurally and thematically equally into male and female halves. Orlando is never androgynous as such, but translates from one sex to another, prefiguring the essentially trans/bisexual model of the artist in 'Anon'. At the moment of Orlando's sexual transition, the narrator suggests that: 'In every human being a vacillation from one sex to the other takes place, and often it is only the clothes that keep the male or female likeness, while underneath the sex is the very opposite of what it is above' (171).[46] While both the metaphor of transvestism and the model of the trans/bisexual suggest a transgressive mutability which challenges prescribed notions of sexuality, the two ultimately provide two divergent modes of thinking about gender identity, a crossroads at which meet, from one direction, the appropriation and undressing of culturally pre-scribed gender and the reinscription of a typically patriarchal, polar, bisexual model of essential gender. Woolf's ideas about gender identity would seem to demonstrate a largely unresolved negotiation, even in her later writing, between divergently essentialist and determinist models.

Orlando, in particular, epitomizes this unresolved negotiation or am-biguity as it fictively explores, questions and plays with gender construc-tions, but finally refuses to pronounce with any certainty on the nature of Orlando's gender transition. To argue in Woolf's favour, the novel is decidedly unambiguous in its clear determination to challenge prescribed sexual constructions. Here, we might consider once again Woolf's rela-tionship to Freud; for the suggestion in the novel of genital mutability certainly challenges the typically Freudian phallocentric association be-tween anatomy and essential identity. Orlando's intrinsically bisexual gender identity further displaces the Freudian notion of bisexuality or same-sex sexual preference as an inversion of normal sexual development; in Woolf's model, gender identity and sexuality are not in conflict, but equally fluid. However, while Orlando's transsexual transition confronts the question of gender and sexual difference, the nature of Orlando's transsexualism remains unclear, the novel offering conflicting portraits of Orlando as essentially gendered versus socially constructed and situated.

At the first moment of Orlando's metamorphosis, a dissociation is suggested between anatomical gender and identity: 'Orlando had become a woman – there is no denying it. But in every other respect, Orlando remained precisely as he had been. The change of sex, though it altered their future, did nothing whatever to alter their identity' (127). This description falls clearly on the side of difference as sociocultural construct, and is central to Gilbert and Gubar's claim that Woolf's concept of gender identity was forthrightly on the side of cultural determinism: '*Orlando*, a work that is nominally about a transsexual, depicts transsexualism through witty costume changes rather than through actual physical transformations . . . Her transsexual, she argues, is no more than a transvestite.'[47] For Gilbert and Gubar, the suggestion in the moment of Orlando's transsexualism is not that costumes are false and selves are true, but that costumes are fluid and interchangeable selves. The clothes make the man, or in this case, the clothes make the man woman; and so the narrator states that had 'they both worn the same clothes, it is possible that their outlook might have been the same' (171). What Gilbert and Gubar fail to mention is that the narrator then goes on to repudiate this position:

That is the view of some philosophers and wise ones, but on the whole, we incline to another. The difference between the sexes is, happily, one of great profundity. Clothes are but a symbol of something hid deep beneath. It was a change in Orlando herself that dictated her choice of a woman's dress and of a woman's sex. (171)

The dialectical conflict presented here between transvestism and essential sexual identity in transition resonates in various moments later in the text as Orlando struggles, quite literally, to dress herself as a woman and to define her identity as a woman. While Orlando discovers that the transition of sexual identity is empowering, particularly when she cross-dresses as a man in the eighteenth century and walks more freely in breeches, she is nevertheless plagued by a limiting and inescapable femaleness emanating, we are at times led to believe, from within herself. What remains undetermined throughout the novel, but particularly in the latter half, is the degree to which Orlando clings to or repudiates traditional, patriarchal ideas of masculinity and femininity. Thus, Woolf's depiction of the transsexuality of Orlando ultimately leaves unresolved the dialectical conflict between traditional and revisionist modes of thinking about gender.

Perhaps Woolf's imaginative and dialectic narrative approach was itself a mode of contesting the authorial authority of patriarchal discourse; but I would argue that, although the novel fails to present a coherent theory of gender, *Orlando* was largely intended to confront and contest gender *privilege*, and at the centre of this conflict stands the male-gendered conception of the artist and the artwork. *Orlando* the-matizes the modernist anxiety coined by Bloom as the anxiety of influ-ence, for only once Orlando has been transformed into a woman does she overcome her anxiety in relation to her once-contemporary literary precursors so as to complete and publish her poem, 'The Oak Tree'. Orlando transforms the patriarchal succession of authorship precisely because she is physically transformed; and yet, despite this transform-ation, we are left to wonder to what degree Orlando's transsexual transformation answers Woolf's plea in *A Room of One's Own* for women artists to think back to their mothers. As the narrative looks back in history, as in other of her works including the essay 'Anon', *Orlando* charts the descent of the artist/spirit figure beginning at a point in the Elizabethan period. The anxiety of patrilinear succession persists in the implied teleology from male author to male author to, finally, one male-turned-female author, and, as in *A Room of One's Own*, the authorial spirit which haunts the work is that of the first precursor, Shakespeare. The shabby man with big, bright eyes and a dirty ruff sitting at a table writing whom Orlando espies as a youth is an image which returns at the end of the novel to haunt her: 'Was it old Mr Baker come to measure the timber? Or was it Sh–p–re? (for when we speak names we deeply reverence to ourselves we never speak them whole)' (281).

The haunting image of Shakespeare as an anxiety-inducing aesthetic patriarch ultimately problematizes the act of writing for a female author like Orlando, as does the coinciding image of the pen as penis, an image which resonates throughout after a sexually charged description of the act of writing used early in the novel. Deliberating upon Orlando's betrayal at the hands of his Russian lover, the narrative proceeds:

Thus it was that Orlando, dipping his pen in the ink, saw the mocking face of the lost Princess and asked himself a million questions instantly which were as arrows dipped in gall. Where was she; and why had she left him? Was the Ambassador her uncle or her lover? Had they plotted? Was she forced? Was she married? Was she dead? – all of which so drove their venom into him that, as if to vent his agony somewhere, he plunged his quill so deep into the inkhorn that the ink spirted over the table, which act, explain it how one may (and no explanation perhaps is possible – Memory is inexplicable), at once substituted for the face of the Princess a face of a very different sort. (74)

The substituted face Orlando then sees is that of Shakespeare, an image which links Shakespeare to an image of the pen as a penis responding with violent orgasm to sexual excitation inspired by a female muse. Though this description occurs early in the text while Orlando is still male, the sexual imagery persists even after her transformation as Orlando the woman sits down to write: 'And she plunged her pen neck deep in the ink. To her enormous surprise, there was no explosion. She drew the nib out. It was wet, but not dripping. She wrote. The words were a little long in coming, but come they did' (238). While the suggestion of writing as sexual excitation persists, as the passage goes on to describe, the orgasm is now of a decidedly different nature, not as dangerously explosive, more sustained and slower in coming. The double entendre implied in the idea of 'coming' here is, I think, quite deliberate. In the late nineteenth and early twentieth centuries, sexologists such as the German Richard von Krafft-Ebing and Woolf's contemporary Havelock Ellis, as well as Freud, began documenting in surprisingly explicit language the physiological and psychological character of sexuality, these predominantly male theorists speculating on the nature of the female orgasm: 'In the female the pleasurable feeling occurs later and comes on more slowly, and generally outlasts that of ejaculation.'[48] More important, however, was the relationship between the female's 'larger and more diffused' sexual impulses and the makeup of her mental character which was seen to reflect her sexuality.[49] In Woolf's writing here as well, Orlando's figurative orgasm would appear to reflect the female side of her bisexuality and, therefore, the feminine quality of her writing. Once again, this is a problematic metaphor, an attempt to reconfigure and feminize what is otherwise an inherently male-gendered association between sex and writing. Woolf's appropriation, while it confronts the pattern of artist, muse and artwork relationship, is nevertheless marked and marred by an anxiety typically characterized in the sexual terms of patriarchal authorship. Though *Orlando* begins in modernist fashion as, both thematically and structurally, a portrait of the artist as a young man, the female artist is ultimately left to wonder how Orlando's ambiguous transsexual change serves to define her own identity as a woman.

FRESHWATER

Apart from being her only properly dramatic text, *Freshwater* is undoubtedly unique in comparison to Woolf's other fictive works, particularly in the manner in which the play imagines and identifies a woman and artist

with whom other women artists might identify. *Freshwater* addresses the
question of female identity in art by discarding a male archetype like
Shakespeare altogether in favour of a genuine mother, the play realizing
the project of 'thinking back' by imagining and dramatizing her life.
Surely the same claim – that Woolf's heroine is a positive role model
for female artists – might be made for many of her other female characters. Lily Briscoe in *To the Lighthouse*, for instance, similarly foregrounds
the construction of a female artistic subjectivity. The play's comic tone
might even be seen to trivialize the 'struggle' for female identity. This is
perhaps why *Freshwater* is rarely taken seriously, so to speak: unlike
Woolf's more sombre and reflective novels such as *To the Lighthouse*
(1927) or *Mrs Dalloway* (1925), *Freshwater* lacks the gravity and depth
which ranks her fiction among the works of contemporary modernists.
For the moment, however, what I am more concerned with is feminist
reading practice. I would suggest that the absence of an anxiety-inducing
patriarch exerting his influence over the text – the kind of influence which
the play's caricaturish male characters fail to exert over Terry – offers the
possibility for a different kind of feminist reading, one which repudiates
the Freudian metaphor of Oedipal anxiety which many feminist critics
seem keen to appropriate and subvert as a way of reconciling Woolf's
status as a modernist with her role as a feminist.

Consider, as an example, the model offered by Gilbert and Gubar. For
these two feminist critics, Bloom's unapologetically male view of authorship provides the basic model for their description of the woman writer
and the nineteenth-century literary imagination. If male writers have male
precursors who symbolize an authority which induces an anxiety of
influence, then the alienation and inferiority experienced by the female
writer in relation to those same symbols of authority is far greater: 'her
fear of the antagonism of male readers, her culturally conditioned timidity
about self-dramatization, her dread of the patriarchal authority of art, her
anxiety about the impropriety of female invention',[50] all function to
inscribe women's works with a similar, though far more debilitating,
anxiety. They describe this process as one of 'inferiorization'. The anxiety
of women writers in relation to their male precursors and contemporaries
therefore casts the idea of influence in the negative framework of inferiority and paranoia, a suggestively Freudian exploitation of the psychological
dimension of the author's writing. When they come to discuss women
writers in the twentieth century, Gilbert and Gubar abandon the mono-
lithic patrilinearity of Bloom's discussion for the complexity of Freud,
choosing instead to characterize the female literary 'psychohistory' by

drawing upon his discussion of the female's psychosexual development in, once again, 'Female Sexuality'. Turning from 'inferiorization' to the female's 'affiliation complex', they conclude: 'When we apply the model that we have been calling the affiliation complex to woman's literary history, therefore, we inevitably find women writers oscillating between their matrilineage and their patrilineage in an arduous process of self-definition.'[51] As I noted earlier in the case of *A Room of One's Own*, the projection of the author as a presence in the text is a narrative convention with phallocentric implications which Woolf both recognized and resisted. So too in the case of the female's 'affiliation complex', however much that model offers a more positive framework for discussing the psychohistory of the female literary imagination, nevertheless, the personal dimension of the female author's anxiety in relation to either her male or female precursors – Freudian echoes of her inferiority complex inescapably inscribed in her writing – reflects what would appear to be the relatively inescapable influence of patriarchal oppression.

Feelings of inadequacy and inferiority in relation to her male contemporaries were certainly some of the fears which Woolf sometimes expressed in her diaries. After her first meeting with T. S. Eliot, for example, Woolf confessed how he had cast a shade over her boldness and self-confidence, causing her to fear that her type of writing was probably being better done by Joyce: 'I kept myself successfully from being submerged, though feeling the waters rise once or twice. I mean by this that he completely neglected my claims to be a writer, & had I been meek, I suppose I should have gone under – felt him & his views dominant & subversive.'[52] The personal dimension of this reflection is a reasonable demonstration of the 'inferiorization' model: Woolf's struggle here is not simply social, but profoundly personal, a struggle between what she inadvertently describes as a typically 'feminine' disposition, her fear of crying and 'going under', versus the not-feminine strength, her not being meek, which she needs to withstand the dominant and subversive views of a strong male author like Eliot. Woolf's feminism, in other words, is in conflict with her socially-prescribed femininity, her fear and inferiority not only the products of, but the obstacles which she struggles to overcome, in her male-dominated social sphere. Arguing in a similar vein, Alice Fox has even suggested that Woolf, in her attempt to model her literary and social criticism after the fashion of her male contemporaries, completely eschewed a feminist position. For Fox, Woolf's two volumes of collected essays and articles, written in a style which Woolf admitted was more casual and less academic than that of her male peers, and both of which she titled *Common Reader* to make this distinction explicit, actually represent self-deprecating attempts by Woolf to write like a man.[53] Fox concludes that regardless 'of how convinced Woolf was that her perception of literature frequently differed from that of men because she was a woman, she finally made common cause with them'.[54] Incidentally, the essay 'Anon' (uncompleted at the time of her death) was intended to begin a third volume of the *Common Reader*. Though the essay was begun much later than the earlier two volumes (published in 1925 and 1932 respectively), Fox's theory – Woolf writing *as* a woman, but *like* a man – offers a potentially interesting interpretation of Woolf's androgynous archetype. The important point here, however, is that Fox's suggestion is also predicated upon Woolf's supposed feelings of inferiority and inadequacy, her feminism compromised by her anxiety to be accepted as a credible and authoritative critic by her male peers.

As a critical practice, feminist reading is not single-minded, and many critics have tried to reclaim Woolf's writing for women by rejecting the negative bias of such models, criticizing in particular the phallocentrism of interpreting the authorial psychology of the text.[55] Rather than read influence as the victimization of female authors, the psychosocial subjugation of the female literary imagination to an anxiety-inducing patriarchy, influence might also be read in the more positive context of willed aesthetic activity with subversive potential, as the ascendancy of a female literary identity (and this is largely the context of Gilbert and Gubar's study of twentieth-century, as distinct from nineteenth-century, women writers). The possibility of a more positive reading might be demonstrated by returning to *A Room of One's Own*. Even in my own earlier reading, I suggested that the presence of Shakespeare as an archetypal author figure reflects a patriarchal influence in conflict with Woolf's call for women writers to think back to their mothers. In one moment, the narrator is critical of the male desire for individual affirmation, what she sees as his need to feel superiority over the female sex, the 'patriarch who has to conquer, who has to rule'.[56] The idea of maternal influence replaces the patrilinear succession of authorship, the isolation and struggle of the male artist, with a more communal identification among women who 'think back' rather than conquer to move forward. At the same time, in this her most conspicuously feminist tract, Woolf receded from any association with the women's movement, even, at times, blaming Suffrage for the increased maleness and hostility of male authors towards women.[57] The isolation involved in inhabiting a room of one's own might therefore appear to efface the project of communal identification among women altogether in favour of a typically male, internalized struggle for self-representation.

The plea for women writers to find a room of their own is at the centre of Woolf's criticism of the predominantly male academic institutions in *A Room of One's Own*. The antipathy she felt towards the academy for relegating women to a relatively minor station in the traditional hierarchy of education was indicative of her negative portrayal of Fernham College, a transparently fictitious conflation of the two women's colleges Newnham and Girton, both established at Cambridge in the mid-nineteenth century to further the cause of women's education and to answer the right of women to enter institutions of higher education, institutions from which they were otherwise barred. The ethos which helped to establish these colleges, local communities of women organized into committees which campaigned tirelessly to raise financial, occupational, political and public support, would later typify the Suffrage cause of the late nineteenth and early twentieth centuries, another movement for which local community support was the basis of its political efficacy. For Woolf, however, the accomplishments of a Newnham or Girton, measured in the poor quality of beef and prunes for dinner, rated poorly in comparison to the men's colleges:

I thought how unpleasant it is to be locked out; and I thought how it is worse perhaps to be locked in; and, thinking of the safety and prosperity of the one sex and the poverty and insecurity of the other and of the effect of tradition and of the lack of tradition upon the mind of a writer, I thought at last that it was time to roll up the crumpled skin of the day, with its arguments and its impressions and its anger and its laughter, and cast it into the hedge.[58]

Muriel Bradbrook was a student at Girton in the years just prior to the publication of *A Room of One's Own*, and she dined in the great hall with 'no reason to complain of human nature's daily food'.[59] Perhaps for this reason, Bradbrook was a formidable critic of *A Room of One's Own*, condemning, not unlike Showalter some years later, what she described as camouflage in Woolf's writing: 'It prevents Mrs Woolf from committing the indelicacy of putting a case or the possibility of her being accused of waving any kind of banner.'[60] For Bradbrook, Woolf's attempt at writing a women's common reader in *A Room of One's Own* failed to be effectively partisan and affective for women readers, to exemplify the ethos of a politically active female community.

At the time of Woolf's drafting of *A Room of One's Own* in 1927 and early 1928, however, disillusion with the Suffrage cause was widespread.

Prior to 1918, internal bickering and conflicting party associations, both multiplied by and within regional associations, had caused numerous rifts within the primary Suffrage collective, the National Union of Women's Suffrage Societies, and had led to the formation of the more reactionary Women's Social and Political Union (commonly referred to as the Suffragettes).[61] Led by the outspoken Pankhurst sisters, the Suffragettes advocated acts of arson and the destruction of property, much to the grief of strictly pacifist Suffragists. Moreover, although public support for women's Suffrage had been consistently high from the time of the movement's inception, the pragmatics of party politics as well as the differing party affiliations of the main Suffrage organizations had fore-stalled any significant political gain, both the Conservatives and Liberals fearing that the new segment of the voting electorate would potentially increase their opposition's base of support. In 1918, the Representation of the People bill was introduced primarily for the purpose of extending the vote to men over twenty-one who had served in the war, but the legislation also included a clause for women's enfranchisement. While most Suffra-gists claimed victory, they were simultaneously disheartened by the age and property limitations which the Act placed on the franchise. In 1928, as women's groups continued to seek support for an unequivocally equal franchise (which they would win in that year), that the many levels of institutionally entrenched gender discrimination would not be immedi-ately corrected by the simple enfranchisement of women was becoming increasingly clear: women realized that they were merely participating in male political systems.[62] This same feeling of disillusionment with regard to women's supposed achievements is undoubtedly the reason for Woolf's negative portrayal of Fernham in *A Room of One's Own*, a disillusion further warranted by the fact that, despite having been established several decades prior to the franchise, women graduates of Newnham and Girton would not be fully recognized by the University of Cambridge until 1947. Given this context, Woolf's dismissal of Fernham reflected the widespread disil-lusion among women in 1928, and especially among 'common' women – working-class or unmarried, unemployed and uneducated women over the age of thirty who remained unenfranchised. Woolf's 'room' was her metaphor for the exclusively and uncompromisingly female domain which she both imagined and desired for writers like herself, one freed from the strictures of class and gender privilege in which her Fernham was mired, a room which was, therefore, positively women-centred.

Woolf's attitude towards the institutional academy was undoubtedly more complex, complicated by her own admitted class bias and by her personal relationships with the intellectually elite, mostly Cambridge-educated male members of her Bloomsbury circle. While she exploited her own fluid, more impressionistic style and her lack of academic training by designating her literary criticism as 'common reading', the point which Alice Fox makes is that Woolf, writing in a well-situated and affluent corner of central London, was decidedly not common and that, privately, she both envied and longed for the status which her male peers such as Roger Fry and Lytton Strachey enjoyed.[63] Accordingly, Fox concludes that Woolf omitted from her criticism the 'feminism which otherwise occupied her thinking at the time and which is everywhere manifest in her fiction'.[64] But if Woolf drew upon her female literary predecessors in writing her fiction, why would she not have been if only partly influenced by her female predecessors who wrote criticism, perhaps the most obvious of whom was Ellen Terry. The anxiety of Terry's influence was clearly an issue for Knights who feared the popularity of her work, though in her criticism, popular as it was, Terry made no claim to being a critical authority. Rather, Terry was following the example set by her nineteenth-century predecessors, female actors and authors like herself who published their personal reflections on Shakespeare's characters. Among these women were Helena Faucit, Mary Cowden Clarke and Annabel Jameson, all of whose early to mid-nineteenth-century books were still in print several decades after their first publication.[65] By the time of Terry's lectures, the book market had demonstrated the viability, if not profitability, of women's informal commentary and fictive exploration of Shakespeare's work, perhaps the kind of 'common reading' which Woolf was evoking for her own criticism.

When she began writing her criticism in the early 1920s, there were few academic precedents for women's literary criticism. A few obscure studies emerged occasionally in the early years of the century, but the two most influential female critics of the period, Muriel Bradbrook and Caroline Spurgeon, would not begin publishing their criticism until the mid-1930s. In 1932, Bradbrook was the recipient of the Harness Prize Essay award for a study which she wrote as a graduate at Girton College.[66] And in 1935, Spurgeon, also Cambridge educated, published her landmark study *Shakespeare's Imagery and What it Tells Us.*[67] Spurgeon's study of the imagery in Shakespeare's plays involved several years' research compiling and collating clusters of images which she culled from the works of Shakespeare and his contemporaries. In 1931, her British Academy Lecture on the subject was published, followed in 1935 with the full-length study. Reviews of her book praised the rigorous methodology of her statistical criticism and the dry, scientific objectivity of her material, her results 'tangible and objective, susceptible of a statistical approach which will rule out such nebulous quantities as the reactions of personal sensibility'.[68] Incidentally, *Shakespeare's Imagery and What it Tells Us* begins with an epigraph from *Orlando* which claims that the secrets of a writer's soul, 'every experience of his life, every quality of his mind, is written large in his works'.[69] There is a wonderful and ironic circularity here in Spurgeon's use of *Orlando* as a preface to her own academic and (arguably phallocentric) psychological interpretation of Shakespeare's imagery.

Nevertheless, though she may have influenced Spurgeon, Woolf herself was not university educated, and the only kind of criticism to which she could have looked for a particularly female precedent was that of her non-academic predecessors like Terry. And Terry's writing was, as Knights noted, not academic, but popular, a term often equated by critics such as Eliot with dilettantism or commonness. So, in the early years of the twentieth century, when Woolf herself was becoming an increasingly popular writer whose works were published by a press over which she had formidable control, there was reasonable evidence to suggest the growing influence of a marketable female perspective, an influence upon which Woolf was able to draw if she chose to do, and to which she would also contribute with her own common reading. Although she may have felt jealously excluded, Woolf was not simply the victim of the male literary academy. Discussing the personal dimension of either Woolf's fictive or critical writing, especially as a woman in the company of men – from the point of view of her 'penis envy' – does little to explain her writing as a woman among other women. This is the more positive woman-centred context for women's writing demanded by *A Room of One's Own*, the idea of women thinking back through their mothers countering the personal dimension of the author's struggle for self-representation, the psychological presence of the author in the text which so often haunts the interpretation of Woolf's writing. The idea of women thinking back to their mothers characterizes their writing in the more positive framework of community and networks of female relationships. Maternal influence implies agency through community, influence as the power of constructive encouragement and the ascendancy of the female literary imagination. This sense of female community pervades Woolf's *Freshwater*, a text inspired by the hope and positivity of the post-equal franchise period.

In writing *Freshwater*, Virginia Woolf drew upon Ellen Terry as a source of maternal influence and creative inspiration, Terry a strong woman with whom Woolf could identify, a talented and versatile artist and writer. This metaphor of literary motherhood implies a number of figurative textual relationships, but Terry was more than simply a figurative mother. She was also a real mother whose children from her second marriage with Edward William Godwin were Woolf's contemporaries. By 1935, Edward Gordon Craig had long abandoned acting and producing in the English theatre and had written the majority of his theoretical, and often chauvinistic, polemic on the art of the theatre. In fact, Gordon Craig was vehemently anti-Suffrage, and so his sister Edith, who could not have been more unlike her brother, carried on her mother's interest in the women's movement. While Terry's string of marriages (though she never married the father of her children) and her choice of profession were still considered morally questionable amongst even liberal-minded women, Terry's periodic commitments to the Suffrage cause were uncommonly significant, no doubt due to her international fame and the substantial income she earned at the Lyceum – she had the highest salary earned by a woman in England in the late nineteenth century.[70] Terry was also an advocate of women's education and she was keen that her daughter should enter Girton College.[71] When Edith Craig failed to meet the entrance requirements, herself a talented actor like her mother, she turned her full attention to the theatre, eventually becoming a reputed costumier and designer as well as the first self-proclaimed woman producer or director of the theatre. Throughout the early twentieth century, Edith Craig was also an active contributor to the women's movement, helping to direct pageants and plays, some of which involved Terry. Edith Craig's most significant Suffrage-inspired productions included Cicely Hamilton's *A Pageant of Great Women* which she first directed in 1909, and in the same year, the debut production of *How the Vote Was Won*, co-written by Hamilton with Craig's lifetime female partner, Christopher St John. By 1935, having completed her directorial work with the largely woman-centred dramatic group which she helped to initiate, the Pioneer Players, Craig still remained steadfastly committed to local amateur and repertory theatre in a host of capacities from designing and directing to teaching and lecturing on the subject of women in the theatre, though her brother is the more remembered of the two for his writing and designs.[72] This almost unbelievable difference between Terry's two children is the difference which the play acts out, contrasting the predominantly male narratives about art to the pragmatic attempts by women to transcend these limiting definitions. Thus, *Freshwater* thematizes the issue of female identity by dramatizing the shift which Woolf's feminist writing prescribed, from woman seen, ordered and framed through the per-spective of the male artist to woman as the self-reflective subject of her own art.

While a host of biographical publications provided the material with which Woolf would fashion her portrait of Terry, Woolf also fictively re-ordered and re-imagined the early events of Terry's life to suit her thematic identity in the play. In her autobiography, Terry expressed none of the disillusionment and discontent of the fictional Terry. Rather than desiring to escape the limiting definitions of femininity imposed upon her by Watts and Cameron, she indicated instead how she remembered her time with Watts as a dream, Little Holland House a paradise of beautiful things where she had been happy being the muse of a great artist who loved to paint her. In the end, Terry did not flee, but was expelled from Pattle society: 'I wondered at the new life, and worshipped it because of its beauty. When it suddenly came to an end, I was thunderstruck; and refused at first to consent to the separation, which was arranged for me in much the same way as my marriage had been.'[73] In her own fantasy of the female artist, Woolf empowered the character Terry by reversing altogether the real Terry's expulsion from her paradise. The events of Terry's early life, her marriage to and separation from Watts, her rela-tionship with Godwin and her return to the stage, are further com-pounded together in the play to compose a host of patriarchal limitations which, in a single gesture of defiance, in leaving Freshwater, Terry is able to reject. No longer framed and subjectified within male art, Terry overturns the patriarchal order of art as she discovers and empowers her own artistic identity, the play thus providing a new literary metaphor for the generation of the female artist.

The question of Ellen Terry's identity proved to be an issue of consid-erable interest for Woolf in her later writing career, and though she saw the necessity to rewrite Terry's early biography for the purpose of *Fresh-water*, Woolf clearly felt a great admiration for Terry. In an essay written in 1941, Woolf began with a glowing tribute to her artistic powers as an actor:

When she came on the stage as Lady Cicely in [Shaw's] *Captain Brassbound's Conversion*, the stage collapsed like a house of cards and all the limelights were extinguished. When she spoke it was as if someone drew a bow over a ripe, richly seasoned 'cello; it grated, it glowed, and it growled. Then she stopped speaking. She put on her glasses. She gazed intently at the back of a settee. She had forgotten her part. But did it matter? Speaking or silent, she was Lady Cicely – or was it Ellen Terry? At any rate, she filled the stage and all the other actors were put out, as electric lights are put out in the sun.[74]

After this tribute, the essay goes on to read Terry's autobiography and to map out the various stages of her life and career – child actor, child-bride, mother, famous professional actor, and finally, writer – as a series of identities or multiple personas, finally asking: 'Which, then, of all these women is the real Ellen Terry?'[75] For Woolf, the real Ellen Terry was not a single, unified identity, but a series of public and private personalities or subject positions which she assumed at different times. Like Gordon Craig in *Ellen Terry and Her Secret Self*, Woolf accepted a division between Terry the wife and mother and Terry the public personality; but whereas Gordon Craig saw his mother's public persona infringing upon Little Nelly, Woolf exploited the metaphor of Terry as an actor of different identities. Terry's strength, so the essay would appear to suggest, was her ability to immerse her own self within the role she was playing, to consume and be consumed by the part: 'When the part was congenial, when she was Shakespeare's Portia, Desdemona, Ophelia, every word, every comma was consumed. Even her eyelashes acted. Her body lost its weight. Her son, a mere boy, could lift her in his arms.'[76] In *Freshwater* as well, the identity of the character Terry is portrayed similarly as polymorphous and changeable, which is the condition that allows her to escape the position in which she has been trapped: the discovery of Ellen Terry, the self-empowered woman, is really the birth of Ellen Terry, the actor. The type of identity which *Freshwater* re-imagines and dramatizes for women artists, then, is non-phallic, more protean and less didactic than the male 'I'. The identity of Terry in life and in the play thus provides a woman-centred metaphor for Woolf's own role as the author of the play.[77] Central to this metaphor for female identity as acted role is the medium of the drama. Unlike the authoritative polemic of the first-person narration of *A Room of One's Own*, the form of the drama provided Woolf with the opportunity to escape the institutional strategies of discourse, allowing her to represent her ideas of female identity in a more dialectic medium, consequently avoiding the proselytizing position of the narrative 'I'. Literally offstage, her personality immersed and concealed within the text, the audience is subsequently less inclined than the reader to make the association between Terry and Woolf, between the author as the self and the character represented as the expression of that self. When Terry declares at the end of the 1935 text, 'I am Ellen Terry', finally appropriating the male

'I', Woolf remains concealed and Terry is seen to empower herself as the author and actor of her own identity.

However, this representation of female identity, which is more fully expressed in the 1935 text, is only a rough sketch in the earlier 1923 text, leaving important distinctions to be made between the two. To begin with, the 1923 draft is much shorter than the completed text. Terry, moreover, is practically absent in the earlier draft except for an early monologue and a late reappearance towards the end. But the humorous caricatures of the 1923 version suggest that Woolf was having more fun ridiculing the pretensions of traditional male art. From the painter Watts, whose work on a portrait of Terry as Modesty at the foot of Mammon is arrested for four months because he is unable to incorporate Mammon's big toe, to the poet Tennyson, who is unable to imagine a fate worse than not being able to hear him recite his ode to *Maud*; these are the men for whom Terry acts as a muse to be transformed into their idealized feminine subject. Particularly in the 1923 version, Woolf's male characters parody outright the woman-as-muse motif which codes the subject of art as essentially feminine and the production of art as a masculine wielding of the phallic pen or brush over the female body. Unlike the subtlety of metaphoric suggestion in *Orlando*, the explicit sexuality of the artist/muse relationship is punctuated by the foppish Tennyson when he invites Terry to sit on his knee:

LORD T. Young woman [*beckoning to* ELLEN], have you ever seen a poet's skin? –
   a great poet's skin? Ah, you should see me in my bath! I have thighs like
   alabaster.
ELLEN It's a very beautiful skin, Lord Tennyson.
LORD T. And you're a very beautiful wench. Get on my knee.
ELLEN I sometimes think you're the most sensible of them all, Lord Tennyson.
LORD T. [*kissing her*] I am sensible to beauty in all its shapes. That is my
   function as Poet Laureate. (61)

Tennyson's playing on the meaning of sensible to mean 'feeling' rather than 'reasonable' reflects the sexual innuendo about which the naive Terry remains unaware. As the episode continues, Tennyson becomes more and more sexually aroused until Terry finally jumps off of his knee kissing him and runs out of the room. Charles Cameron, who has been in the room all the while presumably asleep, then chastises Tennyson for his indiscretion:

MR. C. [*opening his eyes slowly*] Alfred, Alfred!
LORD T. [*much startled*] I thought you were asleep!

MR. C. It is when our eyes are shut that we see most!
LORD T. But there is no need to mention it to Emily. (62–3)

Unlike Tennyson, Watts seems to take little notice of his muse, struggling instead with the grand themes of his art:

WATTS Where is Ellen? Has anybody seen Ellen? She must have slipped from the room without my noticing it. [*Turning to the audience and speaking in rapturous tones*] Praise be to the Almighty Architect! The toe of Mammon is now, speaking under Providence, in drawing. Ah, my dear old friends, that toe has meant months of work – months of hard work. I have allowed myself no relaxation. I have sustained my body on the gristle of beef passed through the kitchen chopper twice, and my soul by the repetition of one prayer – The Utmost for the Highest! The Utmost for the Highest! (63)

Woolf was here parodying Watts' supposedly unusual asceticism which he undertook for the higher cause of Art, while also insinuating the sexual incompatibility between Watts and Terry. His Victorian prudishness towards sex is demonstrated shortly thereafter when he discovers the true meaning of the ancient Egyptian symbolism he employs when depicting the veil of Modesty as the Milky Way:

WATTS Horror! Horror! I have been cruelly misled – utterly deceived. [*He reads aloud.*] "The Milky Way among the Ancient Egyptians was the universal token of fertility. It symbolised the spawn of fish, the innumerable progeny of the sea, and the harvest of the fields. It typified the fertility of the marriage bed, and its blessings were called down upon brides at the altar." Horror! Horror! I who have always lived for the Utmost for the Highest have made Modesty symbolise the fertility of fish! . . . I must start afresh . . . It shall never be said that George Frederick Watts painted a single hair that did not tend directly – or indirectly – to the spiritual and moral elevation of the British Public. (65)

Julia Cameron, although a woman, further affirms the patriarchal attitude towards art typical of Tennyson and Watts, freezing and capturing anyone who walks into her view within the limiting perspective of her camera lens. So she reproduces in the grimly prosaic reality of her photographs the classical and Arthurian themes of her contemporaries, 'Sir Galahad watching the Holy Grail' or 'The Passing of Arthur'. Cameron did, in fact, often dress her servants in fantastic costumes to pose in her allegoric photographs, and the 1923 draft very comically parodies her ambitious artistic endeavours. Cameron, for example, remains distraught throughout the play because she is unable to find a suitable Galahad:

MRS. C. What is the use of a policeman if he has no calves? There you have the tragedy of my life. That is Julia Margaret Cameron's message to her age! [*She sits down facing the audience.*] All my sisters were beautiful, but I had genius [*touching her forehead.*] They were the brides of men, but I am the bride of Art. I have sought the beautiful in the most unlikely places. I have searched the police force at Freshwater, and not a man have I found with calves worthy of Sir Galahad . . . I have sought beauty in public houses and found her playing the concertina in the street. My cook was a mendicant. I have transformed her into a Queen. My housemaid sold bootlaces at Charing Cross; she is now engaged to the Earl of Dudley. My bootboy stole eggs and was in prison. He now waits at table in the guise of Cupid. (64–5)

So in the first version of 1923, the satire is focused upon the typically nineteenth-century apparatus of romantic art which seeks to capture and represent the female muse. The caricatures which result make the 1923 text genuinely funny.

The stylistic deviation from the first to the second text might be compared to the differences which distinguish *A Room of One's Own* from the later tract, *Three Guineas.* Whereas *A Room of One's Own* is more engaging, more imaginative and wittier, and *Three Guineas* more extreme, more politically urgent and focused, so too is the second text of *Freshwater* less entertaining and more overtly discursive than the first. What the 1935 text loses in terms of its dramatic value, it gains in terms of the cogency of its representation of Terry. By the 1935 version of *Freshwater*, the focus has been redirected from the male artists and their strategies of defining and representing femininity, back to their female subject. Accordingly, the later text offers a more dynamic character in Terry, providing her with more opportunities to voice her dissent. Terry begins on the stage locked in her pose as Modesty, a pose which she breaks, rather immodestly, complaining and cursing as she steps out of Watt's frame:

ELLEN [*stretching her arms*] Oh, Signor, can't I get down? I am so stiff.
WATTS Stiff, Ellen? Why you've only kept that pose for four hours this morning.
ELLEN Only four hours! It seems like centuries. Anyhow I'm awfully stiff. And I would like to go for a bathe. It's a lovely morning. The bees on the thorn. [ELLEN *clambers down off the model's throne and stretches herself.*]
WATTS You have given four hours to the service of art, Ellen, and are already tired. I have given seventy-seven years to the service of art and I am not tired yet.
ELLEN O Lor'!
WATTS If you must use that vulgar expression, Ellen, please sound the final *d*.
ELLEN [*standing beside* TENNYSON] Oh Lord, Lord, Lord!
TENN. I am not yet a Lord, damsel; but who knows? . . . (10–11)

In the earlier version, this representative gesture of Terry breaking her pose occurs offstage and she merely recounts this action in a dramatic monologue directed at the men who ignore her. Ironically bemoaning her status as static object of art and expressing her desire for self-representation, she states:

> ELLEN Everybody says how proud I must be to hang for ever and ever in the Tate Gallery as Modesty crouching at the foot of Mammon. But I'm an abandoned wretch, I suppose. I have such awful thoughts. Sometimes I actually want to go upon the stage and be an actress . . . (60)

In the 1935 text, Woolf discards the form of the monologue in favour of a dialectic confrontation between Watts and Terry. Insofar as the monologue as a window on the self reproduces the first-person perspective of narrative, the dialogue, in contrast, allows for Terry to transcend more readily the phallic declaration of the 'I'. Moreover, while the action of the first version occurs in a single act, the action of the third is divided into three acts. The middle act incorporates the meeting between Terry and John Craig, who is simply Mr Craig in the earlier version and whose meeting with Terry occurs offstage. Thus, the second version corrects the omission of the first by inserting into the centre of the drama a scene whose central importance was not originally dramatized there. The second version also downplays the antics of the other characters. Julia Cameron, for example only focuses her camera on Terry, her message less subtle than before as she insists, 'But now you're the Muse' (11). Similarly, the wit and the humorous exchanges which characterize Tennyson and Charles Cameron, the misunderstandings and the innuendos, lose their delicacy, and offered instead are more characteristically nineteenth-century platitudes about art:

> MR. C. All things that have substance seem to me unreal. What are these? [*He picks up the braces.*] Braces. Fetters that bind us to the wheel of life. What are these? [*He picks up the trousers.*] Trousers. Fig leaves that conceal the truth. What is truth? Moonshine. Where does the moon shine for ever? India. Come, my marmoset, let us go to India. Let us go to India, the land of our dreams . . . (14)

The humour and the irony of farce give way to a more propagandic satire of romantic artistic conventions. As a result, although much of the humour of the first version is lost, the later text of 1935 provides a clearly articulated criticism of the conventions which construct and perpetuate female identity; and while the 1923 text might be accused of reproducing a patriarchal perspective by focusing primarily on the male characters, the

1935 text locates Terry at the very centre of the conflict between male discourse and female identity.

The 1935 version of *Freshwater* ends with Terry and Craig's departure, the Camerons' exodus to India, and the entrance of Queen Victoria who grants the peerage to Tennyson and the Order of Merit to Watts. In her real life, Terry's separation from Watts was followed shortly thereafter by her period with Godwin and the birth of her two children to whose adopted surname the character name Craig alludes; but the maternal metaphor which the play explores is ultimately more figurative. The 1935 *Freshwater* rewrites patriarchal history by re-imagining Ellen Terry's life history, rewriting the inherited artistic tradition which is seen to descend through history taking as model and culminating in male archetypes like Shakespeare. Woolf's play offers instead a revisionary historical practice of 'thinking back' to maternal archetypes like Terry, rewinding and rewriting. This suggestion of author as metaphorical mother to dynamic and fluid inter-woven texts, or the idea of mothering the text as a process of 'thinking back', challenges the patriarchal authority and the teleology of the modernist literary narrative. The backward movement, moreover, implies an exponential multiplication of influence – one mother, two grandmothers, four great-grandmothers (even including great aunts), and so on – rather than the artistic tradition which descends through and culminates in the individual talent. Woolf was, of course, childless, but as she might have imagined herself more figuratively as one of a community of literary daughters engaged in a process of 'thinking back' to Ellen Terry, Woolf was simultaneously a mother to Ellen Terry as text. Open-ended and deliberately ambiguous, her metaphor thus offered more fluid ways by which women writers like herself could both re-imagine their relationships with their texts and identify with other female artists and writers. And so, engaged in our own process of 'thinking back' to Woolf, we are left with the question whose answer, although we know the historical facts, needs to be constantly engaged with and rewritten: how many children had Virginia Woolf?

Notes

INTRODUCTION

1 The idea of the author as a function of ideology has been developed particularly by Roland Barthes, 'The Death of the Author' [1968], in *Image, Music Text*, sel. and trans. Stephen Heath (London: Fontana Press, 1977), pp. 142–8; and Michel Foucault, 'What is an Author', in *Textual Strategies: Perspectives in Post-Structuralist Criticism*, ed. Josué V. Harari (London: Methuen, 1979), pp. 141–60. Foucault's author function has been used to great effect by Margreta De Grazia, 'The Essential Shakespeare and the Material Book', *Textual Practice* 2 (1988), 69–86. See also Margreta De Grazia and Peter Stallybrass, 'The Materiality of the Shakespearean Text', *Shakespeare Quarterly* 44 (1993), 255–83. Courtney Lehmann provides a wonderful counterview by noting the persistent tendency in poststructuralist critique to attribute human attributes to the texts, in *Shakespeare Remains: Theatre to Film, Early Modern to Post-modern* (Ithaca: Cornell University Press, 2002).

2 Gary Taylor, *Reinventing Shakespeare: A Cultural History from the Restoration to the Present* (London: The Hogarth Press, 1989). Taylor offers his own counterargument to Foucault in 'What is an Author [Not]', *Critical Survey* 7 (1995), 241–54.

3 This point and the subsequent definition of modernity is offered by Fredric Jameson in his recent *A Singular Modernity: Essay on the Ontology of the Present* (London: Verso, 2002), pp. 17–30.

4 Karl Marx and Fredrick Engels, *The Manifesto of the Communist Party*, in Karl Marx, *Political Writings, Vol. 1: The Revolutions of 1848*, ed. David Fernbach (New York: Vintage, 1974), p. 70.

5 Terry Eagleton, 'Capitalism, Modernism and Postmodernism', *New Left Review* 152 (July/August, 1985), 60–73 (p. 67).

6 Raymond Williams, *The Politics of Modernism: Against the New Conformists* (London: Verso, 1989), p. 34.

7 This distinction is developed in Peter Bürger, *Theory of the Avante-Garde*, trans. Michael Shaw (Manchester: Manchester University Press, 1984). The eventual identification of the avant-garde with European fascism was anticipated both by Walter Benjamin, as elsewhere, in 'The Work of Art in the Age of Mechanical Reproduction', in *Illuminations*, trans. Harry Zohn

(London: Fontana Press, 1973), pp. 211–44 (p. 212); and by Georg Lukács, in 'Expressionism: its Significance and Decline', in *Essays on Realism*, ed. Rodney Livingstone, trans. David Fernbach (London: Lawrence and Wishart, 1980), pp. 76–113.

8 The methodology and terminology here derives from Fredric Jameson, *The Political Unconscious: Narrative as a Socially Symbolic Act* (London: Methuen, 1981).

9 Earlier works include Terence Hawkes' *That Shakespeherian Rag: Essays on a Critical Process* (London: Methuen, 1986); Hugh Grady's *The Modernist Shakespeare: Critical Texts in a Material World* (Oxford: Clarendon Press, 1991); and Richard Halpern's *Shakespeare Among the Moderns* (Ithaca: Cornell University Press, 1997). Building upon the critical methodology of *The Modernist Shakespeare*, more recent studies have begun to articulate the idea of an openly 'presentist' critical practice, including among them Hawkes' recent *Shakespeare in the Present* (London: Routledge, 2002).

10 Jameson, *A Singular Modernity*, p. 13.

11 See, in particular, Walter Benjamin, *Illuminations*; Theodore Adorno, *Aesthetic Theory*, trans., ed., and intro. by Robert Hullot-Kentor (London: Athlone Press, 1997); and Jürgen Habermas, *The Structural Transformation of the Public Sphere: An Inquiry into a Category of Bourgeois Society*, trans. Thomas Burger (London: Polity Press, 1989). These positions have been more recently developed by, for example, Perry Anderson, *A Zone of Engagement* (London: Verso, 1992); and Andreas Huyssen, *After the Great Divide: Modernism, Mass Culture, Postmodernism* (Bloomington, Indiana: Indiana University Press, 1986).

12 Grady, *The Modernist Shakespeare*, p. 20.

13 Ibid., p. 19.

14 I am also indebted to Grady's discussions of modernity in three later works: 'Renewing Modernity: Changing Contexts and Contents of a Nearly Invisible Concept', *Shakespeare Quarterly* 50/3 (Fall 1999), 268–84; 'Introduction: Shakespeare and Modernity', in *Shakespeare and Modernity: Early Modern to Millennium*, ed. Hugh Grady (London: Routledge, 2000), pp. 1–19; and 'Modernity, Modernism and Postmodernism in the Twentieth-Century's Shakespeare', in *Shakespeare and Modern Theatre*, ed. Michael Bristol and Kathleen McCluskie (London: Routledge, 2001), pp. 20–35.

15 Halpern, *Shakespeare Among the Moderns*, p. 11.

16 Ibid., p. 11.

17 Jameson, *The Political Unconscious*, p. 9.

18 Sanford Schwartz, *The Matrix of Modernism: Pound, Eliot, and Early Twentieth-century Thought* (Princeton: Princeton University Press, 1985).

19 Grady, 'Modernity, Modernism and Postmodernity in the Twentieth-Century's Shakespeare', p. 27. Developing from Schwarz, Richard Sheppard gives the socio-cultural matrix further scope by describing modernism as 'a heterogeneous range of responses to the global process of modernization by a generation which had internalized a set of assumptions in conflict with the

values inherent in that process, and which, as a result, experienced modernization as a cultural cataclysm'; 'The Problematics of European Modernism', in *Theorizing Modernism: Essays in Critical Theory*, ed. Steve Giles (London: Routledge, 1993), pp. 1–51 (p. 7).

20 Nietzsche's complete works were published in England between 1909 and 1913 under the title series, *The Complete Works of Friedrich Nietzsche*, 18 vols., ed. Oscar Levy (London: T. N. Foulis).

21 The principal Freudian text under consideration here is *The Interpretation of Dreams*, trans. James Strachey, ed. James Strachey and Alan Tyson (London: Penguin Books, 1976), first published in English translation in 1913.

1   THE SHAKESPEARE REVOLUTION

1 Letter dated 27 January 1897, as cited in Ellen Terry, *Ellen Terry and Bernard Shaw: A Correspondence*, ed. Christopher St John (London: Max Reinhardt, 1949), p. 136.

2 Letter dated 28 August 1896, as cited in Terry, *Ellen Terry and Bernard Shaw*, p. 38.

3 See Edwin Wilson in the Introduction to George Bernard Shaw, *Shaw on Shakespeare: An Anthology of Bernard Shaw's Writings on the Plays and Production of Shakespeare*, ed. Edwin Wilson (Harmondsworth: Penguin, 1961), pp. ix–xxii.

4 *Candida*, written 1894–5, published in George Bernard Shaw, *Plays: Pleasant and Unpleasant* (London: Constable, 1898). Terry assumed the role of Lady Cicely Waynflete in Shaw's *Captain Brassbound's Conversion*, initially in the 1899 copyright reading, and for the Court Theatre production in 1906, which then toured in America; first published in George Bernard Shaw, *Three Plays for Puritans* (London: Constable, 1901).

5 In his letter of 27 January 1897, as cited in Terry, *Ellen Terry and Bernard Shaw*, p. 136.

6 The idea of a Shakespeare revolution in early twentieth-century England has been noted, in particular, by J. L. Styan, in *The Shakespeare Revolution: Criticism and Performance in the Twentieth Century* (Cambridge: Cambridge University Press, 1977), from whose book the title of this chapter derives.

7 As cited in Shaw, *Shaw on Shakespeare*, p. ix.

8 George Bernard Shaw, *Man and Superman*, in *The Bodley Head Bernard Shaw Collected Plays with their Prefaces 2* (London: The Bodley Head, 1971), pp. 490–803, (p. 523).

9 Harold Bloom, *Shakespeare: The Invention of the Human* (London: Fourth Estate, 1999).

10 Harold Bloom, *The Anxiety of Influence: A Theory of Poetry* (Oxford: Oxford University Press, 1973), p. 25.

11 Ibid., p. 10.

12 See Sigmund Freud, *The Interpretation of Dreams*, trans. James Strachey, ed. James Strachey and Alan Tyson (London: Penguin Books, 1991).

13 Cited in Bloom, *The Anxiety of Influence*, p. 50.

14 On the translation and publication history of Nietzsche in England, see David S. Thatcher, *Nietzsche in England 1890–1914* (Toronto: Toronto University Press, 1970), pp. 17–52.

15 On Nietzsche's influence in England see both Thatcher, *Nietzsche in England*; and Patrick Bridgewater, *Nietzsche in Anglosaxony: A Study of Nietzsche's Impact on English and American Literature* (Leicester: Leicester University Press, 1972).

16 Thatcher, *Nietzsche in England*, p. 27; Max Nordau, *Degeneration* (London: Heinemann, 1913).

17 First translated into English by Wm A. Haussmann as 'The Birth of Tragedy or Hellenism and Pessimism', in *The Complete Works of Friedrich Nietzsche, Vol. III*, ed. Oscar Levy (London: T. N. Foulis, 1909).

18 These four currents are noted by John Burt Foster in *Heirs to Dionysus: A Nietzschean Current in Literary Modernism* (Princeton: Princeton University Press, 1981). It should be noted that while the English translation of *The Birth of Tragedy* followed *Thus Spoke Zarathustra*, Nietzsche composed the former in 1871 and the latter between 1883 and 1885.

19 Shaw, *Man and Superman*, p. 688.

20 Ibid., p. 520.

21 As cited in Bridgewater, *Nietzsche in Anglosaxony*, p. 59.

22 Thatcher, *Nietzsche in England*, pp. 216–17.

23 Ibid., p. 203. On Shaw's Fabianism, see also Ian Britain, *Fabianism and Culture: A Study in British Socialism of the Arts c. 1884–1918* (Cambridge: Cambridge University Press, 1982).

24 Friedrich Nietzsche, *The Birth of Tragedy and the Genealogy of Morals*, trans. Francis Golffing (New York: Doubleday, 1956), p. 51.

25 Nietzsche, *The Birth of Tragedy*, p. 52. The explicitly gendered language used here is discussed in chapter 2, pp. 79–81.

26 Freud, *The Interpretation of Dreams*, p. 366. It should be noted that Freud's original discussion of *Hamlet* appeared in a footnote in the German original, and was expanded in the main text of the 1913 English translation.

27 Ibid., p. 368.

28 Ibid., pp. 365–6.

29 Philip Pothen, *Nietzsche and the Fate of Art* (Aldershot, Hampshire: Ashgate, 2002), p. 51.

30 Georg Brandes, *William Shakespeare: A Critical Study, Volume II* (London: William Heinemann, 1898), p 32.

31 Freud, *The Interpretation of Dreams*, p. 368.

32 Walter Raleigh, *Shakespeare* (London: MacMillan and Co., Limited, 1907), p. 1.

33 Ibid., p. 3.

34 This would appear to be the sense in which Terence Hawkes, in *That Shakespeherian Rag: Essays on a Critical Process* (London: Methuen, 1986), discusses Raleigh's lionization of Shakespeare, Raleigh elevating Shakespeare

to the 'stature of cultural superman' (p. 57). In fact, the whole discussion appears under the subheading 'Superman', perhaps referring to Shakespeare and perhaps to Raleigh himself who, Hawkes reminds us, became Sir Walter Raleigh in 1911, four years after his Shakespeare book.

35 Shaw, *Man and Superman*, p. 520.

36 T. S. Eliot, 'Ulysses, Order, and Myth', in *Selected Prose of T. S. Eliot*, ed. Frank Kermode (London: Faber and Faber, 1980), pp. 175–8 (p. 177); first published in *Dial* (November 1923).

37 Ezra Pound, *Selected Poems*, ed. with an intro. by T. S. Eliot (London: Faber and Faber Limited, 1928), p. 158.

38 Eliot, 'Ulysses, Order, and Myth', p. 175.

39 T. S. Eliot, 'The Possibility of a Poetic Drama', in *The Sacred Wood: Essays on Poetry and Criticism* (1920; repr. London: Methuen and Co., 1934), pp. 60–70 (p. 68); first published in *Dial* (November 1920).

40 Eliot, 'The Possibility of a Poetic Drama', p. 68.

41 Eliot, 'Tradition and the Individual Talent', in *The Sacred Wood*, pp. 47–59 (p. 49); first published in the *Egoist* (September and December 1919).

42 T. S. Eliot, 'The Waste Land', in *Collected Poems: 1909–1962* (London: Faber and Faber, 1963), pp. 61–79 (p. 79).

43 T. S. Eliot, 'Marie Lloyd', in *Selected Essays* (London: Faber and Faber Limited, 1976), pp. 456–9 (p. 459); first published in *Dial* (December 1922). Huxley's *Brave New World* first appeared in 1932 and Orwell's *Nineteen Eighty-Four* in 1948.

44 T. S. Eliot, 'The Metaphysical Poets', in *Selected Essays*, pp. 281–91, first appeared in the *Times Literary Supplement* (20 October 1921); 'Four Elizabethan Dramatists', in *Selected Essays*, pp. 109–17, first appeared in the *Criterion* (February 1924).

45 Eliot, 'The Metaphysical Poets', p. 289.

46 Eliot's interest in French social anthropology is charted by Ronald Bush, 'The Presence of the Past: Ethnographic Thinking / Literary Politics', in *Prehistories of the Future: The Primitivist Project and the Culture of Modernism*, ed. Elazar Barkan and Ronald Bush (Stanford, California: Stanford University Press, 1995), pp. 23–41.

47 Bush, 'The Presence of the Past', p. 34.

48 T. S. Eliot, 'The Beating of a Drum', *Nation and Athenaeum* 34 (6 October 1923), 11–12 (p. 12). Richard Halpern, *Shakespeare Among the Moderns* (Ithaca: Cornell University Press, 1997), pp. 24–36.

49 Eliot, 'The Beating of a Drum', p. 12.

50 William Archer, *The Old Drama and the New: An Essay in Re-valuation* (New York: Dodd, Mead and Company, 1926), p. 128.

51 Halpern, *Shakespeare Among the Moderns*, p. 31.

52 T. S. Eliot, 'Shakespeare and the Stoicism of Seneca', in *Selected Essays*, pp. 126–40, originally an address delivered before the Shakespeare Association (18 March 1927) and published in pamphlet form.

53 Eliot, 'Shakespeare and the Stoicism of Seneca', p. 131.

54 For more comprehensive discussions of Eliot's writing on Shakespeare, see William H. Quillian, *Hamlet and the New Poetic: James Joyce and T. S. Eliot* (Ann Arbor, Michigan: UMI Research Press, 1983); and Charles Warren, *T. S. Eliot on Shakespeare* (Ann Arbor, Michigan: UMI Research Press, 1987).

55 Eliot, 'Shakespeare and the Stoicism of Seneca', p. 126.

56 Ibid., p. 128.

57 T. S. Eliot, 'Hamlet and his Problems', in *The Sacred Wood*, pp. 95–103; the article refers to J. M. Robertson, *The Problem of 'Hamlet'* (London: G. Allen and Unwin, 1919) and E. E. Stoll, *Hamlet: an Historical and Comparative Study* (Minneapolis: University of Minnesota Press, 1919).

58 Eliot in the preface to *The Sacred Wood*, p. vii.

59 Eliot, 'Hamlet and his Problems', p. 95.

60 Ibid., p. 96.

61 Ibid., p. 100.

62 J. M. Robertson, *The Shakespeare Canon*, 5 vols. (London, 1922–32); Hugh Grady, in *The Modernist Shakespeare: Critical Texts in a Material World* (Oxford: Clarendon Press, 1991), esp. p. 50, provides a more detailed analysis of Robertson's work in relation to modernism.

63 E. K. Chambers, 'The Disintegration of Shakespeare', in *Aspects of Shakespeare, Being British Academy Lectures* (1923–1931), ed. J. W. Mackail (Oxford, 1933), pp. 23–48.

64 R. A. Foakes, in 'The Reception of Hamlet', *Shakespeare Survey 45* (Cambridge: Cambridge University Press, 1993), pp. 1–13, calls this a process of 'Hamletism'; in a related manner, Adrian Poole also highlights the central significance of Hamlet to the Victorian cultural imagination at several points in *Shakespeare and the Victorians* (London: Thomson Learning, 2004).

65 T. S. Eliot, 'The Love Song of J. Alfred Prufrock', in *Collected Poems*, pp. 13–17 (p. 17).

66 The question of Eliot's politics, and especially his anti-Semitism, has received more critical attention recently. Terence Hawkes discusses the political dimension of Eliot's *Hamlet* essay briefly, particularly in comparison to Eliot's higher valuation of *Coriolanus*, in *Meaning by Shakespeare* (London: Routledge, 1992), pp. 93–6.

67 For a similar discussion, see Lawrence Venuti, *Our Halcyon Days: English Prerevolutionary Texts and Post-modern Culture* (Wisconsin: The University of Wisconsin Press, 1989), p. 40; the phrase 'insurgent middle-class' is cited from T. S. Eliot, 'London Letter', *Dial* 70/4 (April 1923), 448–53 (p. 450).

68 Eliot, 'Marie Lloyd', p. 173–4; and 'London Letter', *Dial* 72/5 (May 1922), 510–13 (p. 511).

69 Eliot, 'Marie Lloyd', p. 458.

70 This point is made by David Chinitz in his persuasive reconsideration of the distinction between high art and mass culture in Eliot's writing, 'T. S. Eliot and the Cultural Divide', *PMLA* 110/2 (March 1995); Chinitz, however, occasionally makes the mistake of implicitly equating Eliot's praise for

working-class or 'popular' culture (in the sense of *Volkskultur* or folk culture) with an emergent mass culture.

71 Amy Koritz demonstrates this point persuasively in *Gendering Bodies / Performing Art: Dance and Literature in Early Twentieth-Century British Culture* (Ann Arbor: University of Michigan Press, 1995), esp. p. 152.

72 Eliot, incidentally, wrote the preface to Knight's *The Wheel of Fire: Interpretations of Shakespearian Tragedy* (Oxford: Oxford University Press, 1930). With regard to Eliot's importance in establishing the English literary academy, see Chris Baldick, *The Social Mission of English Criticism 1848–1932* (Oxford: Clarendon Press, 1983), pp. 109–33; as well as Grady, *The Modernist Shakespeare*, pp. 33–43 and 74–112.

73 See Walter Benjamin, 'The Work of Art in the Age of Mechanical Reproduction', in *Illuminations*, trans. Harry Zohn (London: Fontana Press, 1973), pp. 211–44; and Jürgen Habermas, *The Structural Transformation of the Public Sphere: An Inquiry into a Category of Bourgeois Society* (1962), trans. Thomas Burger (London: Polity Press, 1989).

74 Eliot, 'The Function of Criticism', in *Selected Essays*, pp. 23–36 (p. 69); first published in *Criterion* (1923).

75 T. S. Eliot, 'London Letter', *Dial* 71/2 (August 1921), 213–17 (p. 213).

76 T. S. Eliot, 'London Letter', *Dial* 70/6 (June 1921), 686–91 (p. 687).

77 Charlotte Eliot, *Savonarola: A Dramatic Poem*, intro. by T. S. Eliot (London: R. Cobden-Sanderson, 1926), p. xi.

78 Eliot, 'The Possibility of a Poetic Drama', p. 61.

79 Eliot, 'Four Elizabethan Dramatists', pp. 114–15. 'Most' was included in his later revision in order to note the 'really good' productions at the Old Vic and Sadler's Wells theatres.

2 SEX, LIES AND HISTORICAL FICTIONS

1 In his 1890 edition of *Shakespeare's Sonnets* (London: David Nutt), pp. 56–7, Thomas Tyler quotes a series of letters from the *Chamberlain's Letters during the Reign of Queen Elizabeth* (edited for the Camden Society by S. Williams, p. 100) which shows that Herbert was briefly imprisoned after Fitton's delivery of an illegitimate boy, who died shortly after birth.

2 Frank Harris in the preface to *Shakespeare and his Love: A Play in Four Acts and an Epilogue* (London: Frank Palmer, 1910), p. viii.

3 In his biography of *Bernard Shaw* (New York: Simon and Schuster, 1931), Harris noted that he did in fact attend the play and, moreover, sat in the author's box with Shaw and his wife (pp. 210–11). Harris' play was published not long after the announcement for *The Dark Lady of the Sonnets*, so either Harris' preface was written between the announcement and the performance, or he refused to admit to the irony of Shaw's play, perhaps for the purpose of his own plagiarism narrative.

4 As noted by Shaw in the preface to *The Dark Lady of the Sonnets*, in *The Bodley Head Bernard Shaw Collected Plays with their Prefaces 4* (London: Max Reinhardt, 1972), p. 270.

5 Shaw, *The Dark Lady of the Sonnets*, pp. 312 and 314 respectively.

6 Harris, *Shakespeare and his Love*, p. xiv.

7 Frank Harris, *The Man Shakespeare and his Tragic Life Story* (London: Frank Palmer, 1909).

8 Ibid., p. 6.

9 Ibid., p. 8.

10 Harris in the preface to *Shakespeare and his Love*, p. v.

11 Ibid., p. xiv.

12 Shaw, in his postscript to Harris' *Bernard Shaw*, p. 421.

13 Cited in John F. Gallagher's introduction to Frank Harris, *My Life and Loves* (London: W. H. Allen, 1964), p. xiii.

14 Despite initial reviews which disparaged the crude sexual language and situations, but perhaps due to its shocking lack of morality, *Mr and Mrs Daventry* managed 121 performances at the Royalty Theatre under Mrs Patrick Campbell who also played the title role. On the history of its performance and critical reception, see the introduction to Frank Harris, *Mr and Mrs Daventry: A Play in Four Acts*, with an introduction by H. Montgomery Hyde (London: The Richards Press, 1956).

15 These portraits appear in the first volume alone of Frank Harris, *Contemporary Portraits* (London: Methuen and Co. Ltd, 1915).

16 Frank Harris, *My Life and Loves*, in four volumes between 1923 and 1929, with a fifth volume, based on unpublished material by Harris, published posthumously in 1958.

17 Robert Brainard Pearsall, *Frank Harris* (New York: Twayne Publishers, Inc., 1970), p. 148.

18 Shaw, *The Dark Lady of the Sonnets*, p. 275.

19 William Shakespeare, *Shakespere, Sonnets: The First Quarto, 1609, A Facsimile in Photo-Lithography, by Charles Praetorius, with an Introduction by Thomas Tyler* (London: C. Praetorius, 1886).

20 In his preface to the 1890 edition, Tyler credited the Pembroke theory to the eighteenth-century critic Henry Hallam (*c.* 1837), who had adapted it from the obscure sonnet commentators Bright (*c.* 1819) and Boaden (*c.* 1832).

21 In the introduction to his 1890 edition, p. 1.

22 Arthur Acheson, *Shakespeare and the Rival Poet: Displaying Shakespeare as a Satirist and Proving the Identity of the Patron and the Rival of the Sonnets* (London: John Lane, The Bodley Head, 1903), p. 18.

23 J. M., *Shakespeare. Self-Revealed, in his 'Sonnets' and 'Phoenix and Turtle'* (London: Sherratt and Hughes, 1904), p. 127.

24 Sydney Lee, *A Life of William Shakespeare* (1898; repr. London: John Murray, 1908); F. J. Furnivall and John Munro, *Shakespeare: Life and Work* (London: Cassell, 1908).

25 Shaw, *The Dark Lady of the Sonnets*, p. 271.

26 Ibid., p. 274.

27 Ibid., p. 276.

28 Ibid., p. 275.

29 Harris, *Shakespeare and his Love*, pp. xii and xiii.

30 Shaw, *The Dark Lady of the Sonnets*, p. 292.

31 Shaw's numerous writings on the subject of Shakespeare were not collected until *Shaw on Shakespeare: An Anthology on Bernard Shaw's Writings on the Plays and Production of Shakespeare*, ed. Edwin Wilson (Harmondsworth: Penguin, 1961).

32 Shaw, *The Dark Lady of the Sonnets*, p. 274.

33 C. G. Jung, 'Sigmund Freud in his Historical Setting (1933)', in *Freud: Modern Judgements*, ed. Frank Cioffi (London: MacMillan, 1973), pp. 49–56 (p. 49).

34 Ibid., p. 51.

35 Ibid., p. 52.

36 Frank Harris, *The Women of Shakespeare* (London: Methuen and Co. Ltd, 1911).

37 Walter Raleigh, *Shakespeare* (London: MacMillan and Co., Ltd, 1907); A. C. Bradley, *Shakespearean Tragedy: Lectures on Hamlet, Othello, King Lear, Macbeth* (London: MacMillan, 1904).

38 *The Man Shakespeare*, for example, bears a remarkable resemblance to an earlier 1904 volume, Charles Creighton's *Shakespeare's Story of his Life* (London: Grant Richards), based on two articles published in *Blackwood's Magazine* in 1901, which also endorsed the Pembroke–Fitton theory.

39 James Walters, *Shakespeare's True Life* (London: James Walters, 1890), with a second edition in 1896 (London: Longmans, Green); George C. Bompas, *The Problem of the Shakespeare Plays* (London: S. Low, Marston and Co., 1902); William A. Sutton, *The Shakespeare Enigma* (Dublin: Sealy, Bryers and Walker, 1903), based on articles contributed to the *New Ireland Review*.

40 See, in particular, Chris Baldick, *The Social Mission of English Criticism 1848–1932* (Oxford: Clarendon Press, 1983); Hugh Grady, *The Modernist Shakespeare: Critical Texts in a Material World* (Oxford: Clarendon Press, 1991); and Terence Hawkes, *That Shakespeherian Rag: Essays on a Critical Process* (London: Methuen, 1986).

41 Hawkes, *That Shakespeherian Rag*, p. 57.

42 On Bradley's academic and publishing career during this period, see Katherine Cooke, *A. C. Bradley and his Influence in Twentieth-Century Shakespeare Criticism* (Oxford: Clarendon Press, 1972), pp. 37–42.

43 Somewhat overstating its significance, Hawkes writes: 'Bradley's *Shakespearean Tragedy* is one of those books whose influence extends far beyond the confines of its ostensible subject, permeating the attitudes to morality, psychology and politics of hundreds and thousands of English-speaking people, regardless of whether or not they have ever set eyes on the text' (*That Shakespeherian Rag*, p. 31).

44 Harris, *The Man Shakespeare*, p. x.

45 A. C. Bradley, 'Shakespeare the Man', in *Oxford Lectures on Poetry* (London: MacMillan, 1959), pp. 311–57 (p. 315n).

46 As cited in Philippa Pullar, *Frank Harris* (London: Hamilton, 1975), p. 240.

47 While Bradley's *Shakespearean Tragedy* remains in print, Harris' Shakespeare criticism has all but passed from history. Harris received a short, though derisive, summary in Augustus Ralli's 1932 *A History of Shakespearian Criticism, Volume II* (repr. New York: The Humanities Press, 1959), pp. 269–74 and 303–8. Harris is mentioned in passing in Gary Taylor's more recent *Reinventing Shakespeare: A Cultural History from the Restoration to the Present* (London: The Hogarth Press, 1989), pp. 242 and 262, and is briefly misrepresented in Michael Taylor's *Shakespeare Criticism in the Twentieth Century* (London: Oxford University Press, 2001), p. 83.

48 F. J. Furnivall, in a speech delivered at the opening meeting, in *New Shakespere Society's Transactions Series I* (London: Trübner and Co., 1874), p. vi. Cited in Taylor, *Reinventing Shakespeare*, p. 165.

49 Bradley, *Shakespearean Tragedy*, p. 3.

50 Bradley, 'Shakespeare the Man', p. 316.

51 Frank Harris, 'The True Shakespeare: Part VII', *Saturday Review* (3 September 1898), pp. 304–5; and especially, 'The True Shakespeare: Part VIII', *Saturday Review* (10 September 1898), pp. 335–7, in which he praises Brandes as 'the ablest of Shakespeare's commentators' (p. 335).

52 Georg Brandes, *William Shakespeare: A Critical Study* (London: William Heinemann, 1898) p. 362.

53 Ibid., p. 362.

54 Lee, *A Life of William Shakespeare*, p. 23.

55 Ernest Jones, 'The Oedipus Complex as an Explanation of Hamlet's Mystery: A Study in Motive', *The American Journal of Psychology* 21 (1910), 72–113; Ernest Jones, *Hamlet and Oedipus* (London: Victor Gollancz, 1949).

56 Jones, 'The Oedipus Complex', p. 86.

57 Sigmund Freud, *The Interpretation of Dreams*, trans. James Strachey, ed. James Strachey and Alan Tyson (London: Penguin Books, 1976), p. 690.

58 Ibid., p. 367.

59 Jones, 'The Oedipus Complex', p. 73.

60 Freud, *The Interpretation of Dreams*, p. 368.

61 Sigmund Freud, 'Inhibitions, Symptoms and Anxiety' [1926], in *On Psychopathology: Inhibitions, Symptoms and Anxiety and Other Works*, ed. Angela Richards and trans. James Strachey (Harmondsworth: Penguin, 1979), pp. 227–333 (p. 240); also cited in Philip Armstrong, *Shakespeare and Psychoanalysis* (London: Routledge, 2001), p. 2.

62 In *Shakespeare and Psychoanalysis*, Philip Armstrong considers the correlation between the emergent psychologism of character studies such as those of Bradley with psychoanalysis (p. 15).

63 See, in particular, Frank Cioffi, in the introduction to *Freud: Modern Judgements*, p. 5; see also Edward Timms, 'Freud's Library and his Private Reading', in *Freud: Modern Judgements*, pp. 65–79; and Graham

Frankland, *Freud's Literary Culture* (Cambridge: Cambridge University Press, 2000).

64 Timms, 'Freud's Library and his Private Reading', p. 68.

65 Harris, *The Man Shakespeare*, p. xv.

66 Ibid., p. xvii.

67 Ibid., p. xviii.

68 Shaw, *The Dark Lady of the Sonnets*, p. 275.

69 Harris, *Bernard Shaw*, p. 269.

70 See Shaw in the postscript to Harris, *Bernard Shaw*, p. 429.

71 Harris, *Bernard Shaw*, p. 233.

72 Ibid., p. 233.

73 Frank Harris, *Oscar Wilde: His Life and Confessions*, in two volumes (New York: Frank Harris, 1916).

74 Harris, *Oscar Wilde*, p. 92.

75 Ibid., p. 93.

76 There remain conflicting accounts in the numerous biographies of Wilde as to the nature and extent of Harris' generosity. On the basis of Wilde's letters to Harris, however, it would appear that Harris' contributions, however small, were frequent. See Oscar Wilde, *The Complete Letters of Oscar Wilde*, ed. Merlin Holland and Rupert Hart-Davis (New York: Henry Holt and Company, 2000).

77 Oscar Wilde, *An Ideal Husband* (repr. London: Methuen and Co. Ltd, 1912).

78 Wilde had sold the scenario for the play to several theatre managers. When Harris learned of Wilde's deception, he withheld the remaining 150 pounds and paid off the other creditors. Described in the introduction to *Mr and Mrs Daventry* by Montgomery Hyde.

79 Mary Hyde, in *Bernard Shaw and Alfred Douglas: A Correspondence* (New Haven: Ticknor and Fields, 1982), p. xl; also noted in Merlin Holland, 'Biography and the art of lying', in *The Cambridge Companion to Oscar Wilde*, ed. Peter Raby (Cambridge: Cambridge University Press, 1977), pp. 3–17.

80 Robert Harborough Sherard, *Frank Harris, George Bernard Shaw and Oscar Wilde* (New York: Greystone Press, 1937).

81 Lord Alfred Douglas, *Oscar Wilde: A Summing-Up* [1940], with an introduction by Derek Hudson (London: The Richards Press, 1961), p. 135.

82 Douglas, *Oscar Wilde*, p. 135. Douglas' comments here were in response to Sherard's first biography, *The Life of Oscar Wilde* (London: T. Werner Laurie, 1906).

83 Wilde, *The Complete Letters of Oscar Wilde*. In letters to Harris dated March, August, and September, 1898 and May 1899.

84 Details of publication are recorded in Karl Beckson, *The Oscar Wilde Encyclopedia* (New York: AMS Press, 1998), pp. 286–91.

85 Harris, *Oscar Wilde*, p. 117.

86 *The Trials of Oscar Wilde*, ed. with an intro. by H. Montgomery Hyde (London: William Hodge and Company, Limited, 1948).

87 See Lawrence Danson, 'Oscar Wilde, W. H., and the Unspoken Name of Love', in *Oscar Wilde: A Collection of Critical Essays*, ed. Jonathan Freedman (New Jersey: Prentice Hall, 1996), pp. 81–98. Danson notes that Wilde's paradox here brilliantly challenged the very legal language of 'sodomy' and 'buggery' which otherwise criminalized such love.

88 In *The Wilde Century: Effeminacy, Oscar Wilde and the Queer Movement* (New York: Columbia, 1994), Alan Sinfield has demonstrated how Wilde's writings and trials functioned to associate nineteenth-century effeminacy and dandyism with a twentieth-century understanding of homosexuality.

89 In *The True History of Shakespeare's Sonnets* (London: Martin Secker, 1933), Alfred Douglas, taking up the Willie Hughes theory, expressed his exasperation with Wilde for writing his sonnet theory as if he were 'simply indulging in a piece of clever "leg-pulling"' (p. 34). He traced the theory to the eighteenth-century sonnet commentator Tyrwhitt, whose work was incorporated by Edmond Malone into his 1780 edition of *The Poems of Shakespeare*.

90 Oscar Wilde, 'The Portrait of Mr W. H.' [1889], in *Essays by Oscar Wilde*, ed. Hesketh Pearson (London: Methuen and Co. Ltd, 1950), pp. 189–226 (p. 226). All subsequent references to the text are to this version.

91 See the letter from Wilde, postmark 13 August 1898, in *The Complete Letters of Oscar Wilde*, pp. 1093–4.

92 As cited in Holland, 'Biography and the Art of Lying', p. 9.

93 See the references to Wilde in Michael Holroyd, *Bernard Shaw*, in three volumes from 1988 to 1991 (London: Chatto and Windus Ltd).

94 Pearsall, *Frank Harris*, p. 52.

95 In his introduction to *The Playwright and the Pirate, Bernard Shaw and Frank Harris: A Correspondence*, ed. Stanley Weintraub (University Park: The Pennsylvania State University Press, 1982), Weintraub gives an interesting account of the relationship between Harris and Shaw, particularly the years of their greatest correspondence, following their work together on the *Saturday Review*.

96 Shaw, *The Dark Lady of the Sonnets*, p. 295.

97 See, for example, John Boyd Thatcher, *Charlecote: Or The Trial of William Shakespeare* (New York: Dodd, Mead and Co., 1895); Richard Garnett, *William Shakespeare: Pedagogue and Poacher* (London: John Lane, The Bodley Head, 1904); Wilfrid Blair, *The Death of Shakespeare: A chronicle play in two scenes* (Oxford: Blackwell, 1916); and Clemence Dane, *Will Shakespeare: An Invention in Four Acts* (London: Benn Brothers, Ltd, 1921).

98 All references are made to the original text version of James Joyce, *Ulysses*, ed. and annotated Jeri Johnson (Oxford: Oxford University Press, 1993).

99 Jeri Johnson provides the framework for these two interpretations in her notes to the text of *Ulysses*, p. 834.

100 Roland Barthes, 'From Work to Text' (1971), in *Image, Music Text*, essays selected and trans. Stephen Heath (London: Fontana Press, 1977), pp. 155–64 (pp. 163–4).

101 First published in serial in the *Little Review* in April and May 1919, the episode is usually thought to have been completed in December 1918.

102 Richard Brown, '"Shakespeare Explained": James Joyce's Shakespeare from Victorian Burlesque to Post-modern Bard', in *Shakespeare and Ireland: History, Politics, Culture*, ed. Mark Thornton Burnett and Ramona Wray, pp. 91–113 (esp. p. 104).

103 William M. Schutte's seminal book, *Shakespeare and Joyce: A Study in the Meaning of Ulysses* (Yale University Press, 1957), provides the biographical backgrounds of the historical figures upon whom Joyce modeled his characters (pp. 30–51).

104 James Joyce, 'Ibsen's New Drama', first published in the *Fortnightly Review* (1 April 1900), reproduced in *The Critical Writings of James Joyce*, ed. Ellsworth Mason and Richard Ellmann (Ithaca, N.Y.: Cornell University Press, 1989), pp. 47–67 (p. 63).

105 James Joyce, 'Drama and Life', reproduced in *The Critical Writings of James Joyce*, pp. 38–46 (p. 41).

106 Joyce, 'Drama and Life', pp. 43–4.

107 Ibid., p. 39.

108 Walter Pater wrote 'A Study of Dionysus', published in 1876, which was reprinted in his *Greek Studies: A Series of Essays* (London: Charles L. Sadwell, 1895). Arthur Symons reviewed a French translation of Nietzsche's *The Birth of Tragedy* in 1902 in which he noted the similarity to Pater's discussion; reprinted in Arthur Symons, *Plays, Acting, and Music* (New York: E. P. Dutton and Co., 1903), pp. 9–12. On Nietzsche, Pater and Symons, see Patrick Bridgewater, *Nietzsche in Anglosaxony: A Study of Nietzsche's Impact on English and American Literature* (Leicester: Leicester University Press, 1972), pp. 21–36.

109 Joyce, 'Drama and Life', p. 39. On Eliot's dissociation of sensibility, see chapter 1, pp. 31–4 and 37.

110 Ibid., p. 39.

111 The notes are transcribed in William H. Quillan, *Hamlet and the New Poetic: James Joyce and T. S. Eliot* (Ann Arbor, Michigan: UMI Research Press, 1983).

112 Ibid., p. 37.

113 Richard Ellmann, *The Consciousness of Joyce* (London: Faber and Faber, 1977), includes a list of Joyce's personal library in 1920.

114 Schutte, *Joyce and Shakespeare*, categorizes all of the Shakespeare information according to Joyce's sources (pp. 153–77).

115 Brandes, *William Shakespeare*, p 32.

116 Harris, *The Man Shakespeare*, p. xiv.

117 Freud's theories on 'penis envy' and the castration complex were the basis for his numerous speculations on female sexuality, both cited periodically throughout his early psychoanalytic writing, but especially in 'Three Essays on Sexuality' [1905], in *The Standard Edition of the Complete Psychological Works of Sigmund Freud, Volume VII*, trans. James Strachey (London: The Hogarth

Press and the Institute of PsychoAnalysis, 1953), pp. 125–248; and well after the first publication of *Ulysses*, in the more comprehensive 'Female Sexuality' [1931], in *The Standard Edition of the Complete Psychological Works of Sigmund Freud, Volume XXI*, trans. James Strachey (London: The Hogarth Press and the Institute of Psycho-Analysis, 1961), pp. 225–43.

118 One of the most recent and thorough attempts to demonstrate the Freudian contexts of *Ulysses* is Jean Kimball, *Joyce and the Early Freudians* (Gainsville, Florida: University Press of Florida, 2003). Kimball relies heavily upon Julia Kristeva's concept of 'intertextuality' to explore the extent of textual relationships, which, while provocative, belabours the often thin Freudian correspondences. Luke Thurston, *James Joyce and the Problem of Psychoanalysis* (Cambridge: Cambridge University Press, 2004), responds to Kimball's use of 'intertextuality' by reading Joyce's encounter with psychoanalysis through Lacan's later encounter, all with a view to situating Joyce's broader engagement with 'questions of subjectivity, his complex interpretation and subversion of traditional literary and philosophical ways of articulating the self' (p. 10).

119 Frederick J. Hoffmann, in *Freudianism and the Literary Mind* (Louisiana: Louisiana State University Press, 1967), also asserts that internal evidence demonstrates that Joyce had read most works of Freud and many by Jung by 1922.

120 Kimball, *Joyce and the Early Freudians*, p. 3.

121 Again, see Ellmann's list in *The Consciousness of Joyce*.

122 Kimball, *Joyce and the Early Freudians*, p. 57, also suggests that Joyce would have had access to Otto Rank's 1914 *The Myth of the Birth of the Hero* with its chapters on 'Hamlet as an Incest Drama' and 'Shakespeare's Father Complex', in the Zurich public library.

123 Freud, *The Interpretation of Dreams*, p. 358.

124 Jones, 'The Oedipus Complex', p. 97.

125 Hoffmann, *Freudianism and the Literary Mind*, pp. 129–30.

126 Richard Brown, in 'Shakespeare Explained', p. 92, persuasively relates the development of Stephen as artist-figure to the corresponding stages of Joyce's intellectual development over two decades, first as early Ibsenite, then as fin-de-siècle aesthete and, finally, Shakespearean.

127 Friedrich Nietzsche, *The Birth of Tragedy*, trans. W. A. Haussmann (Edinburgh and London: T. N. Foulis, 1909).

128 Peter Holbrook, 'Nietzsche's Hamlet', *Shakespeare Survey 50* (1997), pp. 171–86 (p. 185).

129 Friedrich Nietzsche, *The Birth of Tragedy and the Genealogy of Morals*, trans. Francis Golffing (New York: Doubleday, 1956), p. 51.

130 Nietzsche, *The Birth of Tragedy*, p. 52.

131 See also Joseph Valente, 'Beyond Truth and Freedom: The New Faith of Joyce and Nietzsche', *James Joyce Quarterly* 25 (1987/8), 87–103.

132 Nietzsche, *The Birth of Tragedy*, p. 21.

3   THE THEATRE AND A CHANGING CIVILIZATION

1   Among these are Robert Hamilton Ball, 'The Shakespeare Film as Record: Sir Herbert Beerbohm Tree', *Shakespeare Quarterly* 3 (1952), 227–36; Michael Chanan, *The Dream That Kicks: The Prehistory and Early Years of Cinema in Britain* (London: Routledge, 1996), pp. 200–1; and John Collick, *Shakespeare, Cinema and Society* (Manchester: Manchester University Press, 1989), pp. 41–2. Given the obscurity of primary sources, I am indebted to secondary sources, and particularly to primary source material reproduced in Robert Hamilton Ball, *Shakespeare on Silent Film: A Strange Eventful History* (London: George Allen and Unwin Ltd, 1968).

2   Ball, *Shakespeare on Silent Film*, p. 74.

3   William Uricchio and Roberta E. Pearson, *Reframing Culture: The Case of the Vitagraph Quality Films* (Princeton: Princeton University Press, 1993), p. 69.

4   Chanan, *The Dream That Kicks*, p. 200, discusses the degree to which the 'exclusive' release and distribution of Barker's film increased its commodity value in the face of American industry dominance.

5   From the *Kinematograph and Lantern Weekly*, as cited in Ball, *Shakespeare on Silent Film*, p. 81.

6   Cited in Ball, *Shakespeare on Silent Film*, p. 79.

7   Described in Kenneth S. Rothwell, *A History of Shakespeare on Screen: A Century of Film and Television* (Cambridge: Cambridge University Press, 1999), pp. 1–3.

8   Cited in Ball, *Shakespeare on Silent Film*, p. 79.

9   Herbert Beerbohm Tree, *Thoughts and After-Thoughts* (London: Cassell and Company, Limited, 1915).

10 Herbert Beerbohm Tree, *Henry VIII and His Court* (London: Cassell and Company, Ltd, 1910).

11 Ball, *Shakespeare on Silent Film*, p. 78.

12 Cited in Ball, *Shakespeare on Silent Film*, p. 231.

13 Michael R. Booth, *Victorian Spectacular Theatre 1850–1910* (London: Routledge and Kegan Paul, 1981).

14 Rachel Low, *The History of the British Film 1906–1914* (London: George Allen and Unwin Ltd, 1949), p. 17.

15 On the censorship of Vitagraph's 1908 *Julius Caesar*, see Uricchio and Pearson, *Reframing Culture*, pp. 65–95.

16 John Drinkwater, *The Gentle Art of Theatre-Going* (London: Robert Holden and Co., 1927), p. 114.

17 The terms 'mass' and 'mass culture' used here and throughout, rather than suggest a specific class association, denote instead the reorganization of class relations in the late nineteenth and early twentieth century precipitated by the increased urbanization, industrialization and democratization of English society and its attendant effect upon the production and reception of culture. Richard Halpern writes: 'Mass culture is not the expression of

some pre-existing social group known as "the masses"; it is, rather, the sum of the conditions that *produce* the historically unprecedented phenomenon of massification and that reorganize the relations of different class cultures as they had developed during the nineteenth century.' *Shakespeare Among the Moderns* (Ithaca: Cornell University Press, 1997), p. 54.

18 Cited in William Archer and Harley Granville-Barker, *A National Theatre: Scheme and Estimates* (London: Duckworth, 1907).

19 St John Ervine, *The Organised Theatre: A Plea in Civics* (London: George Allen and Unwin, 1924), p. 57.

20 Ibid., p. 47.

21 Ibid., p. 13.

22 On the early history of the SMT in Stratford, see Sally Beauman, *The Royal Shakespeare Company: A History of Ten Decades* (Oxford: Oxford University Press, 1982), particularly pp. 68–92.

23 Edward Gordon Craig, 'A National Theatre: Its Advantages and Disadvantages, An International Symposium', *The Mask* 2 (July 1909), 81–9 (pp. 86–7).

24 Cited in Booth, *Victorian Spectacular Theatre*, p. 154.

25 Collick, *Shakespeare, Cinema and Society*, pp. 12–32, traces the history of the Victorian melodramatic tradition through to Tree's performance in Barker's film.

26 Archer and Granville-Barker, *A National Theatre* (1907), p. xviii.

27 P. P. Howe, *The Repertory Theatre: A Record and a Criticism* (London: Martin Secker, 1910), p. 24.

28 T. S. Eliot, 'London Letter', *Dial* 70/4 (April 1921), 448–53, (p. 451).

29 Antonio Gramsci, 'Theatre and Cinema' [1916], in *Selections from Cultural Writings*, ed. David Forgacs and Geoffrey Nowell-Smith, trans. William Boelhower (London: Lawrence and Wishart, 1985), pp. 54–6 (p. 55).

30 Walter Benjamin, 'The Work of Art in the Age of Mechanical Reproduction' [1936], in *Illuminations*, trans. Harry Zohn (London: Fontana Press, 1973), pp. 211–44 (pp. 212–15).

31 Ibid., p. 214.

32 Ibid., p. 218. Ultimately, Benjamin's argument was not strictly critical of mechanical reproduction, but was rather more dialectical, in one moment evoking a nostalgia for a romantic category of art, while also denying the possibility of such a category in a proletarianized or massified society. Benjamin was a socialist greatly influenced by Marx's socio-economic theory, and the implication of his argument is a critique of capitalism: that under capitalist conditions of production, the art artefact was being reduced to an endlessly reproducible, and therefore, commodified, mass culture product.

33 Raymond Williams, in *Culture and Society 1780–1950* (Harmondsworth, Middlesex: Penguin, 1958), supports this claim by suggesting that the Marxist interpretation of culture did not become effective in England until the 1930s (p. 258).

34 Henry Arthur Jones, *The Foundations of A National Drama: A Collection of Lectures, Essays and Speeches Delivered and Written in the Years 1896–1912* (London: Chapman and Hall, 1913), p. 6.

35 Mario Borsa, *The English Stage of Today*, trans. Selwyn Brinton (London: John Lane, 1908), p. 3.

36 See William Archer, 'The Case for National Theatres', in Archer and Granville-Barker, *A National Theatre* (1907), pp. 172–6 (p. 173).

37 With regard to the Fabian critique of culture, see Ian Britain, *Fabianism and Culture: A Study in British Socialism of the Arts c. 1884–1918* (Cambridge: Cambridge University Press, 1982).

38 Archer and Granville-Barker, *A National Theatre* (1907), p. xviii.

39 Drinkwater, *The Gentle Art of Theatre-Going*, p. 20.

40 Howe, *The Repertory Theatre*, p. 22.

41 Gilbert Cannan, *The Joy of the Theatre* (London: B. T. Batsford, 1913), p. 17.

42 Howe, *The Repertory Theatre*, p. 18.

43 Archer and Granville-Barker, *A National Theatre* (1907), p. xviii.

44 Harley Granville-Barker, 'Two German Theatres', *Fortnightly Review* 89 (1911), 60–70 (p. 61).

45 Harley Granville-Barker, *A National Theatre* (London: Sidgwick and Jackson, 1938), p. 27.

46 Loren Kruger, *The National Stage: Theatre and Cultural Legitimation in England, France, and America* (Chicago: The University of Chicago Press, 1992), p. 83.

47 Archer and Granville-Barker, *A National Theatre* (1907), p. 12.

48 Archer, 'The Case for National Theatres', p. 172.

49 Jones, *The Foundations of a National Drama*, p. 4.

50 Howe, *The Repertory Theatre*, p. 25.

51 Thomas H. Dickinson, *The Contemporary Drama of England* (London: John Murray, 1920), p. 206.

52 Tree, *Thoughts and After-Thoughts*, p. 4.

53 Ibid., pp. 46–7.

54 Ibid., p. 49.

55 Benjamin, 'The Work of Art in the Age of Mechanical Reproduction', p. 212.

56 Richard Decordova, 'From Lumière to Pathé: The Break-Up of Perspectival Space', in *Early Cinema: Space Frame Narrative*, ed. Thomas Elsaesser with Adam Barker (London: British Film Institute Publishing, 1990), pp. 76–85 (p. 76).

57 Craig's accompanying commentary is reproduced in Edward Gordon Craig, *Craig on Theatre*, ed. J. Michael Walton (London: Methuen, 1983), pp. 108–15.

58 Peter Brook, in 'The Influence of Gordon Craig in Theory and Practice', *Drama* 5/37 (1955), 32–7 (p. 33), has suggested that the measure of Craig's influence requires a separation between his theory and practice, between the large volume of prescriptive writing on the art of the theatre to which Craig

devoted most of his career and his relatively limited practical work in the English theatre. Peter Holland has also treated the issue of Craig's influence in his introduction to the 1981 reissue of Edward Gordon Craig's 1957 autobiography, *Index to the Story of my Days* (Cambridge: Cambridge University Press).

59 Michel Foucault, in *The Archaeology of Knowledge*, trans. A. M. Sheridan Smith (London: Routledge, 1972), reads influence as a casual rather than rigorously theorized concept which gives a special temporal status to a group of phenomena in the terms of succession, similarity, resemblance, and repetition, all of which link 'at a distance and through time – as if through the mediation of a medium of propagation – such defined unities as individuals, oeuvres, notions, or theories' (p. 21).

60 Edward Gordon Craig, *On the Art of the Theatre* (London: Heinemann, 1911) was expanded from an earlier dialogue titled *The Art of the Theatre* (Edinburgh and Co., 1905); *The Theatre – Advancing* was first published in 1919, but reissued as *The Theatre Advancing* in 1921 (London: Constable). Most of the articles in these volumes had been published earlier in Craig's periodical *The Mask* which was published on and off between 1908 and 1929.

61 Edward Gordon Craig, *Henry Irving* (London: J. M. Dent and Sons Ltd, 1930).

62 Cited in Edward Craig, *Gordon Craig: The Story of his Life* (London: Victor Gollancz, 1968), p. 123.

63 Craig, *Index to the Story of My Days*, p. 213.

64 James Huneker, cited in Edward Craig, *Gordon Craig*, p. 173.

65 For accounts of the production, see Edward Craig, *Gordon Craig*, pp. 175–7; and Christopher Innes, *Edward Gordon Craig: Directors in Perspective Series* (Cambridge: Cambridge University Press, 1983), pp. 97–100.

66 Cited in Edward Craig, *Gordon Craig*, p. 176.

67 Ibid., p. 177.

68 See Edward Gordon Craig's biography of *Ellen Terry and Her Secret Self* (London: Sampson Low, Marston and Co., Ltd, 1931).

69 Craig, *Index to the Story of My Days*, p. 213.

70 Harley Granville-Barker, 'The Heritage of the Actor', *The Quarterly Review* 240/276 (July 1923), 53–73 (p. 67).

71 Edward Gordon Craig, 'The Actor and the Über-Marionette' [1907], in *On the Art of the Theatre*, pp. 54–94 (p. 81).

72 Edward Gordon Craig, 'The Artists of the Theatre of the Future' [1908], in *On the Art of the Theatre*, pp. 1–53 (p. 27).

73 Cited in Amy Koritz, *Gendering Bodies / Performing Art: Dance and Literature in Early Twentieth-Century British Culture* (Ann Arbor: University of Michigan Press, 1995), p. 125.

74 Craig, 'The Actor and the Über-marionette', p. 82.

75 See Heinrich von Kleist, 'On the Marionette Theatre' [Über Das Marionettentheater, 1810], in *Hand to Mouth and Other Essays*, ed. Idris Parry (Manchester: Carcanet New Press, 1981), pp. 13–18.

76 Ibid., p. 18.
77 Edward Gordon Craig, 'Sada Yacco' [1910], in *The Theatre Advancing* (New York: Benjamin Blom, 1963), pp. 261–6 (p. 261).
78 Granville-Barker, 'The Heritage of the Actor', p. 66.
79 See Chapter 1, esp. pp. 27–8.
80 Edward Gordon Craig, 'Symbolism' [1911], in *On the Art of the Theatre*, pp. 293–4 (p. 293).
81 Olga Taxidou lists the issues in which Nietzsche was quoted or which made reference to Nietzsche's writing, in *The Mask: A Periodical Performance by Edward Gordon Craig* (Amsterdam: Harwood Academic Publishers, 1998), p. 26 (n. 7). Taxidou also makes the link between Pater, Symons, Nietzsche and Wagner, demonstrating how the mimetic in representation was displaced in this brand of aesthetic idealism, the symbol becoming a cognitive strategy explaining rather than representing reality.
82 Julian Young, *Nietzsche's Philosophy of Art* (Cambridge: Cambridge University Press, 1993), pp. 66–70.
83 Repr. in Walter Pater, *Greek Studies: A Series of Essays* (London: Charles L. Sadwell, 1895).
84 Repr. in Arthur Symons, *Plays, Acting, and Music* (New York: E. P. Dutton and Co., 1903), pp. 9–12; on Nietzsche, Pater and Symons, see Patrick Bridgewater, *Nietzsche in Anglosaxony: a Study of Nietzsche's Impact on English and American Literature* (Leicester: Leicester University Press, 1972), pp. 21–36.
85 This argument is made of Craig's contemporaries, though not of Craig, by Bridgewater, *Nietzsche in Anglosaxony*, pp. 17–20.
86 Edward Gordon Craig, 'Some Evil Tendencies of the Modern Theatre' [1908], in *On the Art of the Theatre*, pp. 95–111 (p. 111).
87 Friedrich Nietzsche, *The Birth of Tragedy and The Genealogy of Morals*, trans. Francis Golffing (New York: Doubleday and Company, 1956), pp. 36–42.
88 Young, *Nietzsche's Philosophy of Art*, p. 36.
89 Edward Gordon Craig [John Semar], 'Psychology and the Drama', *The Mask* 2 (1909/10), 163–4.
90 Craig, 'The Artists of the Theatre of the Future', p. 21.
91 Edward Craig, *Gordon Craig*, p. 337.
92 Craig, 'The Artists of the Theatre of the Future', p. 31.
93 From the letters of George Bernard Shaw, cited in James Fisher, '"The Colossus" Versus "Master Teddy": the Bernard Shaw/Edward Gordon Craig Feud', in *Shaw Offstage: The Nondramatic Writings*, ed. Fred D. Crawford (The Pennsylvania State University Press, 1989), pp. 199–221 (p. 206).
94 Edward Gordon Craig, 'The Art of the Theatre. The First Dialogue' [1905], in *On the Art of the Theatre*, pp. 137–81 (pp. 140–3).
95 Edward Gordon Craig, 'A Durable Theatre' [1921], in *The Theatre Advancing*, pp. 11–23 (p. 11).

96 Edward Gordon Craig [C. G. Smith], 'Cambridge University and its Ban on Actresses', *The Mask* 4 (1911), 41–2 (p. 41).

97 Craig, 'The Actor and the Über-Marionette', p. 94.

98 From *Scene* [1923], cited in Walton, *Craig on Theatre*, p. 123.

99 Ibid., p. 129.

100 Edward Craig, *Gordon Craig*, p. 254.

101 William Shakespeare, *The tragedie of Hamlet prince of Denmarke* (Weimar: Printed by Count Harry Kessler at the Cranach Press, 1930).

102 Edward Craig, *Gordon Craig*, pp. 267–75; for a full account of the production, see also Laurence Senelick, *Gordon Craig's Moscow Hamlet: A Reconstruction* (Westport, Conn: Greenwood Press, 1982).

103 Theodore Komisarjevsky, *The Theatre and a Changing Civilisation* (London: John Lane The Bodley Head, 1935), p. x.

104 From the title of J. L. Styan's *The Shakespeare Revolution: Criticism and Performance in the Twentieth Century* (Cambridge: Cambridge University Press, 1977). Recent noteworthy discussions of Komisarjevsky's productions include Sally Beauman, *The Royal Shakespeare Company*; Ralph Berry, 'Komisarjevsky at Stratford-upon-Avon', *Shakespeare Survey 36* (1982), pp. 72–84; Susan Brock and Marion Pringle, *The Shakespeare Memorial Theatre 1919–1945* (Cambridge: Chadwyck-Healey, 1984); and Dennis Kennedy, *Looking at Shakespeare: A Visual History of Twentieth-Century Performance*, second edn (Cambridge: Cambridge University Press, 2001). Both Berry and Kennedy in particular have noted that Komisarjevsky's unconventional and eclectic approach to staging Shakespeare anticipated the later English productions of the 1960s and 1970s.

105 Komisarjevsky, *The Theatre and a Changing Civilisation*, p. x.

106 Beauman, *The Royal Shakespeare Company*, p. 110.

107 Brock, *The Shakespeare Memorial Theatre*, p. 45.

108 See Victor Borovsky's family biography, *A Triptych from the Russian Theatre: An Artistic Biography of the Komissarzhevsky Family* (University of Iowa Press, 2001).

109 The accounts of his flight from Russia and subsequent travels are recorded in his 1929 autobiography, *Myself and the Theatre* (London: William Heinemann Limited, 1929).

110 For a detailed account of the production, see Richard E. Mennen, 'Theodore Komisarjevsky's Production of *The Merchant of Venice*', *Theatre Journal* 31 (1979), 386–97.

111 Cited in Beauman, *The Royal Shakespeare Company*, p. 132.

112 *The Times*, cited in Beauman, *The Royal Shakespeare Company*, p. 131.

113 Komisarjevsky, *Myself and the Theatre*, p. 190.

114 Beauman, *The Royal Shakespeare Company*, p. 147.

115 Koltai's designs for the Royal Shakespeare Company's 1982 *Much Ado About Nothing* (again directed by Hands) of painted flying block screens and for the National Theatre's 1967 *As You Like It* (directed by Clifford Williams) of gigantic light-reflecting plastic tubes also suggest immediate influences from Craig and Granville-Barker.

116 Peter Brook, *The Empty Space* (London: MacGibbon and Kee, 1968).
117 Komisarjevsky, *Myself and the Theatre*, p. 108.
118 David Graver makes the distinction between collage and montage and discusses the use of montage in the theatre in *The Aesthetics of Disturbance: Anti-Art in Avant-Garde Drama* (Ann Arbor: The University of Michigan Press, 1995), p. 31.
119 Theodore Komisarjevsky, *The Costume of the Theatre* (1932; repr. New York: Benjamin Blom, 1968). Also of note is his *Settings and Costumes of the Modern Stage*, jointly authored with Lee Simonson (London: The Studio, Limited, 1933).
120 Theodore Komisarjevsky, 'From Naturalism to Stage Design', in R. D. Charques, *Footnotes to the Theatre* (London: Peter Davies, 1938), pp. 77–101 (p. 92).
121 Komisarjevsky, 'From Naturalism to Stage Design', p. 90.
122 Ernestine Stodelle Komisarjevsky in the introduction to Catherine J. Johnson, *The Stage Art of Theodore Komisarjevsky: An Exhibition in the Harvard Theatre Collection* (Cambridge, Mass: Harvard Theatre Collection, Harvard College Library, 1991).
123 Komisarjevsky, 'From Naturalism to Stage Design', p 82.
124 Kennedy, *Looking at Shakespeare*, p. 127, also traces Komisarjevsky's 'synthetic' principle back to Craig.
125 Komisarjevsky, *The Theatre and a Changing Civilisation*, p. 12.
126 Komisarjevsky, *Myself and the Theatre*, p. 63.
127 Komisarjevsky, *The Theatre and a Changing Civilisation*, p 136.
128 Komisarjevsky, *The Costume of the Theatre*, p. 169.
129 On workers' theatre movements, see *Theatres of the Left 1880–1935: Workers' Theatre Movements in Britain and America*, ed. Raphael Samuel, Ewan MacColl and Stuart Cosgrove (London: Routledge and Kegan Paul, 1985).
130 Komisarjevsky, *The Costume of the Theatre*, p. 2.
131 A distinction here between modernism and the avant-garde is perhaps necessary. Peter Bürger, for example, in his seminal *Theory of the Avant-Garde*, trans. Michael Shaw (Manchester: Manchester University Press, 1984), defines modernism as an attempt to separate art from traditional modes of artistic production in order to inscribe a status of aesthetic autonomy. The avant-garde, in contrast, is seen to actualize a genuine disruption from the 'praxis of life' by lashing out against art's institutional status. The avant-garde artwork is thus radically political, disrupting its status as a work of art – an anti-art art. The notion of an anti-institutional art is obviously problematic in the case of the theatre, and acutely for Komisarjevsky given his commercial success. In *The Politics of Modernism: Against the New Conformists* (London: Verso, 1989), Raymond Williams, in contrast, though he is careful to note the difference between modernism's experimentation and the avant-garde's more oppositional orientation, reads this distinction in terms of degrees of extremity, noting instead the ideological continuity between various aestheticisms. Williams' more fluid

definition thus precludes an unnecessarily complicated distinction between the two.

132 In his discussion of the relationship between fascism and modernism in *Fascist Modernism: Aesthetics, Politics and the Avant-Garde* (California: Stanford University Press, 1993), Andrew Hewitt has suggested that, insofar as the various avant-garde movements experience the aesthetic as an alternative to the political realm, 'this alternative begins to present itself as a *political* alternative, and a politics emerges that draws its strength directly from a lack of concern for traditional pragmatics' (6).

133 Komisarjevsky, *The Theatre and a Changing Civilisation*, p. x.

134 Ibid., p. 7.

135 Ibid., p. 13.

136 Benjamin, 'The Work of Art in the Age of Mechanical Reproduction', p. 212.

137 Georg Lukács, 'Expressionism: Its Significance and Decline' [1934], in *Essays on Realism*, ed. Rodney Livingstone, trans. David Fernbach (London: Lawrence and Wishart, 1980), pp. 76–103.

138 Lukács, 'Expressionism', p. 92.

139 Later Marxists have continued to perpetuate the general premise of Lukács' theory, primarily the anti-middle-classness or anti-bourgeois orientation basis of the various avant-garde movements leading to an identification with political extremism. In *The Politics of Modernism*, Raymond Williams in particular has demonstrated the right/left ambivalence of that political identification: after closely comparable denunciations of the bourgeoisie among modernist artists, he argues that their otherwise radically different positions 'would lead eventually both theoretically and under the pressure of actual political crisis, not only to different but to directly opposed kinds of politics: to Fascism or to Communism; to social democracy or to conservatism and the cult of excellence' (55).

140 Komisarjevsky, *The Costume of the Theatre*, p. 165.

141 Ibid., p. 165.

142 Ibid., p. 164.

143 Komisarjevsky, *The Theatre and a Changing Civilisation*, p. 12.

144 Ibid., p. xiv.

145 Lukács, 'Expressionism', pp. 105–7.

146 Komisarjevsky, 'From Naturalism to Stage Design', p. 98.

147 Komisarjevsky, *The Theatre and a Changing Civilisation*, p. 16.

4 SHAKESPEARE'S TEXT IN PERFORMANCE, CIRCA 1923

1 If the idea of isolating a single moment or year to note a significant juncture in the genealogy of Shakespeare's texts sounds familiar, then acknowledgement must be given to Margreta De Grazia's seminal work *Shakespeare Verbatim: The Reproduction of Authenticity and the 1790 Apparatus* (Oxford: Clarendon Press, 1991) in which she notes 1790 as the year in which Edmond

222   *Notes to pages 138–42*

Malone produced his edition of *The Plays and Poems of Shakespeare*. De Grazia identifies this as the 1790 apparatus, the mechanism/event which transformed the cultural status of Shakespeare's texts after that year. Despite her thorough analysis and persuasive argument, De Grazia's methodology has been criticized for overstating the significance of Malone. See, for example, Andrew Murphy, in 'Texts and Textualities: A Shakespearean History', in Andrew Murphy (ed.), *The Renaissance Text: Theory, Editing, Textuality*, (Manchester: Manchester University Press, 2000), pp. 191–210.

2 Alfred W. Pollard, *The Foundations of Shakespeare's Texts*, The Annual Shakespeare Lecture (London: Oxford University Press, 1923), p. 3.

3 Based on six lectures on the Folio given at King's College in 1923 and later published under the title, *Studies in the First Folio*, The Shakespeare Association in Celebration of the First Folio Tercentenary (London: Oxford University Press, 1924).

4 R. Crompton Rhodes, *Shakespeare's First Folio* (Oxford: Basil Blackwell, 1923).

5 Alfred W. Pollard, *Shakespeare's Folios and Quartos: A Study in the Bibliography of Shakespeare* (London: Methuen and Co., 1909).

6 See, in particular, the essays first published in periodicals such as *Egoist* and *Athenaeum* between the years 1917 and 1920 and collected in T. S. Eliot, *The Sacred Wood: Essays on Poetry and Criticism* (1920; repr. London: Methuen and Co., 1934).

7 E. K. Chambers, 'The Disintegration of Shakespeare' [1924], in J. W. Mackail (ed.), *Aspects of Shakespeare, Being British Academy Lectures (1923–1931)* (Oxford: Clarendon Press, 1933), pp. 23–48; J. M. Robertson, *The Shakespeare Canon*, 5 vols. (London: Routledge, 1922–32); see also T. S. Eliot's summary of Robertson's *The Problem of 'Hamlet'* (London: G. Allen and Unwin, 1919) and E. E. Stoll's *Hamlet: an Historical and Comparative Study* (Minneapolis: University of Minnesota, 1919) in *The Sacred Wood*, pp. 95–103.

8 Laurie E. Maguire, in *Shakespearean Suspect Texts: The 'bad' quartos and their contexts* (Cambridge: Cambridge University Press, 1996), notes, however, that while the New Bibliographers introduced a twentieth-century scientific approach to textual analysis, their methodologies were mixed with nineteenth-century presuppositions about authors and texts, the result of which was a combination of material analysis and textual interpretation, the certainty of attitude appropriate to the former being transferred to the latter: 'Wherever one looks,' she argues, 'New Bibliography thus strains against science' (p. 37).

9 Alfred W. Pollard, *Shakespeare's Hand in the play of Sir Thomas More* (Cambridge: Cambridge University Press, 1923).

10 Ibid., pp. 6–11.

11 The 'text' has become an increasingly problematic concept since, most notably, Roland Barthes differentiated the 'text' from the 'work' of the author; the 'work' to mean the immaterial ideal which (the equally immaterial

concept of) the 'author' is thought to have produced, versus the 'text' which is thought to represent the 'work'. See Roland Barthes, 'From Work to Text' [1971], in *Image, Music Text*, sel. and trans. Stephen Heath (London: Fontana Press, 1977), pp. 155–64; and 'The Death of the Author' [1968], in above, pp. 142–8. More recently, W. B. Worthen, in *Shakespeare and the Authority of Performance* (Cambridge: Cambridge University Press, 1997), has suggested how different concepts of the text (text as work, text as textuality, and text as a material object in history) have become compacted post-Barthes in the widespread application of 'textuality' to reading. Worthen also notes how editorial critics often invoke the notion of performance to characterize the relationship between works and texts.

12 The materiality of the text versus an essential idea of Shakespeare is a concept which De Grazia employs in 'The Essential Shakespeare and the Material Book', *Textual Practice* 2 (1988), 69–86. She suggests that the studies of the New Bibliography were only partially removed from the more impressionistic styles of eighteenth and nineteenth-century criticism and editing insofar as the author was revealed to be hidden underneath and redeemed from the physical text. Murphy, 'Texts and Textualities', has also noted 'the deep ironies of the materialism espoused by the New Bibliographic movement' (p. 205).

13 Regarding the history of the various committees associated with the commemoration of Shakespeare and the establishment of permanent Shakespeare and National Theatres, see Sally Beauman, *The Royal Shakespeare Company: A History of Ten Decades* (Oxford: Oxford University Press, 1982); and Janet Minihan, *The Nationalization of Culture: The Development of State Subsidies to the Arts in Great Britain* (London: Hamish Hamilton, 1977).

14 Harold M. Otness, *The Shakespeare Folio Handbook and Census* (New York: Greenwood Press, 1990), pp. 18–23.

15 William Shakespeare, *Shakespeare's Comedies, Histories and Tragedies, Containing a Census of Extant Copies with Some Account of their History and Condition*, supplemented by Sir Sidney Lee (Oxford: Clarendon Press, 1902); updated in Sir Sidney Lee, 'A Survey of First Folios', in *Studies in the First Folio*, pp. 78–105.

16 Otness, *The Shakespeare Folio Handbook and Census*, p. 21.

17 Ibid., pp. 13–14. The most recent catalogue of Shakespeare editions and facsimile reproductions is Andrew Murphy's impressively comprehensive *Shakespeare in Print: A History and Chronology of Shakespeare Publishing* (Cambridge: Cambridge University Press, 2003).

18 Andrew Murphy, in *Shakespeare in Print*, notes that this growth of a mass market for editions of Shakespeare, in addition to nineteenth-century educational reforms, was partly due to the growth of a domestic reading culture in Victorian England (p. 179). Murphy also notes the simultaneous growth of an edition market in America, resulting in a significant cross-Atlantic trade.

19 Randall McLeod, in 'UN *editing* Shak-speare,' in *Shakespeare and the Editorial Tradition*, ed. Stephen Orgel and Sean Keilen (New York: Garland

Publishing, 1999), pp. 60–90, calls this a process of 'unediting': 'For us to witness the vast difference between the evidence of text conveyed by photofacsimiles and what stands revealed as editorial rumours and irrelevant improvements of it, is immediately to unedit Shakespeare' (p. 71).

20 Murphy, in '"Came errour here by mysse of man": Editing and the Metaphysics of Presence', *The Yearbook of English Studies* 29 (1999), pp. 118–37 (p. 132), notes the repeated occurrence of this phrase, especially by Fredson Bowers.

21 Ronald B. McKerrow, *Prolegomena to the Oxford Shakespeare: A Study in Editorial Method* (Oxford: Clarendon Press, 1939), p 6.

22 As photographically reproduced, for example, in William Shakespeare, *The First Folio 1623*, a photo-lithographic facsimile under the superintendence of Howard Staunton (London: Day and Son, 1866), p. A3.

23 Shakespeare, *The Plays and Poems of William Shakespeare*, ed. Malone, p. ix.

24 Pollard, *Shakespeare's Folios and Quartos*, p. 80.

25 Pollard, *The Foundations of Shakespeare's Texts*, p 4.

26 A. W. Pollard and J. Dover Wilson, 'The "Stolne and Surreptitious" Shakespearian Texts' for the *Times Literary Supplement* in 1919 (9, 16 January, 13 March, 7, 14 August).

27 Alfred W. Pollard, *Shakespeare's Fight with the Pirates and the Problems of the Transmission of his Text* (Cambridge: Cambridge University Press, 1917).

28 Chambers, 'The Disintegration of Shakespeare,' p. 42.

29 W. W. Greg, *The Editorial Problem in Shakespeare: A Survey of the Foundations of the Text* (Oxford: Clarendon Press, 1942), p. 42.

30 Cited in W. W. Greg, *The Shakespeare First Folio: Its Bibliographical and Textual History* (Oxford: Clarendon Press, 1955), p. 102.

31 McKerrow, *Prolegomena to the Oxford Shakespeare*, p. 6.

32 J. Dover Wilson, 'The Task of Heminge and Condell', in *Studies in the First Folio*, pp. 53–77 (p. 61).

33 In the General Introduction to *The Tempest*, ed. Arthur Quiller-Couch and J. Dover Wilson (Cambridge: Cambridge University Press, 1921), p. ix.

34 Sir Sidney Lee, 'Shakespeare', in *This Year's Work in English Studies, Volume II 1920–1*, ed. for the English Association by Sir Sidney Lee and F. S. Boas (London: Oxford University Press, 1922), pp. 66–80 (pp. 68–71).

35 Dover Wilson in the Textual Introduction to *The Tempest*, pp. xxxvii–xxxviii.

36 Lee, 'Shakespeare', p. 70.

37 Ibid., p. 68.

38 William Shakespeare, *The Players' Shakespeare* (London: Ernst Benn Ltd), in seven volumes including *The Tragedie of Macbeth* (1923), *The Merchant of Venice* (1923), *The Tragedie of Cymbeline* (1923), *Loves Labour's Lost* (1924), *A Midsommer Nights Dreame* (1924), *The Tragedie of Julius Caesar* (1925), and *The Tragedie of King Lear* (1927).

39 Harley Granville-Barker, 'General Introduction', in *The Tragedie of Macbeth*, p. ix.

40 Harley Granville-Barker, *Prefaces to Shakespeare*, 5 vols. (London: Sidgwick and Jackson, 1927–1948).

41 Dennis Kennedy, in *Granville Barker and the Dream of the Theatre* (Cambridge: Cambridge University Press, 1985), suggests the opposite, that the drawings in the series are 'book illustrations rather than set and costume designs' (p. 154), a point which perhaps demonstrates the impressive beauty of the volumes as commemorative editions.

42 From the 'Publisher's Advertisement', in *The Players' Shakespeare*.

43 William Shakespeare, *Macbeth*, ed. Henry Cuningham (London: Methuen, 1912).

44 De Grazia, *Shakespeare Verbatim*, p. 16.

45 Granville-Barker, 'General Introduction', in *The Tragedie of Macbeth*, p. xxiv.

46 Ibid., p. xvii.

47 Arthur Reed, 'Shakespeare', in *This Year's Work in English Studies, Volume IV 1923*, ed. for the English Association by Sir Sidney Lee and F. S. Boas (London: Oxford University Press, 1924), pp. 74–92 (p. 83).

48 Granville-Barker, 'General Introduction', in *The Tragedie of Macbeth*, p. ix.

49 See, for example, Marvin and Ruth Thompson, 'Performance Criticism from Granville-Barker to Bernard Beckerman and Beyond', in Marvin and Ruth Thompson (eds.), *Shakespeare and the Sense of Performance: Essays in the Tradition of Performance Criticism in Honour of Bernard Beckerman* (Newark: University of Delaware Press, 1989). In *The Shakespeare Revolution: Criticism and Performance in the Twentieth Century* (Cambridge: Cambridge University Press, 1977), J. L. Styan also gives credit to the stage-centred criticism of Poel, Granville-Barker's immediate predecessor (pp. 65–81).

50 Harley Granville-Barker, 'Some Tasks for Dramatic Scholarship', originally a lecture read on 7 June 1922 and later published in *Essays by Divers Hands* 3 (London: Oxford University Press, 1923), pp. 17–38.

51 Ibid., p. 33.

52 Ibid., p. 29.

53 Discussing the idealization of Shakespeare as author, De Grazia, in 'The Essential Shakespeare and the Material Book', turns to Michel Foucault's author function. For Foucault, 'What is an Author?', in Josué V. Harari (ed.), *Textual Strategies: Perspectives in Post-Structuralist Criticism* (London: Methuen, 1979), pp. 141–60, conceiving of the author as preceding the text in a causal relationship requires the creation and projection of an author figure, a projection which serves a classificatory function: 'Such a name permits one to group together a certain number of texts, define them, differentiate them from and contrast them to others. In addition, it establishes a relationship among the texts' (p. 147). Foucault's argument thus establishes the author function as a context for discussing the construction of canonicity.

54 Thorough accounts of Granville-Barker's Shakespeare productions can be found in Dennis Kennedy's *Granville Barker and the Dream of the Theatre* and *Looking at Shakespeare*; and Cary M. Mazer, *Shakespeare Refashioned: Elizabethan Plays on Edwardian Stages* (Ann Arbor: UMI Research Press, 1981).

55 Kennedy, *Looking at Shakespeare*, pp. 73–4.

56 See Simon Williams, *Shakespeare on the German Stage, Vol. I: 1586–1914* (Cambridge: Cambridge University Press, 1990), pp. 172–94; and Styan, *The Shakespeare Revolution*, p. 48.

57 In 1913, William Poel published a full volume, *Shakespeare in the Theatre* (London: Sidgwick and Jackson), which reproduced articles about theatrical practice he had previously written for journals such as *Era* and the *New Age*, and which summarized the principles behind his productions for the Elizabethan Stage Society.

58 Harley Granville-Barker, 'The Heritage of the Actor', *The Quarterly Review* 240/76 (July 1923), 53–73 (p. 53).

59 Ibid., p. 59.

60 Claire Cochrane provides a detailed account of these productions in *Shakespeare and the Birmingham Repertory Theatre 1913–1919* (London: The Society for Theatre Research, 1993), pp. 120–47.

61 Cited in Kennedy, *Looking at Shakespeare*, p. 110.

62 Cited in Cochrane, *Shakespeare and the Birmingham Repertory Theatre*, p. 105.

63 Cochrane, *Shakespeare and the Birmingham Repertory Theatre*, p. 114.

64 Cited in Cochrane, *Shakespeare and the Birmingham Repertory Theatre*, p. 118.

65 Harley Granville–Barker, 'The Theatre: The Next Phase', in *The English Review* 5 (April–July 1910), 631–48 (p. 641).

66 William Archer and Harley Granville-Barker, *A National Theatre: Scheme and Estimates* (London: Duckworth, 1907); Granville-Barker revised and rewrote the scheme after Archer's death, and published it under the title *A National Theatre* (London: Sidgwick and Jackson, 1938).

67 Harley Granville-Barker, *The Exemplary Theatre* (London: Chatto and Windus, 1922), p. 6.

68 Ibid., p. 11.

69 Granville-Barker, 'Some Tasks for Dramatic Scholarship', p. 29.

70 Harley Granville-Barker, 'Shakespeare's Dramatic Art', in Harley Granville-Barker and G. B. Harrison (eds.), *A Companion to Shakespeare Studies* (Cambridge: Cambridge University Press, 1934), pp. 45–87 (p. 83).

71 Harley Granville-Barker, *Associating with Shakespeare*, an address delivered at King's College, London, on November 25, 1931 (London: Oxford University Press, 1932), p. 15.

72 Granville-Barker, 'General Introduction', in *The Tragedie of Macbeth*, p. xx.

5   HOW MANY CHILDREN HAD VIRGINIA WOOLF?

1 L. C. Knights, *How Many Children Had Lady Macbeth?: An Essay in the Theory and Practice of Shakespeare Criticism* (Cambridge: The Minority Press, 1933), p. 64.

2 *How Many Children Had Lady Macbeth?*, p. 5; A. C. Bradley, *Shakespearean Tragedy: Lectures on Hamlet, Othello, King Lear, Macbeth* (London: MacMillan, 1904).

3 Ibid., p. 489.

4 Ellen Terry, *Four Lectures on Shakespeare*, ed. with an introduction by Christopher St John (London: Martin Hopkinson Ltd, 1932).

5 Knights, *How Many Children Had Lady Macbeth?*, p. 3.

6 Ibid., p. 4.

7 Cited in the introduction by Christopher St John, *Four Lectures on Shakespeare*, p. 13.

8 Terry, *Four Lectures on Shakespeare*, p. 80.

9 Amanda Hopkinson, *Julia Margaret Cameron* (London: Virago Press, 1986), pp. 35–7.

10 Julia Margaret Cameron, *Victorian Photographs of Famous Men and Fair Women by Julia Margaret Cameron*, ed. Tristram Powell (London: The Hogarth Press, 1973).

11 Virginia Woolf, diary entry dated 30 January 1919, *The Diary of Virginia Woolf, Volume I: 1915–1919*, ed. Anne Oliver Bell (London: The Hogarth Press, 1977), p. 237.

12 Hopkinson, *Julia Margaret Cameron*, p. 1.

13 Roger Fry, 'Mrs Cameron's Photographs', in *Victorian Photographs of Famous Men and Fair Women*, pp. 23–8 (p. 24).

14 Virginia Woolf, *A Change of Perspective: The Letters of Virginia Woolf, Volume III: 1923–1928* (London: The Hogarth Press, 1977), p. 75.

15 Ellen Terry, *Ellen Terry and Bernard Shaw: A Correspondence*, ed. Christopher St John (New York: G. P. Putnam's Sons, 1931); Edward Gordon Craig, *Ellen Terry and Her Secret Self* (London: Sampson Low, Marston and Co., Ltd, 1931).

16 Christopher St John, cited in the introduction to Ellen Terry, *Ellen Terry's Memoirs*, with notes by Edith Craig and Christopher St John (London: Martin Hopkinson Ltd, 1932), p. v.

17 Harold L. Smith, *The British Women's Suffrage Campaign 1866–1928* (London: Longman, 1998), p. 81.

18 Les Garner, *Stepping Stones to Women's Freedom: Feminist ideas in the woman's suffrage movement 1900–1918* (London: Heinemann Educational Books, 1984), p. 110.

19 Lucio P. Ruotolo provides a detailed summary of what is known about the performance in the Editor's Preface to Virginia Woolf, *Freshwater: A Comedy*, ed. Lucio P. Ruotolo (London: The Hogarth Press, 1976). All subsequent references to the text will be made from this edition.

20 Virginia Woolf, *'A Room of One's Own' and 'Three Guineas'*, ed. Morag Shiach (Oxford: Oxford University Press, 1992), pp. 128–9.

21 Elaine Showalter, *A Literature of Their Own: British Women Novelists from Brontë to Lessing* (Princeton, N.J.: Princeton University Press, 1977), p. 282.

22 Ibid., p. 283.

23 Jane Marcus, 'Thinking Back Through Our Mothers', in *New Feminist Essays on Virginia Woolf*, ed. Jane Marcus (Lincoln: University of Nebraska Press, 1981), pp. 1–30; see also Jane Marcus, *Virginia Woolf and the Languages of Patriarchy* (Bloomington: Indiana University Press, 1987).

24 Marcus, 'Thinking Back Through Our Mothers', p. 9.

25 Harold Bloom, *The Anxiety of Influence: A Theory of Poetry* (Oxford: Oxford University Press, 1973), p. 11.
26 Sandra M. Gilbert and Susan Gubar, *No Man's Land: The Place of the Woman Writer in the Twentieth Century, Volume 1: The War of Words* (New Haven: Yale University Press, 1988), pp. 155–6.
27 Sandra M. Gilbert and Susan Gubar, *The Madwoman in the Attic: The Woman Writer and the Nineteenth-Century Literary Imagination* (New Haven: Yale University Press, 1979), p. 6.
28 Gilbert and Gubar, *No Man's Land, Vol. I*, p. 162.
29 Woolf, *A Room of One's Own*, p. 100.
30 Ibid., pp. 73–4.
31 Beth C. Schwartz, 'Thinking Back Through Our Mothers: Virginia Woolf Reads Shakespeare', *ELH* 58/3 (1991), 721–46 (pp. 721–2).
32 Virginia Woolf, '"Anon" and "The Reader": Virginia Woolf's Last Essays', ed. Brenda R. Silver, *Twentieth Century Literature* 25/5, 356–441 (p. 397).
33 Ibid., p. 382.
34 Schwartz, 'Thinking Back Through Our Mothers', p. 729.
35 Sigmund Freud, 'Female Sexuality' [1931], in *The Standard Edition of the Complete Psychological Works of Sigmund Freud, Volume XXI*, trans. James Strachey (London: The Hogarth Press and the Institute of Psycho-Analysis, 1961), pp. 225–43.
36 Ibid., p. 229.
37 Ibid., pp. 229–30.
38 Ibid., p. 230n.
39 See, for instance, Sigmund Freud, 'Three Essays on Sexuality' [1905], in *The Standard Edition of the Complete Psychological Works of Sigmund Freud, Volume VII*, trans. James Strachey (London: The Hogarth Press and the Institute of Psycho-Analysis, 1953), pp. 125–248.
40 Sigmund Freud, 'On Transformations of Instinct as Exemplified in Anal Erotism' [1917], in *The Standard Edition of the Complete Psychological Works of Sigmund Freud, Volume XVII*, trans. James Strachey (London: The Hogarth Press and the Institute of Psycho-Analysis, 1955), pp. 125–33 (p. 129).
41 Showalter, *A Literature of Their Own*, p. 264.
42 Woolf, *A Room of One's Own*, pp. 128–9.
43 Ibid., p 130.
44 Ibid., p. 73.
45 Ibid., p. 5.
46 All references to the text are made from Virginia Woolf, *Orlando: A Biography* (London: The Hogarth Press, 1928).
47 Sandra M. Gilbert and Susan Gubar, *No Man's Land: The Place of the Woman Writer in the Twentieth Century, Volume II: Sexchanges* (New Haven: Yale University Press, 1989), p. 7.
48 Richard von Krafft-Ebing, *Psychopathia Sexualis, with Especial Reference to the Antipathetic Sexual Instinct*, trans. Franklin S. Klaf (London: Staple Press, 1965), p. 26.

49 Havelock Ellis, *Studies in the Psychology of Sex* (New York: Random House, 1905), p. 249.
50 Gilbert and Gubar, *The Madwoman in the Attic*, p. 50.
51 Gilbert and Gubar, *No Man's Land, Vol. I*, p. 169.
52 Diary entry dated Monday 20 September, in Virginia Woolf, *The Diary of Virginia Woolf, Volume II: 1920–1924*, ed. Anne Oliver Bell (London: The Hogarth Press, 1978), p. 67.
53 Virginia Woolf, *The Common Reader*, 2 vols. (London: The Hogarth Press, 1925 and 1932).
54 Alice Fox, *Virginia Woolf and the Literature of the English Renaissance* (Oxford: Clarendon Press, 1990), pp. 14–15.
55 See Marcus, 'Thinking Back Through Our Mothers'; and Toril Moi, *Sexual/Textual Politics: Feminist Literary Theory* (London: Routledge, 1985), esp. pp. 2–3.
56 Woolf, *A Room of One's Own*, p. 45.
57 See, for example, Woolf, *A Room of One's Own*, p. 132.
58 Ibid., p. 31.
59 Ibid., p. 22.
60 Muriel Bradbrook, 'Notes on the Style of Mrs Woolf', *Scrutiny* 1 (1932/3), 33–8 (p. 38).
61 For a concise history of Suffrage, see both Smith, *The British Women's Suffrage Campaign 1866–1928*; and Sophia A. van Wingerden, *The Women's Suffrage Movement in Britain 1866–1928* (Basingstoke: Macmillan Press Ltd, 1999).
62 Smith, *The British Women's Suffrage Campaign 1866–1928*, p. 1.
63 Fox, *Virginia Woolf and the Literature of the English Renaissance*, pp. 9–10.
64 Ibid., p. 14.
65 Lady Helena [Faucit] Martin, *On Some of Shakespeare's Female Characters* (Edinburgh: Blackwood and Sons, 1885); Mary Cowden Clarke, *The Girlhood of Shakespeare's Heroines, in a series of fifteen tales*, 3 vols. (London: W. H. Smith and Son; Simpkin, Marshall and Co., 1850–2); Anna Bronwell [Annabel] Jameson, *Characteristics of Women, moral, political, and historical [Shakespeare's Heroines]* (London, 1832).
66 Muriel Bradbrook, *Elizabethan Stage Conditions: a study of their place in the interpretation of Shakespeare's plays* (Cambridge: Cambridge University Press, 1932).
67 Caroline F. E. Spurgeon, *Shakespeare's Iterative Imagery: (i) as Undersong (ii) as Touchstone in his Work* (London: Humphrey Milford Amen House, 1931); *Shakespeare's Imagery and What it Tells Us* (Cambridge: Cambridge University Press, 1935).
68 R. G. Cox, 'Statistical Criticism – Shakespeare's Imagery and What it Tells Us, Caroline F. E. Spurgeon', *Scrutiny* 4 (December 1935), 309–11 (p. 309).
69 Spurgeon, *Shakespeare's Imagery and What it Tells Us*, p. 2.
70 Nina Auberbach, *Romantic Imprisonment: Women and Other Glorified Outcasts* (New York: Columbia University Press, 1986), p. 268.

71 Katherine Cockin, *Edith Craig (1869–1947): Dramatic Lives* (London: Cassell, 1998), p. 65.
72 Ibid., pp. 156–75.
73 Terry, *Memoirs*, p. 46.
74 Virginia Woolf, 'Ellen Terry', in *Collected Essays: Volume 4* (London: The Hogarth Press, 1967), pp. 67–72 (p. 67).
75 Ibid., p. 71.
76 Ibid., p. 67.
77 On Woolf's acting metaphor for female identity, see Penny Farfan's recent study *Women, Modernism and Performance* (Cambridge: Cambridge University Press, 2004), esp. pp. 49–64, which covers much of the same material discussed here.

Index